Tales of BADMEN, BAD WOMEN, and BAD PLACES

Four Centuries of Texas Outlawry

Tales of BADMEN, BAD WOMEN, and BAD PLACES

Four Centuries of Texas Outlawry

C. F. Eckhardt

Texas Tech University Press

This book was set in Cheltenham, Snell, and Usherwood. The paper used in this book meets the minimum requirements of ANSI/NISO Z39.48-1992 (R1997). ∞

Design by Melissa Bartz

Printed and bound in Canada by
University of Toronto Press Incorporated

Library of Congress Cataloging-in-Publication Data
Eckhardt, C. F. (Charley F.)
Tales of badmen, bad women, and bad places: four centuries of Texas outlawry / C. F. Eckhardt.
p. cm.
Includes bibliographical references and index.
ISBN 0-89672-412-3 (cloth: alk. paper)
ISBN 0-89672-420-4 (paper: alk. paper)
1. Outlaws—Texas—Biography—Anecdotes. 2. Texas—History, Local—Anecdotes. 3. Texas—Biography—Anecdotes. I. Title.
F386.6.E25 1998
976.4—dc21 98-48223
CIP

03 04 05 06 07 / 9 8 7 6 5 4 3

Texas Tech University Press
Box 41037
Lubbock, Texas 79409-1037 USA

800-832-4042

ttup@ttu.edu
www.ttup.ttu.edu

This book is dedicated to my first grandson,
Stephen Clint Mueller, "MacDuff,"
so he'll have a book that's all his.

Acknowledgments

Without the inspiration or encouragement of these people, somewhere up the line, this book simply would not exist.

J. Frank Dobie
Walter P. Webb
H. Bailey Carrol
"Uncle Frank" Parker
Ralph A. Doyal
G. F. Eckhardt, Jr.
Evelyn H. Eckhardt
Wallace E. Clayton
Joe Austell Small
Alonso G. Schuyler
Eloise Roach
Helen D. Nolen
Wallace O. Chariton
Oren Logan
John L. Tolleson
Ron Filkins
Vicki Walker Eckhardt
Captain Frank Hamer
Sheriff Henry Matysek
Ted Newton
Sgt. Manuel T. "Lone Wolf" Gonzuallas

Contents

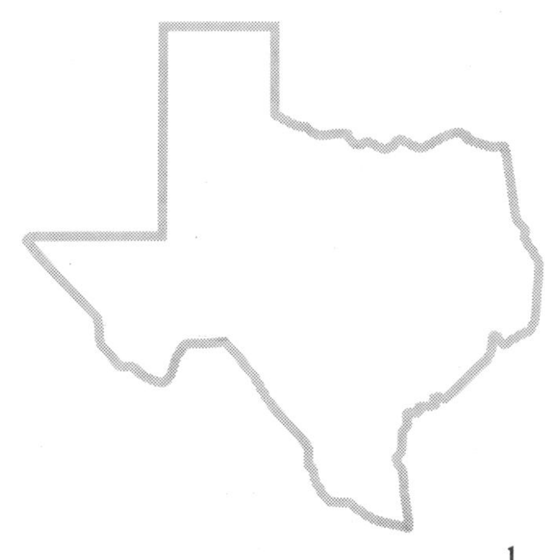

For Starters . . . 1
In the Beginning . . . 3
Texas's First Claim-Jumper 5
The Murder of Juan José Zevallos 22
The Murderous Yocums of the Big Thicket 27
A Lake Called "Haunted" 33
The Man Who Became Judge Roy Bean 39
The Silver at Lockhart 52
How Elgin Got Its Name 57
Gone Like Lottie's Eye 61
Who Was John Wesley Hardin, Anyway—
And Why Do People Say Such Awful Things about Him? 66
The Great Gunfight that Wasn't 83
The Ballad of Sam Bass 87
The Murder of Ben Thompson 110
The Devil's Disciple of Waco 119
The Peculiar Incident of the Public Arch 136
The Wild Bunch in Texas 141
Gregorio Cortez 154
The Unfortunate Circumstances Surrounding the
Moral Motion Picture Film Company 163
The Badman Nobody Knows 168
When Santa Claus Robbed the Bank 173
The Real Story of Bonnie and Clyde 178
Jennifer Is Waiting 204
Where These Stories Came From 209
Index 211

For Starters . . .

What makes a badman, a bad woman, or a bad place? A "bad" man, in today's parlance, can be a "bad man to mess with." In that case, any number of fine old Texas Rangers would qualify as "bad men." However, when "badman" is only one word, it has a meaning all its own. It means a criminal—an outlaw, a killer, a robber, a thief, a swindler, a liver-on-the-law's-fringes, or—sometimes—someone who delights in making the lives of others uncomfortable, if not miserable, though operating entirely within the law. It could even mean, and often did, that the individual was "wuthless"—a bum, a sponger, a petty annoyance not bad enough to kill but not acceptable in the house. Quite often "badmen" never thought of themselves as "bad men."

A bad woman could be one of three sorts of woman. She could be, like her male counterpart, an outlaw, a killer, a robber, or a thief; or she might be a notorious prostitute or madam; or she might be a woman who stepped over the line of accepted "womanly conduct" in her time. In any case, a badman or a bad woman was usually recognized as such by at least the majority of the community in which he or she lived.

But what about a bad place?

There are certain places today you wouldn't want to go into unless you just had to, and then you'd prefer to go in daylight, in company with several people—preferably at least some of them armed—and you'd go in and get out as fast as you could. At one time, in the American West, there were whole towns like that—not as many as Hollywood would have you believe, but they did exist. Bodie, Wyoming, home of the Badman from Bodie. Galeyville, Arizona, hangout of the cattle-rustling Clanton gang. And then there were the Texas towns, like Tascosa and Helena, which were just as bad if lesser known.

It wasn't always the people that made a place bad. Sometimes it had something to do with what happened there in the past and might happen there again. Sometimes it's something you could see, and sometimes it's something you could feel and hoped you wouldn't see.

This book contains all varieties—bad men and badmen, all sorts of bad women, and both types of bad places. They're all part and parcel of the Texas tales the schoolteacher never tells.

IN THE BEGINNING . . .

Texas has been a battleground for people since there have been people in North America. The size and diversity of the place we call "Texas" today is such that no one group of Indians could hold it all or even wanted it all. The historical tribes were a cross section of almost every southern type of Indian found in the United States. The Caddos of East Texas were primarily an eastern woodlands tribe, the Tonkawas of the central hills were nomads who called themselves "brothers to the wolf," and the Apaches of the far western deserts and mountains were the same tribes who lived in Arizona, New Mexico, and northern Mexico.

Right down the middle of Texas came the great southern buffalo range, and every tribe in Texas hunted buffalo when it could. There were more than enough buffalo to go around, but the territorial instinct of the tribes—an instinct all humans have whether they care to admit it or not—made the buffalo range, from east of the Colorado to the Pecos, a battleground almost from the beginning of time.

When the white people moved in, starting in the late 1600s with LaSalle's ill-fated settlement on Garcitas Creek, a tributary of Matagorda Bay, nothing really changed. There was just an added group in the dispute for ownership. Among both groups—whites and Indians—there were individuals and whole groups who were feared and hated because of what they did or were believed to do. No tribe would ally with, for instance, the Tonkawa—because every tribe believed, probably with good reason, that the Tonkawa were eaters of human flesh. The Karankawa of the coast were held in the same disdain.

Then came the white men. No amount of effort could keep the bad men from slipping in with the good. Slowly, at first, and then as a rising tide, white man's crime entered Texas.

TEXAS'S FIRST CLAIM-JUMPER

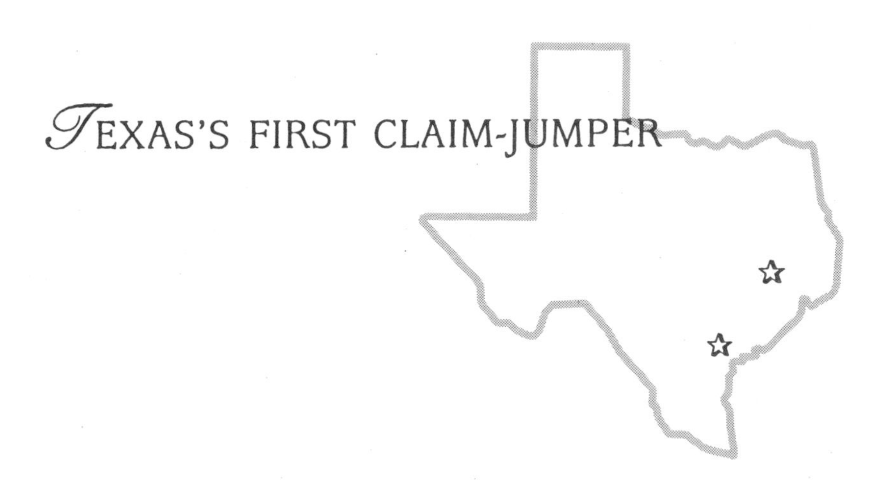

If you had to select a single name as that of the person most responsible for the ultimate settlement of Texas, you wouldn't be at all wrong to select the name René-Robert Cavelier, Sieur de La Salle. Although La Salle's sojourn in Texas was extremely brief, its effects were far-reaching.

Wait a minute here! This is a book about badmen—and, of course, bad women and bad places. René-Robert Cavelier, Sieur de La Salle qualifies as a badman?

You bet he does. Never mind that he is considered one of the great explorers of North America and of Texas. He was a claim-jumper. The Spanish had claim to Texas—ignoring, of course, the Indians, who were here first, but *everybody* ignored them. The Spanish had all sorts of laws to prevent other people—particularly Frenchmen and Englishmen—from settling in lands claimed by Spain.

La Salle *may not* have been trying to settle Texas. He was, at least officially, looking for the mouth of a great river he'd followed down from the French possessions in Canada, which went by a name variously spelled Micipipi, Michipi, and—ultimately—Mississippi. It was there, not on the soil of Spanish Texas, that René-Robert Cavelier, Sieur de La Salle intended to plant a colony when he set sail from the port of La Rochelle on July 24, 1684. Anyway, that's what the French said, and at least part of La Salle's behavior in Texas bears it out.

That's *not* to say that the French didn't have designs on Spanish Texas—they sure did. The French had always been singularly effective in making allies rather than enemies of Indians. The purpose of La Salle's colonial venture was to establish a base in the South from which Indian alliances could be concluded, and from which, in the not-distant future, both Indians and French soldiers could be sent to conquer most of the current American Southwest and northern Mexico and secure its vast reserves of gold and silver for the French rather than the Spanish treasury. That's pretty well clear.

Be that as it may be, the initial, though not the long-range, purpose of La Salle's venture seems to have been to establish a thriving colony in the rich lands surrounding the lower reaches of the Mississippi. However, to do that, the French colonists—who sailed in the thirty-six-gun frigate *Joly* and her sister ships, *L'Aimable, La Belle,* and *Saint François*—had to get there with people and supplies intact. While the *Joly* was a ship-of-war under the command of a French naval captain named Sieur de Beaujeu, the other three were merchant vessels and were heavily laden with the stores and supplies La Salle's colony would need as it was planted in the wilderness.

The voyage across was not a happy one. The *Joly,* a fast and handy sailor, was having to cross-tack and run under minimum sail to allow the slow merchant ships to keep up, much like a spirited racehorse leading a procession of plow mules. In addition, the two knights—"Sieur" means "Sir" or "Knight" in French—apparently took an instant dislike to one another. They very nearly came to the crossing of swords on several occasions, and both were noted swordsmen. Cooler heads were able to separate them each time, but the upshot was, Sieur de Beaujeu was more than glad to see the last of this Sieur de La Salle, and apparently he didn't much care *where* he saw the last of him.

The Atlantic crossing took two months, and the first landing—according to Sieur de Beaujeu—was to be Martinique. La Salle vetoed the idea. A lot of ships called at Martinique, and some of them were Spanish. The little French flotilla would be sailing into the "Spanish Lake," the Gulf of Mexico (called, by the Spanish, *Seno Mexicano*). The Spanish considered everything in or on the borders of that body of water Spanish territory, and—in spite of La Salle's claim to being the first to discover the Mississippi's mouth—that included present-day Louisiana, Mississippi, Alabama, Georgia, and Florida, as well as Texas, Mexico, Central America, and all of South America except Brazil.

Martinique and half of Saint Domingue—present-day Santo Domingo, which is still divided pretty much down the same line that was established in the seventeenth century, with the Dominican Republic speaking Spanish and Haiti speaking French—were French possessions, as were some smaller islands. Spain at best tolerated the French in the outer edge of the Gulf, without welcoming them beyond Cuba.

The French ships finally made landfall at Saint Domingue, and as they did, word came that the *Saint François* had been lost to Spanish privateers working out of Puerto Rico. Not only had supplies and equipment vital to the success of the colony been lost, but the very real chance existed that the whole enterprise was known to the Spanish, and that Spanish men-of-war might swoop down and destroy the three ships, or that Spanish soldiers might await them as they disembarked at their destination. In addition, La Salle and about fifty others were suffering from a peculiar ailment of some variety that combined high fever with near-insane tantrums and actions. The flotilla had to stay in harbor at Petit Goave for several weeks while they recuperated. In the meantime, several of the soldiers consorted with the local women of Petit Goave, many of whom were of Taino Indian ancestry and—though immune themselves—carried the syphilis spirochete. Others jumped ship and went over to the French pirates who made Petit Goave their hangout.

It was not until mid-November that the company was well enough to proceed, and then there was a problem, and its name was longitude. La Salle had the latitude of the mouth of the Mississippi pretty well down pat, but when he got there in 1682, he'd been unable to fix the longitude precisely. That wasn't unusual. Nobody had ever fixed longitude with any reasonable certainty, and nobody would be able to for the next 150 years—at least—until timekeeping improved a great deal.

There was a standard solution to the problem, and it was called "running down the latitude." You simply found your latitude and then you sailed along it, investigating every landfall until you found the one you were looking for. It worked fairly well—unless the appearance of your desired landfall had changed, or you happened to sail past it in the dark. That seems to be what happened to La Salle. He and his three ships sailed better than 400 miles past the Mississippi's delta to what is now known as Matagorda Bay on the Texas coast. Here the French colony landed on February 20, 1685. Here also, the *L'Aimable* ran aground—or was possibly deliberately grounded by her master, Sieur d'Aigron. He and La Salle didn't like each other, either.

A storm blew in before *L'Aimable*'s cargo could be salvaged, and most of it was lost, leaving the colony with only the supplies aboard *La Belle,* the smallest of the three supply ships. Nearly everyone was down with dysentery from the bad food and bad water, syphilis was claiming men regularly, and now the whole bunch, it seemed, was stuck in the middle of nowhere with some not-too-friendly Indians in immediate bowshot. On March 12, the armed frigate *Joly* departed for France, and scarcely a week later *La Belle* ran aground, drowning most of her crew and a goodly number of colonists in the process.

Shortly thereafter, La Salle took the strongest and most able-bodied men and set out in search of the Mississippi. After exploring the borders of Matagorda Bay and the coastline for several miles above and below it, he came to the conclusion that he had missed his target, but he didn't know by how far or in which direction he'd missed it.

In July of 1685, the French pirate Michel de Grammont and the Dutch pirate Laurens de Graff (called Lorencillo by the Spanish) made a massive raid on the Port of Campeche. All through July and August the pirates and Spanish sailors and troops fought over the town, with the pirates retreating in the end. Among the captured items the Spaniards recovered was a ship named *Nuestra Señora de Regla,* which the pirates had renamed *Reglita.* A member of the crew of *Reglita* was a young man named Denis Thomas, who had been one of the La Salle colonists who jumped ship in Saint Domingue the previous year.

Denis Thomas was a Frenchman who just wanted to go home. He told the Spanish everything he knew about the man they then called "Monsieur de Salaz" and his enterprise of settling the "Micipipi." After he told all he knew, the Spaniards hanged him.

But what was this Micipipi? Nobody had ever heard of it. Spanish officials decided it might be what earlier explorers had called *Bahía del Espiritu Santo*—Holy Ghost Bay. There was just one problem with that. Nobody had sailed to Espiritu Santo Bay in at least fifty years, and nobody knew for sure where it was.

The Spanish weren't any better at longitude than La Salle.

The Spanish didn't know where Espiritu Santo Bay was, but they had a fair idea where it wasn't. It wasn't any farther down the Mexican east coast than Tampico, and it wasn't any farther up the Florida west coast than present-day Apalachicola, which the Spanish called Apalache. If you'll pick up a map of the southern coast of North America and give it a once-over, you'll find that there was quite a lot of space in which it could be. In fact, it had been in quite a few places, none of which were Matagorda Bay, where the French colony actually was. Around 1519, the Spanish explorer Alonzo Alvarez de Piñeda had given the name to the main channel of the Mississippi as it emerges from the delta; De Soto had given the name to what is now called Tampa Bay; and yet another explorer had so christened Mobile Bay.

Gaspar de Palacios, admiral of the Spanish navy and the most competent navigator Spain had in the New World, put together all the known writings about Espiritu Santo Bay and concluded that it was 145 leagues from Tampico, 190 leagues from Vera Cruz, 120 leagues from Apalache, and 280 leagues from Mexico City. The points within the search area that actually correspond to those distances from those points are, in order, Corpus Christi Bay, the mouth of the Rio Grande, the Mississippi delta, and—surprise!—Matagorda Bay.

Not that there weren't enough descriptions of Espiritu Santo Bay, that mysterious body of water that was rapidly taking on ghostly proportions of another sort. It was supposed to be vast, though landlocked, with a deep channel surrounded by fertile land with heights suitable for the building of forts, and fed by two major rivers, one of which drained *La Mobila* (Alabama), the other draining *Nuevo Mejico*, which is present-day Texas, New Mexico, and Arizona, with parts of Colorado and Nevada thrown in. The simple truth is, the Espiritu Santo Bay the Spanish were seeking never existed.

The French, however, did exist—but that was about all they did. They certainly weren't thriving in this obscure corner of what they hoped to convert to *Nouvelle France.*

La Salle's one great obsession seems to have been to find, once more, the great river. He sent out at least four expeditions looking for it. One apparently reached the Rio Grande. At least some

Frenchmen from somewhere reached the lower Rio Grande near the vicinity of present-day Eagle Pass sometime around 1685. If they weren't La Salle's we don't know whose they were, but they definitely were there and they left traces. And when the Spanish found those traces a couple of years later, it scared them silly.

Back at the colony, things weren't going all that well. The initial site picked on Matagorda Bay proper proved prone to flooding and "miasmic," which means it was humid and the air often stank, so the colony was moved overland about three or four miles to what we now know as the mouth of Garcitas Creek on Lavaca Bay.

La Belle, run aground in the storm that drowned most of her crew, was left on the beach with most of her rigging intact. Only the colony's supplies, meager as they were, had been unloaded—along with those two essentials without which no colony in a strange land could survive: chickens and pigs.

A small fort was built, and it was supplied with a number of small cannons—some small-caliber ships' guns and field guns, and several swivel guns or "murthering pieces" as the English called them. (It was an apt name. They were short shotguns with a bore of about one and one-half inches, and they were usually loaded with "langrage"—nuts, bolts, nails, broken glass, chopped-up chain, what have you.) Around the fort were several small family huts. La Salle brought families as well as soldiers, and the soldiers were expected to start families by marrying—by both tribal and Christian customs—local Indian women. It was this intermarriage by soldiers with local Indian women that laid the foundation for nearly all successful French settlements. Fields were broken and crops were planted.

In the meantime, La Salle was still out looking for the Mississippi. On one of his forays he found himself in need of boats, and some local Indians had some *pirogues*—dugout canoes, in English. The Indians seem to have been Karankawas, who were a nasty bunch to be on the wrong side of, unless you had them both outnumbered and outgunned.

La Salle wanted the *pirogues,* and he tried to trade several things for them, including some steel axes. The Indians either actually didn't understand what La Salle wanted or they were deliberately being obtuse, holding out for a better price. At any rate, La Salle finally decided enough time had been wasted with the pigheaded redskins and had his men fire a volley over their heads. The Indians scrammed and La Salle and his men took over the *pirogues.* This act probably sealed the fate of the colony.

In the summer of 1687, the Spanish sent an overland expedition to look for La Salle's colony, and it actually got as far as the Rio Grande. It not only found evidence that Frenchmen had been there; it found a Frenchman. (La Salle's men, too, found a couple of Frenchmen living among the Indians, though who they were and where they came from is still a mystery.)

His name, he said, was Jean Gery, which the Spanish translated "Juan Enrique." Nobody, to this day, knows where he came from, how he got where he was—he wasn't one of La Salle's men—or how long he'd been living among the Chichimec Indians when the Spanish found him. He was a *cacique*—a sort of combination chief and medicine man—and the Chichimecs treated him like a semideity. He was also, apparently, a gifted liar and stark, staring nuts to boot.

He had a story to tell, though. Brother, did he have a tale! It scared the Spanish silly.

According to Jean Gery, the French started their colony nearly fifteen years before, around 1670. It was a big one, too—a fort with twenty guns, protected by six companies of soldiers. There was a church and a monastery, with six Capuchin priests. The church was so big it had six bells. French vessels regularly called at the settlement, and three merchant ships stayed in port all the time to load out the produce of the colony for France. The colony raised corn, wheat, tobacco, and sugar cane, and herded cattle, sheep, horses, and mules. A great many Indians were allied with the colony and lived at peace with it. The settlement was near the mouth of a large river, on a big bay. The colony possessed seven locally built barques, small ships propelled by either sails or oars; by boat it was a one-day journey to the sea, while it required three days by horse.

Jean Gery came among the Indians, he said, to reduce them to obedience to the King of France. Last year he had been visited by sixteen French soldiers, and just two months ago seven came to see him. He told them the wonderful success he was having enlisting the Indians as subjects of the King of France.

This scared the Spanish right out of their underwear. Their worst nightmares had come true. The French were not only settling in New Spain, they were doing so in force, making allies of the Indians, and preparing to invade and annex northern New Spain. Jean Gery was sent to Mexico City, where a number of holes began to appear in his story and he began to contradict himself. It rapidly became obvious to the Spanish that Jean Gery was a mental case, and that what he said could not be trusted.

The problem was, the stories he told and the description he gave of the site of the French settlement fit the mythical Espiritu Santo Bay almost precisely. In addition, he was definitely French, and—according to the Indians where he lived, who *weren't* out in cloud-cuckoo land—he had, in fact, been visited on two fairly recent occasions by groups of white men who wore armor and carried guns and who spoke with him in a language both they and Gery understood but the Indians did not, which definitely was not Spanish. That meant only one thing—the French were somewhere fairly close, and they might be in force.

The French *were* fairly close—about 180 miles up the coast—but they not only weren't in force, things were not at all going well with them. By the time La Salle set out on his final and fatal journey in search of the Mississippi, only about 30 of the original 250-odd colonists survived. The Spanish, however, had no way of knowing this, and continued reports from Indians coming out of Texas's interior mentioned strange white men who wore armor and carried guns. These men, at least in the Spanish mind, could only be Frenchmen.

In addition to expeditions by land, the Spanish sent expeditions by sea in search of the French colony. One of these actually found the mouth of the Mississippi—or at least the largest channel emerging from the delta—but didn't recognize it for what it was. It was choked with logs, apparently from upriver flooding, so the Spanish named it "River of the Logs" and sailed on past looking for the French. Other expeditions coming out of Florida explored Mobile Bay, the area around Biloxi, Mississippi, and Barataria Island. Those coming out of Mexico City explored the almost-uncharted upper coast of Mexico north of Tampico, the mouth of the Rio Grande, the Barrier Islands of the Texas Coast, present-day Baffin Bay on the King Ranch, Corpus Christi Bay, Aransas Bay, and—at long last—Matagorda Bay.

It was in Matagorda Bay that the Spaniards found *La Belle,* aground but still apparently seaworthy.

At that point they were less than five miles from a point where the blockhouse La Salle grandiosely named Fort Saint Louis would have been clearly visible, and when the ship was found, the French colony was still very much alive, though—again—by no means thriving. For reasons unknown, the Spanish did not put a shore party out to search for whoever left a full-rigged ship of unquestionably French design sitting aground in a bay on an uninhabited—though Spanish-claimed—coast. It would be more than two years before the French settlement—whose cooking-fire smoke should have been clearly visible from the decks of the Spanish ship—was found.

In the meanwhile, La Salle was off again, this time on the expedition that ended his life. Factions had developed within the exploring party, and a plot to murder the leader took place. In East-Central Texas, at a place generally agreed to be along the Navasota River, one of La Salle's men shot him from behind. This person was then shot by a supporter of La Salle, who was in turn shot by another of the plotters, who was in turn shot by another La Salle supporter. Somewhere along in there the survivors decided that regardless of which side they were on in the plotting, if they continued to shoot one another in the back, sooner or later there wouldn't be anyone left. The band agreed to suspend hostilities and to search not for the Mississippi, but for the French settlements to the northeast. That they happened to be a lot farther from French Canada than from the Mississippi, and that they'd have to cross the Mississippi to get to French Canada, they seem not to have known. At any rate, the explorers completely abandoned the colony at that point and headed northeast.

At least two of the anti-La Salle plotters, Jacques Grollet and Jean L'Archeveque, either voluntarily went to live with Indians or fled the rest of the party and were captured. Sometime shortly afterwards, two Indians delivered to the Spanish at El Parral, inside present-day Mexico, a piece of parchment with a painting of a European ship on it. On the parchment, both Grollet and L'Archeveque had written messages in French, but because the Spanish could not read the messages, they remained untranslated for 250 years. Grollet's was mostly illegible by then, but L'Archeveque's read:

> Sir
>
> I do not know what sort of people you are. We are French. We are among the savages. We would like very much to be among Christians such as we are. We know well that you are Spaniards. We do not know whether you will attack us. We are sorely grieved to be among the beasts like these who believe neither in God nor in

anything. Gentlemen, if you are willing to take us away, you have only to send a message, as we have but little or nothing to do. As soon as we see the note we will deliver ourselves up to you.
Sir, I am your very humble and obedient servant,
Jean Larcheveque of Bayonne

Both L'Archeveque and Grollet were eventually rescued from their semi-captivity among the Tejas Indians, being found at a Tonkawa encampment where Tejas chiefs—together with their white slaves—were visiting. The encampment was in the vicinity of present-day Smithville. The pair were questioned by the Spanish and revealed that they had returned to the site of Fort Saint Louis after leaving the La Salle expedition—both being very careful to avoid saying why they'd left the expedition—and found it destroyed. When confronted with the madman, Gery, both denied ever having seen him before, and both denied any knowledge of a town called "Xeble" in France, which Gery claimed as home. This upset the Spaniards even more—it was obvious now that there was not just one group of Frenchmen in New Spain, but two. Otherwise, where had Gery come from? (For the record, that question has never yet been answered.) An overland expedition under General Alonso de León, consisting of eighty-five soldiers including himself, an historian named Juan Bautista Chapa, a French-speaking Spaniard named Francisco Martínez, Father Damian Massanet (the expedition chaplain), twelve armed mule-drivers, thirteen servants—and Jean Gery—set out from Presidio de San Francisco (now Monclova) on March 23, 1688, to find the devilish French once and for all. There were also a number of Indian guides, 720 horses and mules, and a number of cattle to be slaughtered for meat as the need arose, as well as eighty-five mule loads of provisions. This was a serious expedition. On the thirtieth of March the expedition crossed the Rio Grande. At about the same time, the final disaster fell on Fort Saint Louis.

Remember those canoes? The ones La Salle got tired of trying to trade for and stole? The Indians he stole them from were the Karankawa. Kronks were not good people to fool with.

Probably it was early morning. The Kronks always liked to attack then. Several Karankawa came out of the brush, making signs and talking trade. The French came out to greet them. There weren't many French left—maybe twenty or thirty. A rumored epidemic of smallpox may have killed a great many, but, other than hearsay evidence, there's no proof that smallpox hit the colony.

It was, of course, a ruse. A large force, perhaps as many as a hundred Karankawa warriors in full war regalia, were hidden in the brush. As soon as the French were outside, all unawares, the Kronks rose out of the brush and attacked.

If there was a fight at all it wasn't much. Most of the corpses later found—skeletons by then—were away from the fort, with their backs to it and arrows protruding from them. At least one of the skeletons was identified, by clothing remains, as a woman.

It was probably all over in an hour. Whether or not any of the French captives received an invitation to a Karankawa banquet—at which French cuisine in the form of barbecued Frenchman would be featured—we don't know, but it seems likely. Even the animals—the chickens and the pigs—were butchered. The houses were looted, but a lot of things were left behind. The Indians broke the guns and took no powder, not knowing how to make the white-man thundersticks work. They took all the jewelry and most of the cloth they could find, buckets and axes, and a lot of books, but virtually nothing else. It was the spring of 1688, and the French flag had flown on Texas soil for only four years.

On the morning of April 23, 1688, General de León's expedition arrived on the west shore of Matagorda Bay. There they found the wreckage of *L'Aimable*, along with some scattered and ruined cargo, but—it seems—no sign of *La Belle*, which had been found apparently seaworthy the previous year. As they skirted the bay, they found an abandoned Indian encampment with, among other things, a broken wine case and a book in French. Obviously, they were getting close.

Another expedition, led by Francisco Martínez, was just now crossing the Rio Grande. They received a letter borne by some Indians, apparently from some survivors of the massacre. It was signed by the same Jean L'Archeveque whose first plea for help would go unread for 250 years. With him, or in the immediate vicinity, were James Heins, an English buccaneer who'd signed on with La Salle at Saint Domingue, and a man named Ruter—both of whom had been involved, with L'Archeveque and Grollet, in the plot to murder La Salle. Also in the group were Pierre Meunier and a thirteen-year-old boy named Pierre Talon. (Louis L'Amour fans, now you know where he got that name for his character.) The Martínez expedition eventually rescued L'Archeveque, Grollet, Meunier, and Talon, together with Talon's younger brother; two other Talon children were never found. Heins and Ruter chose to remain with the Indians.

On the morning of April 28, 1688, de León's expedition finally reached Fort Saint Louis. He found a strongly built blockhouse fort of five rooms, four on the bottom floor and one on top. Over the door was carved the date 1684—the date of establishment—and 168_, which was apparently intended to be completed with the date of abandonment. The end had come too suddenly for the completion. The construction was apparently from ships' timbers, and it had a high, steeply-pitched roof for shedding rain.

Inside the fort de León found eight pieces of artillery, three swivel guns, and the broken stocks of some hundred arquebuses. The Indians had apparently carried off the barrels and locks for the metal in them. A considerable quantity of shot was found, which was removed to Mexico and evidently later was melted down and made into nails and hinges for a church in the village of Santiago de la Monclova. Broken bottles and wooden cases and books were about all the Indians had left.

Near the fort were some twenty to thirty dwellings, mostly made of mud and wattle and roofed with buffalo hides. There were fields of vegetables and some pens for animals. Out in the saltgrass, a hundred yards or more from the fort, de León's men found the skeletons of those who'd been killed last.

The swivel guns and artillery pieces were buried on the spot. Then de León went back to Mexico, carrying the news.

The following year, 1689, Father Damian Massanet established a mission called *Espíritu Santo de la Bahía*, on the site of La Salle's fort, after having burned the French structure to the ground. It was later—much later—moved inland. It gave the name La Bahía to the town Texas knows today as Goliad. This marked the beginning of the real Spanish settlement of Texas. A line of missions was planned and, by 1718, Father Morfi (pronounce it "Murphy"—that's what he called it) was establishing a mission and town along the tiny Rio San Antonio. First called San Fernando de Bejar, it would later become known as San Antonio.

The Spanish also found something very strange. Among the Tejas Indians there were Christians—of a sort, anyway. Though no priests had ever visited them, they had proper Catholic shrines, including crucifixes and images of saints with candles—or at least lights of some sort—burning in front of them. Where had they learned this?

"From the woman in blue," the Indians told them.

"What woman in blue?"

"The young, attractive woman in blue who came among us and taught us these things."

That revived a tale from early in the century. Between 1621 and 1629, the Jumano Indians from near El Paso sent repeated messages to Father Alonso de Benavides in Santa Fe about a young, attractive woman in blue who had come among them teaching

Christianity. Father Benavides established missions for the Jumano. Upon seeing the blue habit of a Poor Clare nun, the Jumanos agreed that the dress was the same as their woman in blue, but that their woman was much younger and prettier than the nun Father Benavides pointed out.

On his return to Spain in 1631, Father Benavides heard of the youngest Mother Superior in Spain, Sister María de Jesús de Agreda of the Poor Clare order, who insisted that, in spirit, she had left her convent in Spain many times and gone preaching to the Indians of the New World. She gave accurate descriptions of the customs, appearance, and dress of the Jumanos, which Father Benavides believed she could not have known unless she had seen them. He, at least, was convinced that Sister María de Agreda was the woman in blue of the Jumanos, and when he returned to his New World parish with a painting of Sister María, the Jumanos agreed.

Without getting into metaphysics and similar diversions, if the woman in blue wasn't Sister María, who was she? Nuns didn't go wandering around like itinerant priests sometimes did. Poor Clare nuns especially—they were a cloistered order who never left the convent after taking their vows. The Jumanos—and now the Tejas—had definitely talked to somebody who knew a lot about Catholic ritual, and in both cases they insisted the person who taught them—in their own languages, not in Spanish—was a "woman in blue." Sister María was the only woman in blue who ever claimed any contact with these Indians, although—at least physically—she set foot outside her convent in Spain only once from the time she took her vows at age eighteen until she died, many years later. And that was to establish her own convent outside the Agreda city wall.

There were other French incursions into Spanish territory, and within a few years Sieur de Bienville was to settle on the banks of the Mississippi a few miles upstream from where it enters the

Gulf and call his settlement *Nouvelle Orleans*. The existence of this colony would drive a wedge between Spanish Florida and the Spanish possessions to the west, establishing a vast territory the French called *La Louisiane*. Their title would be continuously disputed, and lead would fly on widely spaced occasions—leading, in one case, to what is known as the Chicken War. In it, a French commandant in Louisiana, hearing that one of the interminable wars between Spain and France had broken out in Europe and determined to strike a blow for *La Belle France* in the wilderness, attacked a Spanish mission. Nobody was home—the priests and the five or six soldiers detailed to protect them were warned by their Indian converts of the French invasion and hid in the woods. The French, determined not to go back empty handed, took a pig and a dozen or so chickens and returned to Louisiana. The war lasted about a week and involved maybe forty people, none of whom got hurt, but it's still on the books as a "French-Spanish conflict in Texas."

The French were far more successful in making allies of Indians than were the Spanish, and for years French military advisers aided tribes that gave the Spanish trouble. The Indians who destroyed the mission on the San Saba near present Menard may have been French led. And those who met and whipped the expedition of Spanish out to revenge the massacre were flying a French flag. The village of Spanish Fort, Texas, on the Red River, was not a Spanish fort at all—it was a Wichita village with white residents, and all the white-man artifacts found in it have been identifiably French.

Still, the French never invaded Texas in force again, and never established regular settlements in it. The reason?

Try Texas's first claim-jumper—René-Robert Cavelier, Sieur de la Salle. His four-year failure on Matagorda Bay so thoroughly scared Spain that it began to push settlement—and never backed off.

THE MURDER OF JUAN JOSÉ ZEVALLOS

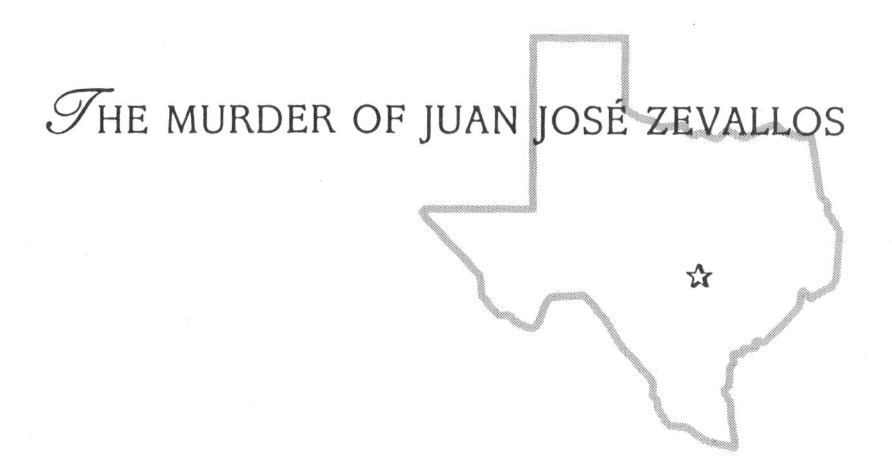

In the mid-eighteenth century, the little village of San Fernando de Bejar had grown into the thriving military-religious-civilian complex that formed the nucleus for present-day San Antonio. If it could be done once, the Spanish wondered, could it be done again? Plans were laid and a site selected for a new multi-mission-and-presidio complex to the north and east.

The site selected was on the banks of what is now known as Brushy Creek, near present-day Rockdale. It was fertile and well-drained, and its deep soil produces excellent crops even today. There was—and is—abundant timber in the area for the building of rough structures, and considerable sandstone in a number of outcroppings for building. The site received the grandiose name of Ranchería Grande. It was intended to be the second of a line of rancherias—mission/presidio/town complexes—to extend from San Fernando de Bejar all the way to Florida, consolidating the Spanish claim to the entire southern half of North America.

Three missions were established, and the names they are generally known by today are San Ildefonso, Candelaria, and Dolores.

A presidio was set up, called San Xavier. A nearby river was also named for Saint Xavier, though today it is known as the San Gabriel. Typically, the missions served different tribes. One served some eastern-fringe Apaches, one the local Tonkawas, and one some northwestern-fringe cousins of the Karankawa. The presidio was established with fifty soldiers, and there were two priests in each mission. Ground was broken, crops were planted, and a total of some two hundred Indians gathered voluntarily at the missions to be Christianized and turned into farmers. It was a good start—very promising. More promising, at the beginning, than San Antonio itself. The missions were started in 1748.

By June of 1752 it was all over. The missions and presidio were in ruins, the Indians scattered, and the fields overgrown with weeds. Ranchería Grande was a failure. For generations the failure was blamed on the Indians—they were "too warlike to be civilized" or "too lazy to work." In fact, the Indians were not to blame. The murders of a presidio soldier named Juan José Zevallos and a mission Candelaria priest named Ganzabal, on May 11, 1752, killed Ranchería Grande.

When a rancheria or mission/presidio complex was to be established, a commander had to be chosen for the soldiers to be stationed at the new fort. Command of a presidio or frontier fort was an extremely lucrative position. The *comandante de presidio* received, into his own pocket, all of the money necessary to run the presidio—the money to pay the men, to buy them clothing and arms and feed them, to maintain the condition of the fort, to buy and maintain horses for the fort, and to pay his own salary, which was known in Spanish as a "hardship" because it was very low. Whatever money he could save out of the presidial allowance—by cheating the soldiers, making them wear rags, buying substandard arms and ammunition, letting the fort run down, and buying inferior horses in insufficient numbers—he could keep for his own and no one, under normal circumstances, would ever say anything about it. The post of *comandante de presidio* was a route to riches for a man mean enough and crooked enough to take advantage of it.

Felipe de Rabago y Terán was just such a man. When he was appointed *comandante de presidio* at the fort on Brushy Creek, he was determined to enrich Felipe de Rabago y Terán in as short a time as possible. He was also a man of lusts, and women were his target. As a Spanish aristocrat he knew he had nothing to fear from the Spanish bureaucracy if he indulged those lusts on Indian women, and from the day his presidio was established he encouraged his soldiers to make free use of the Indian women at the missions, without regard for native or Christian marriage vows. It apparently kept the soldiers happy enough that they didn't notice the commandant's various swindles.

If that was all that happened, probably nothing would have been said. Spaniards had been making free and easy with Indian women since Columbus first hit the Caribbean in 1492. The result is an entire sub-race in southern North America, Central America, and South America, known as *mestizos*, or mixed-bloods.

One of the soldiers, Juan José Zevallos, had a wife, and her name was María. He took her from Bejar to Ranchería Grande with him. We don't know what she looked like for sure, but there are rumors that she was young, at least attractive if not beautiful—and of a temperament that didn't reject the flirtatious ways of so many men around one woman.

At some point, perhaps even before the expedition left Bejar, María Zevallos attracted the notice of Felipe de Rabago y Terán. So the story goes, before the garrison was halfway from Bejar to the new fort, María had abandoned Juan José and moved, bag, baggage, and body, into the commandant's blankets. Zevallos was not happy with the situation, but there was nothing he could do about it.

As soon as the garrison and the priests arrived at Ranchería Grande and began to construct their homes, the Indians began to gather. Almost immediately, the commandant turned the soldiers loose on the Indian women, apparently with no more instructions than, "Have fun, boys." The priests protested via letter to Mexico City, but the mail was a military responsibility, and, as military commander, Felipe de Rabago y Terán opened and read each of them. Their letters were accompanied, therefore, by letters from Rabago y Terán denying every charge and suggesting that there were actually very few Indians at the missions and the priests were trying to cover their failure to attract converts by claiming the soldiers were driving the Indians away. The *comandante* had what *he* wanted—María—safely ensconced in his quarters.

Poor Zevallos, who was married to the woman, went to the padres for help. In retaliation, Rabago y Terán had the man arrested and chained to the wall of the guardhouse. At nightfall, he had a cot, a table, and a candle brought in. Then he brought in María—wearing a blanket but nothing else. The blanket went on the cot, María got on the blanket, and the *comandante* got on María. For the rest of the night, the *comandante* enjoyed himself with his mistress while her anguished husband looked on, chained to the wall, tightly gagged, and unable to interfere or even protest. At dawn, the *comandante* and María left, and sometime later, Rabago y Terán had the husband released.

This little demonstration of his power by Felipe de Rabago y Terán was to be the beginning of the end of Ranchería Grande. Zevallos went to the priests, and particularly to Padre Ganzabal. The padre protested vigorously to Mexico City, detailing what Rabago y Terán had done and taking a deposition under oath from the soldier, detailing how the commandant humiliated him and debauched his wife. Zevallos immediately had to seek sanctuary in the chapel at the Candelaria mission to prevent Rabago y Terán from taking vengeance on him.

It didn't help much. On May 11, 1754, both Padre Ganzabal and Zevallos were murdered inside the church, the padre shot with an arrow and Zevallos with a musket. Though the murders were blamed on Indians by the commandant, everybody knew the Spanish never let mission Indians have firearms. Some weeks later, an Indian turned up in San Antonio and confessed—without being tortured, or so the record says—to putting an arrow in the priest. He apparently named his confederate who fired the shot into Zevallos as well. Both the Indian and a soldier he named as his accomplice were hanged, and somehow the Zevallos deposition disappeared in the confusion.

The Indians, who—up until the murder—had been pretty much taking the Spaniards' antics in stride, decided enough was enough. When the Spaniards took to murdering their own kind in the very house of their God, there was something wrong with the whole situation. Within a matter of a few days the whole rancheria was virtually deserted except for the Spaniards. In addition, according to various reports, there were signs and evil portents in the sky, the creek dried up, the crops failed, and the cows went dry. In fact, even today you will hear more than occasional reports of mysterious lights and signs in the night sky in the valley of Brushy Creek near the sites of the missions.

The Spanish commandancy in Mexico City ordered an investigation. As a result, Felipe de Rabago y Terán was relieved of his command and jailed, though ultimately no action was taken against him. The presidio and missions along Brushy Creek were ordered abandoned. The presidial establishment was removed to the San Marcos river and later to the San Saba at present-day Menard. The missions were reestablished elsewhere. The entire attempt to establish missions in Central Texas was abandoned. Never again were missions erected in the rich farmlands along the eastern San Gabriel.

What became of María we don't know. Capitan Felipe de Rabago y Terán, according to legend, died very unpleasantly, having syphilis, gonorrhea, and several other similar ailments.

THE MURDEROUS YOCUMS OF THE BIG THICKET

Away down in the southeast part of the state, a little to the north and west of Houston, there's a vast wilderness—vast even now, after generations of attempts to clear or tame it—called the Big Thicket. It has long been known as a haven for outlaws, and perhaps the most vicious outlaws ever to inhabit the Big Thicket were the Yocum family—today occasionally referred to as the Bender Gang of Texas.

The actual Benders were notorious mass murderers of the late nineteenth century. At their "hotel" in Kansas, the Bender family—using young, attractive Kate Bender as bait—murdered and robbed at least fifty travelers, perhaps more. The bodies of the victims were severely mutilated, and in one case the Benders murdered not only a male traveler but his five-year-old daughter who was traveling with him.

What became of the Benders no one knows—at least not officially. Writers of fiction and semi-fiction have had field days reviving the Benders almost anywhere you look, and there are at least five jails in Kansas, Nebraska, and Colorado in which Old Man

Bender is supposed to have sawed a foot or a hand off to escape once he had been identified. By my tally, Old Man Bender left behind both hands and three feet, which is a neat trick if you can manage it.

According to those who knew, the Bender family was followed and overtaken by a posse, which dispensed rough but appropriate frontier justice to the lot and then cremated the bodies on a pyre made of the family's wagon and possessions. Supposedly, the original intent was to kill all but Kate Bender, who was the worst of the lot. She was to be taken to Mexico and sold into slavery in a house of prostitution. When she learned what her fate was to be, she fought so savagely that she had to be killed, and her body was burned with the rest.

This story, which has been around at least since the 1890s, has formed the basis of at least one novel. It's also very likely true.

The Yocums were much earlier than the Benders—the 1830s—and didn't get the publicity. The Yocum family, so the story goes, was involved with the John Murrel gang of criminals operating in Alabama and Mississippi in the early 1800s. It was, in fact, John Murrel who plotted the great slave revolt of the early 1820s, which—though it was discovered and prevented—resulted in the executions of dozens of slaves thought to be part of it. Murrel's intention was never to free the slaves, as has been alleged, but, by his own statement, to take advantage of the "great tumult" a slave insurrection would create to loot homes and towns for his own profit.

Sometime around 1821 the Yocums were living at Many, Louisiana, when a member of the notorious family began to court a proper young lady named Susan Collier. Susan had an uncle, James Collier, who was married to one of the Yocum women. Susan's father, Robert Collier, ran Matthew Yocum, her criminal suitor, off his place—some say with a horsewhip—and promoted marriage to a man named Charles Chandler.

Matthew Yocum and James Collier then murdered Robert Collier and attempted to kill Charles Chandler, but seem to have bitten off more than they could chew. When the smoke cleared, both Matthew Yocum and James Collier had fatal holes in them, and Charles Chandler was reloading his pistols.

Shortly afterwards, the Yocums murdered a Louisiana white man (name unknown) who was legally married to a free black woman, then kidnapped the woman and the mulatto children with the intent of taking them to Texas to sell. Neighbors followed the Yocums and rescued the woman and children in a gun battle in which several members of the Yocum gang were killed. The surviving Yocums then migrated to Texas.

That Yocums were definitely here in 1830 is attested by a letter from Matthew G. White, then *alcalde*, or mayor, of Liberty, to Stephen F. Austin. White informed Austin that "two certain men"—Thomas D. Yocum and a brother—who were wanted in Louisiana for various crimes, including the murder of a man and the theft of a "whole family of colored persons," had been burned out and driven across the Sabine. He said the men were now attempting to relocate in his district, and asked that Austin "afford us some clue . . . by which we may rid ourselves of such persons as are a great pest and annoyance to our settlement."

Thomas D. Yocum built an inn, or combination saloon and lodging house, near Pine Island Bayou, between Beaumont and Sour Lake. This inn stood right alongside the cattle trail to Louisiana.

Though it was illegal, Texas settlers drove longhorn cattle to Louisiana as early as 1825. There were literally thousands of the beasts. They were unbranded, they roamed at will, and they were extremely destructive to farmsteads and fields. The early settlers coming from the United States, not yet having adapted to cattle-raising as a way of making a living, were trying to farm—and these wild cattle were invading the fields and eating up the corn as fast as it sprouted.

In Texas the cattle were worthless. In Mexico they were worthless—Mexican *rancheros* had thousands of them. Across the Sabine in the United States, they were worth upwards of a dollar apiece, hard U.S. money—and there was very little hard money, United States or any other kind, in Texas. A herd of 500 to 1,000 head of these wild cattle, simply there for the taking, could make a man a fortune several times greater than one he could earn by farming over many a year.

Mexico, of course, had a law against it—but, then, Mexico had a law against anything that turned a profit for anyone but a government official, it seemed. Besides, there never was a Mexican law that couldn't be gotten around with some hard money, and hard money was what New Orleans paid. Law or no law, the cows went east—and the money came west.

As cattle drovers went eastward toward New Orleans they stopped and were warmly welcomed at Yocum's Inn. When they returned with money belts filled after selling their cattle, they stopped once more at Yocum's Inn—and were never seen again. In company with these mysterious disappearances, the Yocums acquired a fine stock of horses.

A slave girl named Turner's Lou—a slave's owner's name was always given first, in the possessive form—was a troublesome girl, and was often whipped for her misbehavior. One night, after being whipped, she ran away. Deep in the Big Thicket she came on Thomas D. Yocum—hiding gold coins in a small but sturdy brick vault built in the woods. The story goes that she was caught by Yocum, but after she swore never to tell about the vault, Yocum returned her to her owner for a reward.

Shortly afterward, an organ-grinder and his trained monkey appeared in the area. The monkey was wearing a green velvet suit and a red satin cap. When the organ-grinder cranked his instrument the monkey danced, then held out his cap for coins. The novelty filled the organ's coin box with money. A few days later, near the Yocum Inn, someone spotted the organ-grinder's old dappled-grey horse grazing in a field. A search of the area turned up a smashed crank organ and a blood-stained green velvet suit and red satin hat that were recognized as the monkey's. No bodies, though, were found.

Exactly how many people the Yocums might have robbed and murdered no one knows. Their downfall was sealed in 1841, when a man on a fine horse appeared at the Yocum Inn asking for directions. He was well-dressed, and allegedly wore a heavy gold watch and chain. Thomas D. Yocum agreed to ride with the man and show him the place he was hunting. A few hours later Yocum returned—leading the fine horse. Yocum's wife asked, "How much did he have?" When Yocum replied that the latest victim had only six bits on him, she said that any man who rode a horse like that, wore such fine clothes, carried a gold watch and chain, and had only had seventy-five cents in his pocket, certainly deserved to get killed. Another potential victim, staying at the hotel, overheard the conversation. He slipped out the back way and went to the local Regulators, an illegal but widespread vigilante group in the area.

In October of 1841, apparently the month of this last murder, a Regulator posse went to Yocum's Inn, ordered him and his family to pack up and quit the country, and then torched the building. Shortly after the family left, a black man who'd been a witness to some of the goings-on at Yocum's Inn showed the posse the bones of one victim in a well and the bones of another on the prairie. The posse then set out after the Yocums, catching up to them a day or so later. They shot Thomas D. Yocum, and might have killed more of the family.

At least one member—Christopher, Thomas D.'s son—was not killed. Christopher was known, locally, as the "good Yocum," though "good," in this case, might have been a relative thing. He was, at least, legally married to a young woman of fairly good family, and he had not been caught in any criminal acts or in possession of the fruits of a crime.

In 1842, Christopher Yocum returned to the Big Thicket country to get his wife. He was recognized and a mob began to form. The local law locked him in the Beaumont jailhouse to prevent a lynching. The effort failed. The next morning, Christopher Yocum was found hanged in his cell, a large square nail driven into the top of his head. No one was ever arrested or indicted for this murder.

Whether Turner's Lou was telling the truth when she told of having seen Thomas D. Yocum hiding money in a mysterious "brick vault" in the Big Thicket, or was simply spinning a yarn to avoid yet another whipping, no one knows. The Yocums weren't given the chance to recover any hidden loot, no gold was rumored to have been found in the burned inn, and no rumors claim that any great amount of money was found among their possessions after they were shot. Did Thomas D. Yocum really have a brick vault filled with bloodstained gold hidden deep in the pines and cypresses of the Big Thicket? If he did, no one's found it yet.

A LAKE CALLED "HAUNTED"

There are only three "natural" lakes in Texas. One—very well-known these days—is in northeast Texas. It's called New Caddo Lake today, at least by those of us old enough to remember when Old Caddo Lake, the original Caddo Lake—which was much larger than the present version—was only a memory. The original Caddo Lake can be called a natural artificial lake, and that's not a contradiction. Over across the Louisiana line on Cedar Bayou there was once a beaver dam. It wasn't a particularly large one, but in 1811, when the most powerful earthquake ever recorded to hit North America devastated the entire central portion of the continent, a great many trees were knocked down. A lot of these trees floated down Cedar Bayou and stopped at the beaver dam, and as a result a vast but shallow lake was formed over much of northwest Louisiana and northeast Texas. It lasted until 1874, when the U.S. Army Corps of Engineers dynamited the logjam and drained it.

A second lake, called Lost Lake or Hidden Lake, is actually a part of an underground river, the roofing cavern of which collapsed millennia ago. It's located in the Davis Mountains of far West Texas, and at one time—though the lake was only about a hundred yards long and thirty yards wide—it was renowned for the black bass to be caught in it.

The third is far less well-known. It lies in the brush country of South Texas, not far from the Nueces River. It is, in fact, a *resaca*—an oxbow lake formed in the bed of the old Nueces when the river—for one reason or another—changed its course millennia ago. It's spring-fed, which is what keeps water in it. It's called Espantosa Lake. Espantosa, as you might gather, is Spanish. It means haunted—but in a special way: "haunted by horrors," or something very like that.

I've long been fascinated with the story of Espantosa Lake. The problem with writing about it was, for a long time anything I wrote would be a mere rehash of J. Frank Dobie's stories in *Coronado's Children*. I needed a new angle on the story.

The story of Espantosa Lake holds that sometime very early—the exact date is not specified—a group of immigrants from Mexico camped on the banks of a small lake not mentioned by any guide and not found on their maps. The next party of immigrants found wagons and gear on the lake's banks, but no people and no animals. The wagons had not been burned or looted, as Indians would have done. The living things had simply disappeared. It was as though the earth had opened and swallowed them up.

Well, the lake was on early Spanish maps—as Lago de los Lagartos. Alligator Lake. Guides mentioned it—but mostly what they said was "stay away." Even before it got the name that means "horribly haunted," the lake near Crystal City had an evil reputation.

When the alligators left, no one knows, but it was probably between the late 1700s and early 1800s. As late as the 1740s and 1750s, Spanish explorers penetrated the limestone hills of Central Texas and described the banks of El Río de San Xavier—now the

South San Gabriel River—as being "black with alligators." By the time English-speaking explorers moved into the area, there were no alligators mentioned in their accounts of the San Gabriel. If the riverbanks had still been "black with alligators," as the Spaniards wrote a century earlier, surely somebody would have written something about it. Apparently, then, there was a severe drought or some exceptionally severe winters—or something equally devastating to alligators—between the 1740s and the 1840s, which killed off the alligators on the San Xavier/San Gabriel and at Lago de los Lagartos/Lago Espantosa as well.

One of the tales about Espantosa insists that at night, when the moon is full, you can hear the voices of women screaming in terror and the sounds of babies crying coming from the water. Both sounds have possible natural explanations.

Either through reading, or through personal, hair-raising experience, most people know that the scream of a hunting panther sounds almost exactly like the shriek of a woman in mortal pain or terror. (Truth told, it's probably not a hunting call—it's probably Mamma Panther in heat hollering, "Here I am, boys!")

The *brasada* of South Texas has long been home to what our old-time ancestors called "painters"—North American lions, also called panthers, pumas, cougars, catamounts, or mountain lions. They're still there, and there are more of them there—and in other places—than almost anybody suspects. Even if you've spent much of your life in the deer woods, it isn't likely that you've seen one—but it's dead certain that one or more have seen you. That's why you didn't see them.

Although it's less widely known, the wail of a beaver kitten, one that's lost or hungry or wants its mamma, sounds almost exactly like the crying of a human baby. Historically, there were beavers on the upper Nueces as late as the 1830s.

Less easy to explain is the ghost wagon of Espantosa Lake. As J. Frank Dobie tells the tale in *Coronado's Children*, a group of cowboys were camping alongside the trail leading from Espantosa Lake to a little store along the main road. They were out of tobacco—which was (and is) a plumb serious situation among cowmen. Worse, the little store didn't have any tobacco on hand and wouldn't have any until the supply wagon arrived—and it wasn't expected for a couple of days at least.

The first night the cowboys camped they heard, distinctly, the rattle of a wagon and the whuffling and clopping hooves of its horses going down the trail from the store toward the lake. They breathed a sigh of relief—the supply wagon had come early, and tomorrow the store would have tobacco. When they went to the store next morning they were told that no such wagon had arrived. What was worse, no one on the main road had seen or heard a wagon. The following night the cowboys again heard the distinct sounds of the wagon. One decided to step into the trail—though lined with heavy, tangled brush on both sides, it was brightly lit by an almost-full moon—and stop the driver to see if he had any tobacco he could spare. He stepped into the trail—and though he and all the rest of his companions could hear the wagon plainly, there was nothing visible in the moonlight. The brush was difficult to penetrate even afoot—for a wagon to crash through it was impossible. The wagon sounds grew louder with the approach until they abruptly stopped—at a point, by the sound, about twenty yards in front of the cowboy standing in the trail. There was a pause—and then they resumed behind him, slowly headed down the trail for the lake. The very familiar sounds of the wagon—sounds any cowboy knew well—were no less clear, says Dobie, than the thunder of the three vain shots from his Winchester the by-now-a-mite-jumpy cowboy threw after it.

Doubt this? Tell Albert H. Love of Seguin that you doubt it.

Back about 1930, Mr. Love camped on the banks of Espantosa Lake. Mr. Love, then about thirteen or fourteen, had a daddy who was a huntin' and a fishin' man. If you told him about water that might have fish in it, he went to find out. In the summer of 1930, his dad took the family to fish at Espantosa Lake. How his dad found out about Espantosa he doesn't recall—either a relative or a friend seems to have told him. They stopped at the little store on the main road, then went to the lake to camp. Almost at first sight, Mr. Love says, he felt "something's wrong with this place."

The water was still and almost black, but sweet, not stagnant. His dad intended to seine minnows for bait, and sent Albert out into the water with the end of the seine. They caught no minnows. The water was deep, Mr. Love says, up to his chest—and the large black water snakes that swam uncomfortably close kept him from keeping his mind on the job.

Almost as soon as they camped, the Loves had an unpleasant visitor—an old dun horse that had one shoulder almost eaten away by screwworms. You could see the bones working, picked clean of flesh, as the horse walked. They had no gun big enough to shoot it, but a two-rope temporary fence kept it out of camp.

They caught no fish. None at all. Young Albert took the .22 and went looking for squirrels in the trees around the lake, but he didn't find any. The place, except for the snakes and the dying horse, seemed bare of life.

That night, as he and his father slept, his mother heard what she described as "a bunch of horses" running toward camp. The sounds stopped abruptly, then resumed. When she told her husband the next morning, he said it was the wind in the cottonwoods—but the night was dead still. The next night Mrs. Love heard the same sounds of horses. The second night was as still as the first. The Loves didn't spend a third night on the banks of Espantosa. That fall, after he returned to school, Albert Love read J. Frank Dobie's newly published *Coronado's Children*—and read, for the first time, of the hauntings of Espantosa Lake.

Espantosa Lake is still there. Today, or so the locals claim, there may not be any alligators in the lake, but there are alligator gars of almost mythical size. Few people go there, and almost no one goes after dark. It's a spooky place, even in the daytime. Besides, the gars ate all the good fish, so why go? Or maybe there's a better reason—but they'd rather not talk about it.

THE MAN WHO BECAME JUDGE ROY BEAN

There was a feller in Langtry who got to messin' around with one of "those" women—the kind his mamma and pappa told him to stay away from. Eventually, as tends to happen in cases like that, she let daylight through him with a six-shooter and the hole wasn't worth patching. The local justice of the peace, acting in his capacity as coroner, was called to make a ruling on the cause of death.

"This here feller," he announced, "went and committed suicide, that's what he done. That's my rulin'," the J.P. said.

There happened to be a lawyer in the crowd. "Judge," he objected, "you can't rule suicide here! That woman shot him. This was murder."

"I kin an' I did. I tole that damfool if he kept messin' aroun' with that chippy he'd be committin' suicide, an' he kept messin' around with her, and by God he committed suicide. That-air's my rulin', an' that's the way she stands," the J.P. replied.

The J.P. in the story is, of course, the notorious Roy Bean, Law West of the Pecos. The story might or might not be true, but it is as likely to be true as any of the other "Roy Bean ruling" stories, and any number of them have historical documentation—like the ruling on a man found dead with a bullet hole between his eyes, where Bean ruled: "The deceased met death at the hands of a person unknown who was a helluva good pistol shot."

Who was this feller Roy Bean, anyway? Where did he come from? Where had he been and what had he done before he showed up at the little trackside town of Langtry, Texas, to pronounce himself justice of the peace and the "Law West of the Pecos"? Or did he just spring, fully grown and grey-bearded, pet bear and all, from the rocks and cacti of the Chihuahuan desert?

Phantly Roy Bean, Jr.—Fauntleroy Bean?—was born sometime between 1825 and 1830, in a small cabin alongside the Ohio River, in Mason County, Kentucky. His parents were Phantly Roy and Anna Bean, and he was the youngest of five children. His oldest brother, Joshua Bean, went west to California in 1845 to become the first Anglo mayor of San Diego and the major general commanding the California State Militia. He was murdered—assassinated, in fact—in 1852. The next oldest boy, Sam, became high sheriff of Doña Ana County, New Mexico, when Doña Ana County stretched from the present western border of the Texas Panhandle to the Gila River, which currently serves as the state line between Arizona and California. What became of sister Molly and brother James we have no immediate information. Yet, in spite of the older Bean boys' accomplishments, few people outside California or New Mexico even know there was but the one Bean—Judge Roy Bean, the Law West of the Pecos.

Sam Bean the elder—not to be confused with Sam Bean, Roy's son—went out to Californy with his big brother Josh in 1845, and three years later he returned to the Bean cabin on the Ohio. When he left to go west again he took baby brother Roy, somewhere between fifteen and twenty years old, with him. The brothers went into the freight-hauling business—wagons and mules—out of Santa Fe, New Mexico.

The Bean boys were, of course, nicknamed Los Frijoles by the locals, and both of them seem to have picked up a fair mastery of colloquial Spanish. For a time they freighted between Santa Fe and Chihuahua City. Unfortunately, a Chihuahua City badman decided to have some fun with Los Frijoles. Since Sam was known as a man with a hot temper and the sand to back it up, the bad-hat decided he'd pick on Roy.

It was a bad choice. Exactly how it happened, no one knows, but the badman wound up with a hole in his head—smack between his eyes—that hadn't been there when the argument started. It was probably a fair fight, but in the minds of the locals, the wrong man won it. The Beans left town at a high lope, heading for the United States. They got as far as a place called Jesús María, where the local folks caught up with them. There was a fight—involving not just the Beans but every other Anglo in town—with the result that all the Anglos in that part of Chihuahua had to pull freight for the other side of the Bravo.

All but one. Sam stayed behind. He had a girlfriend—a sixteen-year-old beauty named Petra Querquer. Her father was an old Mexican hand named Santiago Querquer. At least, that's how their names are spelled in Mexican records. We know Sam's daddy-in-law-to-be better as James Kirker, the most notorious and bloodiest of the Apache scalp-hunters.

Roy eventually reached California, where he found big brother Josh doing himself proud as San Diego's mayor and as a high muckety-muck in the militia. Even with brother Josh's local influence, it didn't take Roy long to get into trouble.

The trouble involved a Scotsman named Collins, who thought he was quite a pistol shot. Roy figured he was quite a pistol shot, too. Collins challenged Roy to a shooting match. Collins suggested that they fire from horses, moving at a gallop. Roy suggested that the targets be each other. The local folks loved the idea—it beat the local bullfights all hollow.

There was an immediate culture clash. Spanish custom not merely tolerated but encouraged dueling, and not just as a matter of settling personal differences, but as an art form. Americans—particularly Yankees, of which there was an oversupply in California—had long distrusted the *affaire d'honneur*, and ever since Aaron Burr put a richly deserved hole in Alex Hamilton's hide they'd been trying to ban it. The San Diego County high sheriff, a Mexican-born Hungarian named Agustin Haraszthy, merely insisted that if the boys were going to shoot one another, they should take precautions to make sure no bystander got hit with a wild shot.

The duel, as it turned out, was non-fatal. Roy hit Collins in the leg, then shot his horse from under him, and was on the verge of finishing the job when Sheriff Haraszthy stepped in and arrested both participants. Both were charged with attempted murder—of each other. Collins was also charged with challenging Bean to a duel—it was, after all, illegal—and Bean with accepting the challenge. Both were sent to jail in lieu of bonds of $1,000 each.

According to Major Horace Bell—whose source was Roy Bean—dozens of young women "stormed the jail" with basketsful of flowers, fine foods, wine, and cigars for Bean, but none, of course, for Collins. Apparently they brought him a little something else, too, because on March 6, 1852, Roy left the jail without benefit of key or legal release.

According to Major Bell, the lovelies brought Roy picks and shovels under their skirts, and he dug a tunnel to escape. Roy later claimed that he didn't need a pick and shovel—the jail was, after all, a public-contract job. He tunneled his way out with a tin cup and a pewter spoon. In San Diego they'll tell you he went out a window, aided by a half-dozen intoxicated Indians. In any case, Roy quit San Diego for less hostile climes—the Headquarters Saloon in San Gabriel, California (nine miles from Los Angeles), owned by Major General Joshua Bean of the California Militia, lately mayor of San Diego.

Josh, being a practical sort, decided that baby brother Roy should pull his weight. He put the lad in an apron, gave him a bungstarter, and put him behind the bar. It was the beginning of a lifelong career for Roy Bean—from then until the day he died, he was seldom far from a saloon, and when he was in one he was usually behind the bar, not in front of it.

In November of 1852, someone—quite possibly the nebulous and notorious *californio*, Joaquín Murieta—ambushed and assassinated General Josh Bean. Three men were eventually hanged—lynched is the more accurate word—for the murder, one of them an illiterate shoemaker named Cipriano Sandoval, but it was, and still is, believed that Joaquín was behind the murder if he didn't pull the trigger himself. The upshot was that Roy Bean, as only surviving available kin, inherited the Headquarters Saloon.

Roy remained in California for seven years or thereabouts, and the last glimpse we have of him there is through Horace Bell's writings. The year is 1854. Roy, in red-topped boots and a claw hammer coat, packing a silver-hilted bowie knife, was the prosperous and successful proprietor of the Headquarters Saloon. In late 1858 or early 1859, Roy turned up in Las Cruces, New Mexico, county seat of Doña Ana County. According to big brother Sam, who took him in, he had "barely enough clothes for decency and none to spare," and he was riding a rawboned, swaybacked, spavined, half-starved *rocinante* for a saddlehorse.

What happened to Bean's California prosperity, no one knows for sure. Roy, of course, had a tale. It involved a beautiful (naturally) Spanish girl who was deeply in love with the dashing *gringo* who owned the town's most prosperous saloon—one Roy Bean. The girl's parents, on the other hand, favored the suit of a former Mexican government official who was—of course—a coward, a dastard, and a poltroon, and besides he was too old for her and only after her money anyway. No doubt Roy had several more pejoratives to heap on the unfortunate suitor.

At any rate—according to Roy's story—the villain called Bean to the field of honor, having some nefarious plan to do in his rival, and got permanently plugged for his trouble. The deceased's friends then lynched Roy, who was saved because the rope was just long enough that he could balance himself on his toes to keep from strangling until the beauty appeared with a knife and cut him down. She provided him with a horse, they bade a passionately tearful farewell, knowing that they were parting forever—and here he was on Sam's doorstep.

We know for a fact that between 1854 and 1858 there was a small but severe depression in southern California, and a great many businesses went broke. That, serious historians insist, is what really happened to the Headquarters Saloon.

Be that as it may, oldtimers who knew Roy personally recalled that his neck was stiff for most of his life, to the point that he either couldn't turn his head or it was extremely painful for him to do so. He had the habit of cutting his eyes to look to the side rather than turning his head, which many folks said made him appear "shifty-eyed," when in fact he simply couldn't—or wouldn't, because it was painful—turn his head. Some who knew him very well testified that he bore a permanent scar—like a rope burn—on his neck, and that's why he always wore a high collar or a bandanna around his neck.

Sam was doing well in Las Cruces. Not only was he high sheriff of a county bigger than most eastern states, but he owned a general store/gambling house/saloon and a freighting business besides. He put little brother Roy to work behind the bar. There Roy Bean stayed until 1861.

The Bean brothers, being Kentuckians, favored the South. Roy insisted that he recruited and outfitted—at his own expense—a scout company he called the Free Rovers. The Free Rovers did in fact exist, and are recorded as a scout or spy company for General John Baylor's Texas Confederate troops in New Mexico. New Mexico historians refer to them not as the Free Rovers, but as the Forty Thieves.

As to how Roy actually financed the Forty Thieves, Sam had his own opinions. Sam, in addition to being sheriff and providing Las Cruces's sporting crowd a place to play, acted as the banker for the professionals. Each night the gamblers entrusted their operating capital to Sam's safe, retrieving it each morning. Roy, who was night barkeep, had the responsibility of seeing to it that all the gamblers' pokes were inside the store's safe and the safe was locked before he went home.

One morning Sam opened the safe and there was no money. There was also no Roy. Within a week the Forty Thieves began to ride. Sam had to make good to the gamblers, and relations between the brothers Bean were on the coolish side for several years thereafter.

By 1862, the Confederacy had lost any chance it ever had of controlling New Mexico Territory—which included both New Mexico and present-day Arizona—and Roy headed southeast to San Antonio. He acquired—by means probably best left unprobed—several dozen wagons and teams, and went into the extremely lucrative business of freighting cotton to Mexico. In later years, he used to brag that he lit his cigars with five-dollar bills in those flush times—but if he did, you can bet they were Confederate paper fivers. Bean was too canny a crook—even then—to burn money that had any real value.

In 1863, Pat Milmo, an Irish storekeeper in San Antonio, hired Roy Bean to take some cotton—either forty bales or forty wagonloads of bales, depending on which version you believe—to Mexico for him. Milmo's brother Dan, the son-in-law of the governor of Coahuila, would then pick up the cotton in Eagle Pass, pay Roy the freight charges, see to it the cotton got across, and ship it to

Vera Cruz to be transshipped to Europe and sold. Roy took his wagons to Harrisburg (now part of Houston), loaded the cotton, and freighted it to Eagle Pass as per contract.

The Milmo brothers' agent in Eagle Pass insisted he'd never heard of Roy Bean and knew nothing about any cotton Pat Milmo was having freighted from Texas. Roy was kept waiting for thirteen days until someone who knew about the arrangement showed up from the interior and authorized the unloading of the cotton. Roy was then paid—but only the contract price for carrying the cotton. The Milmo agent did not offer anything for the thirteen days of delay.

That made Roy mad. As soon as his wagons were empty he loaded up all the Milmo-owned equipment and supplies he could find and left town, selling the stuff on the way back to San Antonio.

This, of course, annoyed the Milmos. They immediately began trying to prosecute Roy for theft or to sue him for damages or whatever they could do to recover the value of what he took. Finally, in the fall of 1866, after the courts in San Antonio were run by the Union Army, Pat Milmo sued Roy in civil court for $350.

Roy instantly countersued—for $2,000. He insisted that the Milmos had kept him waiting from December 28, 1863, until January 10, 1864, tying up 8 wagons, 180 mules, and 13 employees for thirteen days, which had a value of $12 per wagon per day, for a total of $156 per day, or $2,028.

The Milmos were beaten. Pat Milmo tried to have civil authorities attach $350 worth of Roy's property, but the simple truth was, Roy didn't have $350 worth of property to seize. Milmo gave up, and Roy didn't pursue his suit any farther.

Roy had wagons, but—being Roy Bean—he hadn't paid for them. In March of 1866, Julien Romain and Rafael Quintana, who had financed Roy's venture into the hauling business, seized eight of his wagons for nonpayment of debts. They seized the wagons in March, held them until August—during which time Roy made no effort to pay his debt on them—and then began to sell them. They sold four. Roy then calmly went to the wagonyard, hitched up the other four, and took off for parts unknown. The wagons were never returned. Romain and Quintana sued Bean for $304, but—though the case was still supposedly under litigation as late as 1870—they got nothing.

Sometime in late 1866, Roy moved into a small house on the banks of San Pedro Creek in San Antonio. It's still there. A lawyer lives in it these days.

Trouble was, Roy didn't own the house—a man named Lively did. Somehow Roy neglected to mention to Mr. Lively that he was living in the house, and of course he never paid any rent on it. Subsequently, a Mr. Wells made Mr. Lively an offer on the property, which Lively accepted. When Wells arrived to take possession, he found Roy Bean living in the house—and Roy insisted it was his and not Lively's at all. Wells and Lively took Roy to court, got an order to vacate, and a judgment against Bean for sixty-four dollars. Bean not only didn't move out, he didn't pay the sixty-four dollars. He also went to district court with a deed of some variety, causing both Mr. Lively and the judge who'd ordered him out no end of trouble when they were required to explain themselves. The deed, of course, was phony, but Roy claimed—naturally—that he'd bought the house in good faith from a person representing himself as Mr. Lively's agent.

Roy finally agreed to move out if Lively would pay his expenses and throw in a jug of whiskey. He then sold Wells his freighting business for $3,000 cash and took up residence on South Flores Street in San Antonio, an area that rapidly became known as—and is still known as—Beanville. There he remained for sixteen years.

In Beanville, Roy took a wife. He was at least thirty-six, possibly as old as forty-one. He was thick of body, coarse of manner—and possessed of $3,000 cash. At least this latter seems to have appealed to Señor Leandro M. Chávez, who owned a sizable ranch not far from Beanville. Why a descendant of the Canary Islanders would be interested in having a daughter marry someone like Roy Bean one has to wonder, but it is cold fact that on October 28, 1866, Señorita María Anastasia Virginia Chávez became Mrs. Roy Bean.

It was apparently a stormy marriage, for eight months later Virginia Chávez de Bean filed charges on her husband, who she alleged "the life of a human being (hers) did seriously threaten to take. . . ." Roy succeeded in getting a change of venue to Boerne, and in December of 1868 the charge was dismissed.

It wasn't the only time Virginia went home to Mamma. According to at least one legend, Roy came home late at night to find her asleep instead of waiting on him. He grabbed a blazing stick from the fire, jerked the covers off the sleeping girl, and applied it to her bare backside. She ran home screaming and filed on him for felonious assault. Supposedly this went to court, and Bean's lawyer caused the case for the prosecution to fall apart by requesting that the judge order the accuser to present proof of her supposed injuries by showing the jury the scars. The damage must not have been permanent, however, because about a year later Roy Bean, Jr., was born—the first of several young Beans.

Roy engaged in the wood business in San Antonio. The freight line of Wicks and Hickman owned most of the wooded area around Beanville, and—since Roy occasionally did a little (very little) work for Wicks and Hickman—they asked him to keep an eye on their woodlots and keep people from stealing wood. This Roy did—mostly by stealing wood from Wicks and Hickman himself. He was so enthusiastic a protector of Wicks and Hickman's property that for almost two years he held an exclusive contract with the George Holmgreen & Sons ironworks to supply their furnaces with wood.

Not all of the wood came from Wicks and Hickman property. Roy got chased out of several other folks' woodlots, and this gave him an idea. There were a lot of charcoal-burners in the area, and Roy knew they were occasionally poaching on woodlots—both Wicks and Hickman's and others. He set himself up as the Beanville woodlot police, and when he found charcoal-burners—most of whom were Mexican—coming out of either "his" woodlot or one he'd been chased out of, he "confiscated" their wagonloads of wood and sold them to Holmgreen. He got so good at it that the poaching charcoal-burners were paying him off at two bits a load not to confiscate their loads of wood—when he had no right to any of the wood and he had, in fact, been run off the very woodlots they were poaching.

Somewhere along the line Roy acquired legal title to a shack and two city lots. An Atascosa County man wanted the property and offered to swap thirty milk cows for it. Roy agreed—if, of course, the cows proved healthy and good milkers.

The swap was made, Roy milked the cows and sold the milk—and never fed the cows. They got weak, sickened, and died. When the Atascosa County man came to take possession of the property, Roy refused to surrender it. The cows, he insisted, had up and died on him, which meant the Atascosa County man had tried to cheat him by attempting to swap diseased cows for good property.

After the dairy business ended, Bean went into the beef business—other people's beef, of course. He stole and butchered unbranded cattle on other folks' land, and either peddled the meat door-to-door or sold it from his combination shack, saloon, and store in Beanville. At one time he had a standing offer of five dollars to any boy who would bring him a "stray" horse or cow, so long as the stray was unbranded. The horses he sold; the cattle he butchered.

When all else failed, Bean got back into the freighting business. Using his own wagons or other people's, he hauled freight from

San Antonio south and west, as far away as Chihuahua City and El Paso. It wasn't long before he quit hauling into Mexico, though, saying, "My horse don't like the water there." An unprovable—but very probable—story has him being smuggled out of Chihuahua City under a load of cowhides after a killing.

In 1872, a Mexican freighter named Anastacio González camped near Howard's Well, in what is now Pecos County. Near the well was an encampment of U.S. soldiers, commonly called Fort Howard, though it was not even a permanent encampment. Roy Bean's wagons were also camped near Howard's Well, and Roy himself was at Fort Howard, enjoying army hospitality. Just about dawn somebody looked up and reported a large fire blazing up near the well. Everybody quieted down—and heard the unmistakable pop of rifles in the early-morning stillness. "Indians!" Roy yelled, jumping on his horse and heading for his wagons.

With typical Bean luck, Roy's wagons were unraided. González and eight of his men were murdered, their wagons looted and burned, their mules stolen. Just after daybreak, a man and a woman turned up at Roy's camp. They had survived the massacre, but were very reluctant to talk about how they'd survived it until they discovered that everybody in González's camp had been killed.

The man was González's mule wrangler—and the person who was supposed to have been on guard. The woman was the wife of one of the muleskinners. They'd slipped off from camp together just before dawn to do what men and women who slip off from camp together just before dawn do—and while they were in the process of doing it, the Indians killed everybody but them. Roy ordered the woman into his wagon—and turned the unfortunate muleskinner loose on the prairie to make his way to the soldier camp the best way he could.

By 1880, Roy was pretty well down-and-out in San Antonio. He had no money and—since most of San Antonio had grown wise to his schemes—he had no way of cheating anyone out of any money. He also had virtually no freighting equipment left, for Roy never maintained his equipment and was famous for working horses to death and never feeding them. He wanted to leave—but how? It would take money to move.

Into the picture stepped T. E. "Ted" Conner. Conner had the most successful business in Beanville—a store and wagonyard—and was known, unofficially, as "the mayor of Beanville." He didn't mind Roy Bean, but his wife did. She was a Yankee, and—frankly—Bean scared the life out of her. She wanted to be rid of him—quickly and permanently. She offered to have her husband buy him out.

Strangely enough, Bean balked. He might be broke and on his last legs in Beanville, but he was in Beanville—the place named for Roy Bean. It was "his" town, and as long as he was the "Bean" of "Beanville," he was a man of at least *some* distinction, if of little *but* distinction. As sure as he left, he told her, she'd change the name of it to "Connersville."

It was not until Mrs. Conner personally promised Bean that the place would remain Beanville and she would even use Beanville as a return address on her mail, that Roy agreed to sell out. The Conners got everything Roy Bean owned for $900 cash.

Roy Bean invested the $900 in a wagon, a team, a tent, some barrels of whiskey, and some firearms. He put his children in the care of Mr. and Mrs. Simon Fest, Jr., of San Antonio and headed westward along the Galveston, Harrisburg, and San Antonio Railroad line for end-of-track. It was his intent to establish a moving saloon that would follow end-of-track as it moved.

Bean first settled at the camp of Vinegaroon, a place once described as "so quiet we haven't had a killing in four hours." He established his saloon there, and when the tracks moved, so did he—to Eagle's Nest Camp, shortly renamed Langtry. The rest of the story is available any number of places, usually entitled "Judge Roy Bean."

THE SILVER AT LOCKHART

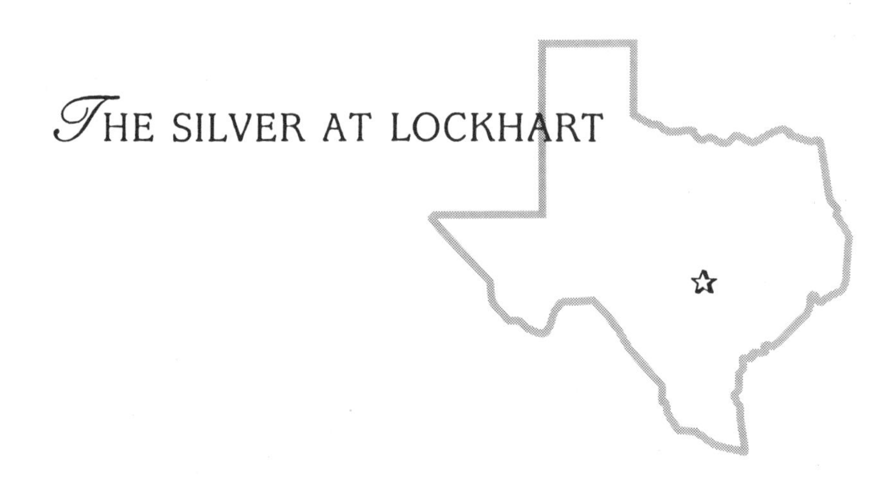

If Lockhart, Texas, seems a strange place to hold legends of buried wealth, it is. To no one's knowledge has any great mineral wealth—other than oil—come out of the ground around Lockhart, and there are certainly no legends of lost mines there. There is, however, the tale of a wagonload of silver—coins, plate, cutlery, candlesticks, what-have-you.

The years immediately prior to the War between the States (which I refuse to call the American Civil War because that would endorse the North's definition of a nation) were not pleasant ones in Texas. Virtually all memoirs of the era, written about that part of Texas that lies west of the Colorado River, are filled with accounts of Indian raids, murders, thievery, and kidnappings. It was during this period—and the period immediately after the war, which was just as unsettled—that two of Texas's most celebrated Indian captives met their fates. Herman Lehmann was taken by Comanches, and Frank Buckelew was captured by the Lipan-Apaches.

For the record, and for those who read Lehmann's memoirs, old Herman had a bad habit of making up stories if he didn't know the answer to a question. When he was asked how the Comanches made their flint arrowheads, he told the questioners that the Comanches heated flint flakes, then dripped water on them to cause the flint to flake away. For several generations this was repeated in Texas schools as gospel—after all, Herman Lehmann said it, and he was there.

By the time Lehmann was taken by the Indians, the Comanches had all but given up using flint arrowheads. They either traded for ready-made strap-iron arrowheads, or traded for or stole pieces of strap iron—barrel hoops were a favorite—to make their own iron arrowheads. In a point the movies nearly always miss, anytime the Comanches found a barrel when they raided, they immediately smashed it and pulled the hoops off.

It took a long time before anyone tested Herman's way of making arrowheads, and when they finally did, they made a discovery— if you drop cold water on a hot piece of flint rock, it doesn't flake neatly. It explodes! You wind up picking flint flakes out of your hands and belly. We now know, of course, that the Comanches—like every other primitive people worldwide who used flint for projectile points—shaped the initial flakes by percussion (a good whack with a hammer-stone) and then finished the flake into an arrowhead by pressure-flaking the sides.

Herman's memoirs make excellent reading if you realize that on anything technical—like "how to make arrowheads"—he was likely to use his overactive imagination. Buckelew's memoirs are much better, and since he was the only captive ever taken by the Lipans who actually lived among them for a time and then managed to return to his own people, his memoirs are the only actual eyewitness record we have of the customs of the Lipans.

Now, the Indians in this story are alleged to be Comanches—the same tribe who captured Herman Lehmann—but if they were, they were almighty peculiar Comanches. Bear in mind, though, that to a Texian of the 1850s, any horseback Indian of hostile demeanor was a Comanche until proved otherwise.

Allegedly, they swept down from the north, raiding, burning, stealing, killing, and kidnapping as they came. They seem to have been about twenty in number, which—frankly—is an awfully small war party for the Comanches. Comanches tended to raid in big numbers—50 to 200—though they did occasionally split up into small groups to strike many locations at once.

This bunch apparently picked up a wagon somewhere in which to carry their plunder, and that's very un-Comanche. The Comanches despised wheeled vehicles—they were too slow. Besides, they could be tracked easily by pursuers, which a Comanche didn't like at all.

According to the story, the wagon was loaded with plundered silver. Why Comanches would take silver is anybody's guess, and any guess is probably going to be wrong. A Comanche might take a few coins to hammer out flat so he could make ornaments of them and a few more to swap to the bootlegger for some firewater, but Comanches really had no use for the sort of stuff the story says was in the wagon—not just coins, but silver tea services, silver cutlery, candlesticks, and what all else one might imagine.

In or on the edge of Lockhart, they kidnapped a white woman, then turned south to follow the east bank of Clear Fork Creek, which lay about two miles west of the pre-1860 limits of Lockhart. Local men immediately took up the pursuit, and—finding the wagonload of silver too heavy to move fast—the Indians unhitched the horses, overturned the wagon into Clear Fork Creek, dumped the silver, set the wagon back upright along the creekbank, and continued their flight south.

The pursuers from Lockhart saw the silver being dumped and passed the empty wagon, but continued the chase. At a point about seven and a half miles southwest of Lockhart, approaching

Round Top Mountain, the Indian carrying the woman simply knocked her in the head with his tomahawk and dumped her body. The Comanches then disappeared into the steep valleys, broken hills, and brush that surrounded Round Top.

The pursuers gave up the chase, returned to the woman, and carried her body almost to Lockhart, where they buried her. Years later, when the Lockhart-to-Prairie Lea road was laid out, it passed very close to the grave. As late as the 1950s—and perhaps even now—a mound of rocks said to mark the grave of the woman killed by Indians lay about a mile and a half out of old Lockhart on the Prairie Lea road.

So the story goes, it was then nearly night, so the men from Lockhart didn't return to seek the treasure the Indians abandoned in Clear Fork Creek until the next day. When they did return they found the wagon—but no silver. The pursuers, though, insisted that they did in fact see the silver dumped into the creek, and some of them lived into the early years of the twentieth century, still insisting that they'd seen the silver. Clear Fork Creek has been probed, dredged, and seined, but no trace of the silver has ever been found.

Local legend diverges here—one group insists that the Indians slipped back by night and recovered the treasure, while another group insists that the silver sank into the boggy bottom of the creek and remains to be found. What *nobody* seems to have commented on is the fact that these were about the most un-Indian-acting Indians ever to raid anywhere in Texas. Using a wagon. Plundering for silver. And taking the time to unhitch the horse and dump the silver. Indians didn't, as a rule, do that sort of thing—they didn't like to lose time when they were being chased, and if they had anything to drop that they felt would delay the pursuers, they left it in plain sight.

All of which leads to this: these fellers might have been dressed like Indians, but they acted like white-men bandits. There's almost nothing in their behavior—except the murder of the captive—that says "Indian." Even that could be doubtful—if the woman could identify them as white men rather than Indians, a white-man bandit would have no more qualms about murder than a marauding Comanche, and a great deal better reason for it.

There's no question, apparently, that the incident happened. The question is the identity of the raiders. If they were in fact Comanches—or any Indian tribe—they were the white-man-bandit-actingest Indians ever to raid in Texas.

*H*OW ELGIN GOT ITS NAME

In Bastrop County, just over the Travis County line on the old Houston highway, there's a little town called Elgin. Note that name—E-L-G-I-N. There's a watch by that name, and you pronounce the name of that watch "Eljin," with a soft *g* sound. There are also a couple of towns in other states—one in Ohio that I know of in particular—that have the same name. They're also pronounced "Eljin."

Elgin, Texas, is pronounced "Elgin." With a hard *g*. Like in "gun."

Why is the town pronounced with a hard *g*, while every other Elgin is pronounced "Eljin"?

So the story goes, the name of the town wasn't, originally, going to be "Elgin." It was going to be "Helgin." The United States Post Office, though, turned down "Helgin" but approved "Elgin," so the townsfolk kept the distinctive pronunciation to indicate that there was something different about their little town.

Why Helgin? There are those—those disreputable members of the Shadetree Historical Society who tell stories like they oughta be told 'stead of like the little ol' ladies want 'em told—who insist that Helgin came from Hellagin, and the place was actually named for a sandy hill to the east of town, along the railroad tracks, which is called—to this day—Hellagin Hill.

That self-same Shadetree Historical Society claims there was once a cowman who had large holdings east of where Elgin now stands. His name may have been I. Prentice "Print" Olive, but that's not for sure. Whoever he was, he was a man of strong convictions, and one of those convictions was that his land was his and nobody, by God, better mess with him on it.

Unfortunately, he did get messed with—by the Houston & Texas Central Railroad, which built westward from Houston in the 1870s. It either crossed his land or ran along the edge of it, and it ran right alongside a nameless sandy mound.

Somehow, our cowman became convinced that the H&TC's "steam cars" were doing him harm. Likely he lost some cows to it. That thing which railroad people call a "pilot" on the front of the steam engine—which most of us who grew up when engines were big and black and puffed smoke and steam still call a "cowcatcher"—wasn't there for decoration. Cattle wandered onto railroad tracks. Sometimes they wandered off. Sometimes they were converted to hamburger by a Baldwin 4-4-0 before they got the chance. In addition, the sounds of the puffing, snorting steam engines, the long, lonesome wail of the whistles, and the rattling and banging of a train of cars frightened animals—cattle, horses, or what have you.

"That train," he said—or so folks say he said, "has got to go." He decided to chase the railroad away.

Chasing a railroad away isn't all that easy. Railroads have investments in land and tracks and roadbeds, and they're reluctant to abandon them. The cowman got nowhere in his first attempts to chase them stinkin', snortin' steam cars somewheres else.

Then he got an idea. He got two of his cowboys—both of 'em pretty good shots—and armed each one with a Winchester repeater that shot fifteen times. He also bought 'em a couple of cases of cartridges. "You boys," he told 'em, "yawl go get on 'at li'l ol' sandy rise 'longside 'em tracks, an' ever' time one 'nem railroad trains comes by, yawl shoot out ever' winder-light an' piece a glass in 'er. 'At'll larn 'em 'bout skeerin' mah cows."

And, so the story goes, that's exactly what they did. The two cowboys with their Winchesters—and all the ammunition they could carry—stationed themselves atop the sandy hill, and every time a train came by, they cut loose.

It didn't take the railroaders long to realize what was happening, and since the train couldn't take an alternate road, as soon as the engineer saw the sandy rise coming up through the post oaks, he gave a series of short blasts on the whistle, which is the standard alarm signal for a train. The conductor and brakeman then ran through the passenger cars yelling, "Ev'body lay down on the floor, we fixin' to have Hell agin!" Before long, the train crews began to call the sandy rise "Hell Agin Hill."

How long this went on is anybody's guess, but the railroad tracks are still there and the cowman isn't, so it's pretty obvious who finally won. When the railroad built a switch and a siding near Hell Agin Hill, a station and finally a small town grew up around it. Eventually, so they say, the town needed a name, so the folks suggested Hellagin, from Hell Agin Hill. That was rejected, as was the subsequently suggested "Helgin." When the postmaster general approved "Elgin," the townsfolk kept the hard *g* pronunciation as a reminder of the unique source of their town's name.

That's the story the Shadetree Historical Society tells. It definitely isn't the one the official histories tell, and it isn't the one you'll hear from the li'l ol' ladies of the garden club. What they'll tell you—almost invariably—is that the town was named for a Mister Elgin. Somehow, though, they've never gotten his first name straight—I've heard Tom, Bob, Jim, and Raymond—nor have they ever gotten straight who Mister Elgin worked for. I've been told he worked for the railroad, the post office, the telegraph company, and an express company. Officially, I believe, his name was Robert Elgin and he was an official with the H&TC.

Now—who do I believe?

When Roy Bean, later to achieve notoriety as "Judge Roy Bean, Law West of the Pecos," lived in San Antonio, he once had a dairy of sorts. He sold milk door-to-door from large cans on a mule-wagon, and there were those who insisted that Roy had a bad habit, when the milk supply ran low, of stopping at the San Antonio River and "stretching" the supply a mite. When one of his customers actually found an eight-inch catfish in the milk, he confronted Roy with the evidence.

"Well, I swan," said Bean. "I'm gonna have to quit waterin' 'em cows in 'at-air San Antone River. Looky thar—one of 'em done went an' swallered a catfish."

Forty years ago or so you could climb to the top of the sandy rise that's still called Hellagin Hill, and with a minimum of scraping around in the sand, fill the entire crown of a size 6 7/8 pima straw dime-store cowboy hat with empty .44 Winchester shells. I know. I did. I sure don't think they got there because a cow swallowed them.

Gone Like Lottie's Eye

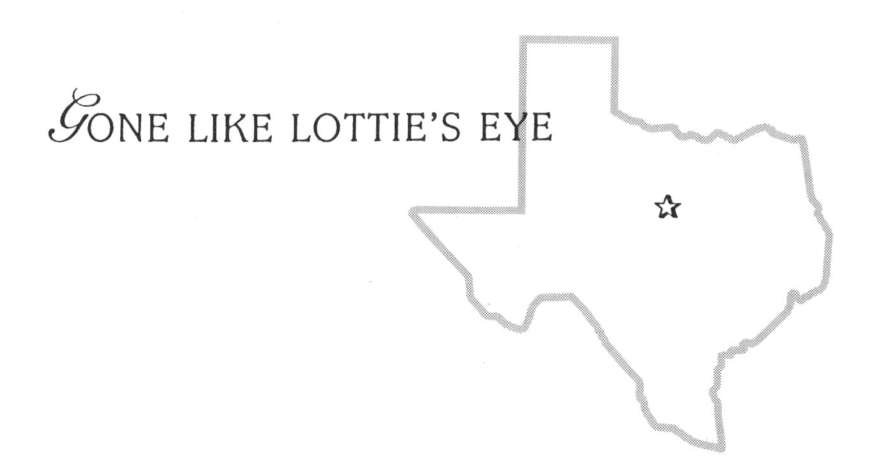

She swept into the Flat, and it took one heckuva strange sort of feller not to notice her. She was tall for a woman—statuesque, they call it—red-haired, and nothing short of gorgeous. She gave her name as Lottie Deno.

Fort Griffin sat high on Government Hill above the upper Brazos, between present-day Albany and Throckmorton. The Flat—also known as Fort Griffin Flat or Hidetown—was on the riverbank below it. If you ever go there and look, you'll see why it was called the Flat. Between the foot of Government Hill and the Brazos, about half a mile to the north, the ground is so flat if you dropped a marble it'd lose its mind trying to decide which way to roll.

The Flat was first founded to supply the soldiers of Fort Griffin with those things the Army didn't issue—rotgut liquor, an opportunity to lose their meager thirteen dollars a month pay to gamblers, and the solace of women who had "gone to the dogs"—that is, to the soldiers. It wasn't much to begin with and never got much better—a collection of wooden shacks, some of them permanently roofed but others simply topped with canvas, which contained saloons, brothels, and shops selling overpriced gewgaws that competed for the soldier's dollars.

Then came the buffalo hunters. For a short period—less than ten years—a man could, if not get rich, certainly make a better than average living by shooting buffalo for their hides. Hides by the literal millions were shipped east, as the boom of Sharps, Remington, and Springfield rifles all but exterminated the North American plains bison. Why?

Well, some say Uncle Sam wanted it that way. Some even go so far as to point to a speech made by General Phil Sheridan to the Texas legislature, in which he praised the buffalo slaughter for being more effective than the army in bringing the Plains Indians to heel. There's just one problem with that—Phil Sheridan never made that speech.

The Texas Congress and legislature kept track—and still keeps track—of every outside speaker who ever spoke to either House or to both Houses in joint session, the date of the speech, and the subject the speaker elaborates on. The records are complete from 1836 to the present. Phil Sheridan's name isn't there—and there are also no reports in Austin newspapers that he made such a speech to a civic group. He probably believed that way, but the "smoking gun" of buffalo extermination as an official policy of the United States government—Major General Phillip H. Sheridan's speech to the Texas legislature acknowledging the policy at least semi-officially—unlike the actual guns of the buffalo slaughter, smokes only in myth.

With the rise of the lucrative but short-lived trade in buffalo hides, the Flat became a thriving metropolis where millions of "flint," or untanned hides, were sold to buyers for tanneries in the eastern United States. There was, for a short time, money—a great deal of money—to be made in Hidetown. Who paid it?

Buffalo-hide leather, frankly, wasn't much good for what you need leather for. There were only so many buffalo robes and buffalo coats to be sold, and there were only a few thousand Concord coaches—which used buffalo-leather "thoroughbraces" for springs—ever made. However, the very properties that made buffalo leather useless for most purposes—the fact that it was thick, spongy, and elastic—made it ideal for one purpose: there was not a single other material available that made better drive belts for machinery than buffalo hide. The entire eastern United States and all of western Europe rode into the machine age propelled by buffalo-hide drive belts.

Into the Flat, shortly after the buffalo men, came the woman who gave her name as Lottie Deno—but she didn't come to make her living on her back, as did most of the women who came to Hidetown. By no means. Lottie came to make her way at the card tables. She was a poker player. And according to at least some of those who played with her and lost, she might have had the face of an angel, but she had ice water in her veins.

Lottie was deadly—a cutthroat at the poker table who asked no quarter and offered none. Doc Holliday is said to have played against her; Wyatt Earp might have tried his hand; even young Bat Masterson certainly saw the gorgeous redhead, if he didn't try his luck with her. They were all there when she was.

When you tried your luck with Lottie, you tried it only one way—at cards. There is absolutely no record or rumor that any man ever got lucky with Lottie any other way, and it seems precious few ever got lucky with the pasteboards. Lottie amassed something of a fortune at the poker tables of Fort Griffin Flat.

Who was she? Nobody knew then—and nobody knows now. It was as if she was suddenly born, fully mature and with the skills of a cutthroat gambler, on the stagecoach coming in. Not that there aren't rumors enough—she was the widow of a murdered gambler, the wife of an army officer ruined by drink or gambling, the daughter of a rich man destroyed by ill fortune. But of certain knowledge there is none whatever. Gorgeous Lottie Deno just appeared in Fort Griffin Flat, rented a shack to live in, sat down at the poker tables, and started winning money.

Ice water in her veins? That's what the men who gambled with her believed. In the midst of a game, lead started to fly. The seasoned gamblers hit the floor. When they peered over the edge of the table to see if the shooting was over, there sat Lottie, not a single flame-red hair out of place, not a speck of dust on her dress. "Gentlemen," she is supposed to have said, "I came to play poker, not to roll around on the floor."

She was dealing during another fight, when someone flung a spittoon. The heavy object struck Lottie in the side of the head, knocking her unconscious and onto the floor. When she was brought to by the anxious gamblers, she resumed her place at the poker table and started dealing again. It was not for several hours that anyone learned that the blow from the spittoon had cost her the sight in one eye. It gave rise to an expression—"Gone like Lottie's eye"—that you'll still hear occasionally in West Texas.

Then one day she didn't turn up at her usual table. After a while, the owners of the saloon where she dealt, fearing foul play, went to the shack she'd rented. Inside, pinned to the bedclothes, they found a note telling them to sell the contents of the shack and give the money to poor children to buy food and clothing. That was all. No "Good bye, it's been fun," no "I've done what I came to do and I'm going home," no nothing. Lottie Deno was simply gone—she'd vanished as mysteriously as she came.

Nor did she ever turn up elsewhere. To this day, no positive trace of the woman known as Lottie Deno has ever been found. It was as if she'd vanished from the face of the earth—just as it seemed she'd suddenly appeared on earth one morning with a deck of cards in her hand.

Who was Lottie Deno? Where did she come from? Where did she go? Why did she come to Fort Griffin Flat? Where did she learn to play poker like a cutthroat? What happened to the money she won? WHO WAS SHE? In nearly a hundred and twenty years, nobody's answered a single one of those questions. All we know for sure is that one morning a gorgeous redhead who could handle cards with the best of 'em turned up at Fort Griffin Flat, and one night she left—and left the mysterious legend of the vanishing gorgeous gamblin' gal of Griffin behind her.

WHO WAS JOHN WESLEY HARDIN, ANYWAY—AND WHY DO FOLKS SAY SUCH AWFUL THINGS ABOUT HIM?

"That feller Wes Hardin, one time he up an' shot a feller—just 'cause the pore feller was a-snorin' too loud to suit him."

John Wesley Hardin did, in fact, kill at least forty-two men and possibly as many as fifty-one, depending on who's doing the counting. Out of the forty-two known and historically documented killings, only one could not have been considered, by the standards of nineteenth century Texas, a "fair fight"—both men armed and facing one another, either a known quarrel between them or one openly threatened the other, and one or both had previously announced the intention of killing the other. It was usually, in the latter case, a situation in which the other feller announced he'd "come to kill Wes Hardin" and didn't quite turn out to be the man-killer he thought he was. In spite of the "snoring" tale—still being perpetuated by Time-Life in television advertisements for its American West books—Wes never in his life shot anyone "for snoring too loud."

John Wesley Hardin was born May 26, 1853, in Bonham, Texas, and grew up in Trinity County, Texas. His parents were

John G. Hardin, a lawyer, schoolteacher, and Methodist minister, and Elizabeth Dixon Hardin. He is known to have had two brothers: Joseph G. Hardin (his middle name may have been Gibson) and Jeff Davis Hardin, (obviously born during the War between the States). John Wesley, the oldest son, was named by his preacher father for the founder of the Methodist church. So far as is known, there were no girls born to John and Elizabeth Hardin.

John Wesley Hardin was related to a number of families in the De Witt County area, among them his mother's people, the Dixons, as well as the Clementses, Dowlearns, and Taylors. Those families formed the nucleus, around the Taylors, of one side of Texas's most famous feud, the Sutton-Taylor Feud or De Witt County War.

There are anywhere from several to a couple of hundred stories about how the De Witt County War got started, and some folks can tell two or three or even more, depending on who's listening and how much the teller has to drink before starting the story. This is the story I heard. If you've heard another, it's probably as close to right as this one, or at least neither closer to nor farther from the facts.

After the War, East Texas was shy on saddlehorses. The Confederate government "requisitioned" so many saddlehorses between 1861 and 1865 that most of the state east of the Brazos—and not a small part of it west of that river—was virtually afoot. A man who had horses for sale could just about name his own price—quite often in hard money—for his animals. They didn't have to be "good" horses, either—horses with bloodlines going back to the horse Adam rode. All they needed was a leg on each corner and the ability to get to town and back without dropping over dead.

William "Buck" Taylor made up a herd of semi-broke range horses to take east and sell for hard money. A neighbor, William

"Bill" Sutton, asked Taylor to take along five or six spare horses he happened to have on hand and sell them, too. Buck agreed.

Taylor was selling horses in the vicinity of Marlin when the high sheriff showed up and clapped him in irons. It seems some of Buck's horses—specifically identified as the ones he got from Bill Sutton—had been positively identified by their legal owners as stolen from near Marlin in the not-distant past.

How Buck got out of the Marlin jailhouse I don't know—my informant sort of glossed over that part—but when he got back to De Witt County he was foaming at the mouth. He went all over De Witt County naming Bill Sutton as a "damned horse thief." As a result, on Christmas Eve, 1868, Bill Sutton and one or more of his family or friends ambushed Buck Taylor and his close friend Dick Chisholm in Clinton (then the county seat of De Witt) and murdered both of them.

Apparently the Taylors went to the law, but the law was unable to get an indictment against Sutton and his party. Friends and relatives of the Taylors, though, weren't quiet about their feelings for the Suttons and their friends. One of the loudest was a Karnes County rancher named Crockett Schoate. In August of 1869, a party of men, Bill Sutton among them, murdered Schoate at his home. Shortly afterwards, they also murdered Mart Taylor and his father-in-law, Dave Morris.

Bill Sutton tanked up on busthead and raised a ruckus in Hallettsville, not far from Clinton. Henry Kelly, whose wife was a Taylor, was deputized to help arrest him. Within a few weeks, Henry Kelly and his brother were arrested by Jack Helms, a De Witt County deputy sheriff and a known Sutton partisan. (Helms later became a captain in the hated "Davis Police.") Although the Kelly brothers were charged with disorderly conduct—certainly never a capital offense in Texas, or we'd be without either a state government or the sport of football—both were shot and killed by Helms and his posse while "trying to escape."

Pitkin Taylor, whose daughters had married the Kelly brothers, went to the law about the murders. Shortly afterwards, in the middle of the night, Pitkin heard a cowbell in his corn patch. He went out in his nightshirt and unarmed, thinking one of his cows was in the corn. Hidden gunmen, believed—with good reason—to be Suttons or Sutton partisans, shot him down on his front porch.

Young Jim Taylor, Pitkin's twenty-year-old son, vowed on his father's open grave that he'd "wash my hands in old Bill Sutton's blood," and the war was on. He gathered his kin—Bud Dowlearn, Scrap Taylor, Al Day, Bill Taylor, Wes Hardin, and others—and went on the hunt for Suttons and Sutton partisans. The Taylor party was six killings behind and determined to make up the difference.

Apparently Wes's first killing was caused by nothing more than the fact that he happened to be related to the Taylors. Jack Helms deputized two black men to arrest Wes. Wes was in a small roadside store in De Witt County when Helms's two deputies came in, loudly announcing that they were on the hunt for Wes Hardin and Helms had told them not to treat him gently.

"Are you really looking for Wes Hardin?" a small, light-haired man, hardly more than a boy, asked.

"We sure are," they said.

"You found him. I'm Wes Hardin."

When the smoke cleared, one of Helms's deputies was dead and the other was making a flying dash for the tall and uncut, a bullethole through his cheek. He remains one of the few men Wes Hardin ever set out to kill and didn't. Years later, in 1873, Wes and Jim Taylor cornered Helms in a blacksmith shop near Gonzales. While Wes held spectators at bay with his six-guns, Jim chased Helms round and round inside the shop, shooting him until he fell dead. Although it has been alleged that Helms was armed with only a knife at the time, those who knew the man said he was never without at least one pistol and often carried as many as three.

In Texas, between the early summer of 1865 and the fall of 1874, it was tantamount to suicide for a white man to kill a black, regardless of what prompted the killing. Texas was under Yankee military rule from 1865 until 1870, and from 1870 until 1874, under the thumb of Edmund J. Davis, the radical republican governor who'd been a Yankee brigadier and hated all ex-Confederates and their families. In spite of the fact that the black deputies had announced they were out to take Wes Hardin—who had not, at the time, ever committed a crime or even been charged with one—dead or alive on the orders of a man known to be a partisan of a faction dedicated to killing Taylors and all their kin (of whom Wes was one), the young man was wanted by Reconstruction law. From that time until his capture in Florida in 1876, John Wesley Hardin was a wanted man in Texas.

The Clements brothers, also Taylor kin, had, so far, no direct part in the feud. They asked Wes to go with them to Kansas with a trail herd. The oldest, Emanuel Clements, Jr., known as "Manny" (usually called Manning or Mannen in the New-York-published true western fact magazines, with his last name misspelled: Clemens, Clemmens, Clemons, or Clemmons) was the trail boss. Hardin agreed, and from that time until he left Texas "for good" in 1874, his regular line of business was trailing cattle north. In the meantime, the feud had broken out in open war all over South Texas, and whenever Taylor partisans spotted Sutton partisans—or vice versa—nobody bothered to talk. The guns came out and people died.

Wes was still in his teens when he took the trail north with his Clements cousins, but he seems to have been a dependable and resourceful young man. He had a lot of responsibility placed on him by Manny Clements, and he apparently carried out his duties well.

Somewhere in southern Kansas, a trail herd began to crowd the drag of the Clements herd. Wes rode back and warned the other trail boss off several times, but the other man, thinking he was dealing with a mere boy, continued to press the drag. Finally fighting words were passed and Wes told the other man to stay back or die. Then he rode back to his own herd.

Very shortly, the other trail boss was seen coming at Wes at a gallop, six-shooter in hand. Wes was armed with an old, almost worn-out percussion navy Colt, which had a condition known to Colt shooters as a "rocking cylinder." The hole in the center of the cylinder, through which the rotating pin passes, had become oversized with use and the cylinder of the revolver would "rock" back and forth, making it difficult to fire. Wes had to hold the cylinder back against the frame to make it fire.

Wes dismounted for a steady shot, held his horse, raised his six-shooter, pulled the trigger—and it snapped. By this time the other man was getting uncomfortably close and beginning to shoot. Wes tried again—and again his revolver misfired.

"Turn loose your goddamn horse and hold the goddamn cylinder!" Manny yelled at him. Wes released the horse, grabbed the cylinder, and dropped the man from his horse with a single shot.

While he was in Kansas—still not yet eighteen and with a price of $500 on his head back in Texas—Wes served as a deputy sheriff in a Ford County (Dodge City) posse, running down a man wanted for murder. In his autobiography, which he wrote while still in prison, he commented on this with some irony.

No purpose would be served here in recounting all the men Wes Hardin actually killed, is supposed to have killed, maybe killed, or is rumored to have killed. Any number of books, from Hardin's autobiography (which gives the total as better than fifty—among others, he claimed to have been the actual killer of Jack Helms) to Eugene Cunningham's *Triggernometry*, in which he is credited with forty-two, each one carefully documented as to time and place, will do better. We'll discuss one—the famous "snoring" case—and then fast-forward to the last known Hardin killing—the unquestioned murder of Deputy Sheriff Charles "Charlie" Webb of Brown County on the town square in Comanche, Texas, on May 26, 1874.

The "snoring" shooting is a nebulous one, though apparently somebody did shoot a sleeping man and it was later blamed on Wes. The man hanged for that shooting was Wes's brother-in-law, Brown Bowen. It is recorded fact that Wes's father-in-law pleaded with his daughter's husband to confess to that murder, and that Wes told him he'd own up to his own killings, but "let Brown take his medicine like a man." At that point, Jane Bowen Hardin's father disowned her, and it was at about that same time that the "killed for snoring" story started.

Wes's closest friend was a German cowboy named Frederick Duderstadt. Fred Duderstadt's nephew, Ernst Duderstadt, known as "Mister Duder," was a long-time acquaintance of mine in Seguin. I asked him one time if his Uncle Fred had ever mentioned the "killed for snoring" incident.

"All Uncle Fred ever said about it," Mister Duder told me, "was that on the night it happened, he and Wes were with a herd about fifty miles north of there. They rolled out their blankets side by side next to the wagon. Come daybreak, Wes was still there, he didn't act tired, and there weren't any sweaty horses in the remuda." The facts of the Charlie Webb killing are simple enough. Wes, Jim Taylor, and Bud Dixon were drunk and looking for trouble. Allegedly, Webb had arrested the son of one of Wes's acquaintances and "mistreated" him. Hardin, Taylor, and Dixon cornered Webb in front of Wright's Saloon. There were words passed, Webb said, "I'm not afraid of you," and went for his gun, and when the smoke cleared, the sidewalk had a hole in it where Webb's gun fired prematurely. Webb had holes in his head, belly, and hand. It was murder, pure and simple—nothing but. According to Eugene Cunningham, Webb was Wes's forty-second—and final—notch. The killing of Webb ranks as the only out-and-out murder Wes is known to have committed.

Wes apparently realized what he'd done. Up to the killing of Charlie Webb, he'd had the sympathy—at times the outright support—of a great many people in Texas. Charlie Webb, though, was no Reconstruction bully. He was a fair, popular, honest, well-liked lawman. All of Comanche—and much of Texas—turned against Hardin for the killing. Wes's brother Joe—a lawyer in Comanche who had no part whatever in the killing of Webb and wasn't present when it happened, and Bud Dixon, who was in on the killing—were lynched by a mob in Comanche. So strong was the feeling about the killing of Charlie Webb that no indictments were ever returned against any member of the mob that lynched them.

Wes immediately took off for parts unknown. But Texas was so jumpy about Wes Hardin that in November of 1875—Wes was long gone by then—a man named Monroe was shot and killed by police in Dallas on the unsupported accusation that he was John Wesley Hardin.

Wes, in fact, was in Florida. In the summer of 1874 he went to New Orleans, where he met with his wife, Jane Bowen Hardin, and their daughter. The three of them went by ship to Cedar Key, Florida. Hardin took the name John H. Swain. He settled with his family in Gainesville, Florida, where he opened a combination liquor and grocery business. He later moved to Micanopy, Florida, where he operated a saloon, and then to Jacksonville, where he had another liquor and grocery store combination—and where his son was born.

In the meantime, detectives were busy. Wes got wind of people snooping around and asking pointed questions. The Hardins moved once again, this time to Pollard, Alabama. Jane's uncle, Neil McMillan, a local deputy sheriff, lived in Pollard, and they lived with him. Wes traded in horses and eventually got involved in a logging business. Shortly afterwards, Brown Bowen, Jane's brother—wanted in Texas for a particularly cold-blooded murder of a sleeping man—joined the Hardins at McMillan's residence in Pollard.

As of November of 1874, Texas was back under conservative rule. The new governor, Richard Coke, assigned two men to clean up the Hardin business—Texas Ranger Sergeant John Armstrong and Texas Ranger Private Jack Duncan. Duncan went undercover, befriending Jane's father.

At length Duncan became a trusted friend of the elder Bowen, and—by abusing the friendship and snooping in the house—found a letter from Brown to his father. It was postmarked Pollard, Alabama, and in it Brown wrote: "Sister sends her love." The only sister Brown had who wasn't living at home was Jane. Therefore, Duncan reasoned, Jane had to be either with or near Brown. Where Jane was, Wes wasn't far away.

Eventually John H. Swain, a.k.a. John Wesley Hardin, was located in the Florida Panhandle. Wes had been captured by law before and almost murdered by the Davis Police. He had vowed he'd never be taken alive—a vow which had cost more than one carpetbagger lawman his life.

Armstrong and Duncan went to Florida and shortly had good information telling them that Wes would be on a westbound Pensacola Railroad passenger train passing through Pensacola. They contacted the president of the railroad and the Pensacola police, and made arrangements to arrest Hardin on the train. According to the plan, Duncan, whom Wes had never seen, would board the train and sit down behind the outlaw. At Duncan's signal Armstrong would enter the coach from the opposite end and throw down on Wes. At the same time Duncan grabbed Wes from behind, a Pensacola officer would reach through the open window and grab Wes by the gun arm and other Pensacola officers would throw down on anyone aboard the train who was trying to help Hardin.

No one knows why, but the Pensacola police officers never showed up. As Armstrong entered the coach at Duncan's signal, his big Texas hat on his head and a long-barreled Colt in his hand, Wes yelled, "Texas, by God!" and grabbed for a six-shooter stuck in the waistband of his pants. Duncan grabbed Wes from behind. Two of Hardin's friends stood up and went for guns. Armstrong shot one down and the other made a dive out the train window and disappeared.

In the meantime, Duncan had his hands full in a wrestling match with an infuriated Hardin on the floor of the train coach, and Wes was having troubles of his own that didn't include Jack Duncan. He got his hand on his six-shooter—a model 1860 Colt—but when he pulled on it, the hammer hung in his suspenders. The harder he pulled, the tighter the gun hung. By his own words, "I nearly pulled my trousers off over my head." The comedy stopped when Armstrong "buffaloed" him—whacked him between the ears with the long barrel of that Colt.

The two Texas officers had their man—but all they had was a Texas warrant, which, in Florida, was just a piece of paper. They had to get rendition papers signed by the governor of Florida to take Hardin to Alabama, more rendition papers from the governor of Alabama to get him to Mississippi, the same to get him into Louisiana, and then papers from the Louisiana governor to get him across the Sabine and into Texas. Meanwhile, Wes was screaming at the top of his lungs that he was John H. Swain, a respectable businessman, he was being kidnapped, and he had no idea who this John Wesley Hardin might be. All the while, his friends and Jane's relatives were gathering to prevent his removal, legally if they could, by gunfire if no other way.

Rendition papers or no, the rangers bullied their way out of Florida and into Alabama. In the short stretch of railroad between Florida and Mississippi, the train filled up with Hardin's pals. Armstrong took out that long-barreled Colt, put the muzzle to Wes's temple, cocked the hammer through the four chilling clicks that have brought folks to say, "A Colt spells its name," and said,

"I don't know who'll fire the first shot, but I'll fire the second one." That ended attempts to rescue Wes by force.

By dint of numerous pieces of paper, most of them of extremely questionable legality, the two rangers brought Hardin across four states and into Texas. He was lodged in the Travis County jail in Austin, where his father-in-law visited Wes and tried to persuade him to confess to the murder of the sleeping man with which his son was charged. Wes refused. "Let every tub stand on its own bottom," he's quoted as having said. Brown Bowen was eventually captured, returned to Texas, tried in Gonzales County, and hanged for the "snoring" murder. Bowen's father never forgave Wes, and apparently disowned his daughter for remaining loyal to her husband. At any rate, she seems to have had a hard time getting back to Texas from Alabama, and she apparently had to sell most of the family's property—including Wes's guns—to get the money to come home.

What might have been one of those guns, a Smith & Wesson .32 rimfire revolver made in 1868—the same year as the "Colt navy with the rocking cylinder" incident—was found on the junk table at a gun show in southwestern Georgia about twenty-five years ago. My good friend George W. Olney, then living in southern Georgia, was a Smith & Wesson collector, and he picked up the old piece for a small sum.

When he got it home he disassembled it to clean it up, and on the inside of the wooden grips he found carved the initials JWH. There are several authenticated Wes Hardin guns, and all are marked with the initials JWH carved on the inside of the grips.

Wes was tried for the murder of Deputy Sheriff Charlie Webb in Comanche. A force of twenty-five Texas Rangers were assigned to guard the prisoner and the trial in the Comanche courthouse to prevent a lynching. He was found guilty and sentenced to serve twenty-five years in the Texas penitentiary.

Of that twenty-five years, Wes actually served nearly seventeen. For the first three years he concerned himself with trying to escape—seven attempts, by his own statement—and spent a lot of time in solitary confinement. Eventually he resigned himself to the fact that he was in prison and he wasn't getting out until the State of Texas was ready to let him out. He began to study—first theology, then law. After he'd served nearly seventeen years, Wes was granted a gubernatorial pardon on February 17, 1894, and walked out of Huntsville a free man. His freedom was marred by the fact that his beloved wife Jane was killed in a disastrous fire only a few weeks before his release.

Wes applied to take the bar examination and was admitted to the Texas bar as an attorney in 1894. He immediately returned to his old stomping grounds and set up a law practice in Gonzales, in the next county north of De Witt.

The Sutton-Taylor feud was still simmering, though a Texas Ranger lieutenant named Lee Hall, leading Captain L. H. McNelly's old company, had turned down the heat under it considerably. Hall and his men arrested and jailed a number of Sutton partisans and Judge Henry Clay Pleasants saw most of them convicted in his courtroom, but a large number were released on technicalities. Most of the political control in the area had passed out of the hands of Sutton partisans in the 1874 election, and while the officeholders weren't all Taylors or Taylor partisans, the De Witt and Gonzales County law wasn't actively out to exterminate the Taylors and their kinfolk any more. Still, there was a lot of the old Sutton crowd still around. There was gunpowder all over the ground, and all it would take to set it off would be a careless match. Wes Hardin was determined he was not going to be that match.

In a hotly contested election, Wes backed a candidate for Gonzales County sheriff. He would, he said, leave the county for good rather than take a chance on old troubles being stirred up if his man lost. His man did lose, and Wes was true to his word—he left the area completely and never returned. He moved over 100 miles to the west, to Junction, where he established his law practice. There, in 1895, he married seventeen-year-old Callie Lewis. Whether Wes was trying to regain his lost youth or Callie was rebelling against her parents we don't know—both versions have been circulated— but the marriage only lasted a few weeks.

Wes was in Junction only a few months when one of his cousins, Jim Miller, was the intended victim of an attempted murder in Pecos. Jim had two nicknames. He was called "Preacher" Miller, because he could preach one of the finest hellfire-and-brimstone Methodist sermons ever heard. He was also called "Killer" Miller, because he'd kill almost anybody for fifty dollars. No one knows whether the assassination attempt was justified or not, but Wes was asked to come help the local prosecutor in the case. He did, and when the case was concluded, his Clements cousins—Manny, in particular—asked him to move to El Paso. The Clements brothers were well established in El Paso, with several businesses, saloon-keeping being one, and they felt they needed a lawyer who was also family.

Wes was drunk when he killed Charlie Webb, and he insisted later that, had he been sober, the killing would never have happened. From the time he went to prison he never ceased to harp on the evils of excessive drinking. After his release, in Gonzales and Junction, he was known for drinking nothing stronger than beer, and not much beer. When he got to El Paso—a wide-open town if there ever was one—the liquor, the gambling, and the women attracted him once more.

Wes opened a law practice in El Paso, and several of his El Paso business cards are available—at *very* high prices, of course— on the antiques market there. He also went to the El Paso Saddlery Company and had a pair of shoulder holsters made. Into one he shoved a Colt model 1877 double-action revolver in .38 caliber—a "Lightning"—and into the other, a "Thunderer," which was the same gun in a .41 caliber. El Paso Saddlery, for the record, still makes shoulder holsters to the same pattern as the ones they made for Wes, and if your urge is strong enough they'll make one for you. Properly outfitted—though it had been illegal to carry a pistol on one's person since 1894—Wes began to hit the tables and the saloons.

It's recorded that Wes drank heavily in El Paso, and when he was in his cups he leaned very heavily on the "I'm Wes Hardin—I've killed fifty men" reputation. It didn't take much leaning. Very few people cared to go nose-to-nose with Texas's most legendary gunman—a man who'd killed somewhere between forty and fifty men, most of them face-to-face. Wes was also known to call, "Cheat!" in perfectly honest card games and rake in the pot at gunpoint. He did not endear himself to the El Paso sporting crowd. There was a young woman—a prostitute part-time, if not full-time—who was "married," either by license or by common law to a very-much-wanted horse thief by the name of Martin Morose. Martin Morose was Polish, not Celtic, by heritage. Mr. Morose was spending most of his time in Juárez, where the Texas law couldn't touch him, and his wife Beulah, known as Betty, was spending most of her time keeping company with John Wesley Hardin. Mr. Morose didn't like it one bit.

Late one night Mr. Morose came sneaking back across the Rio Grande on the catwalk of the Mexican Central Railroad bridge. Somebody was waiting in the shadows. Mr. Morose very quickly became the late Mr. Morose, and Mrs. Morose, the widow Morose. Who shot Martin Morose off the bridge into the Rio Grande no one knows to this day—but there are those who, if you say, "Wes Hardin did it," will answer, "I won't argue with you on that."

Rowdy John Selman was a tough and shady character all over West Texas, and in 1895, he was a constable in El Paso. He was also an "enforcer" for various would-be hoodlums, an investor in numerous questionable enterprises, including houses of prostitution, a pretty fair cowboy when he wanted to be and no slouch with a six-shooter. Alice Abbott, who called herself the "Best Madam in the Whole World" in her photo album, kept a photo of Rowdy John that contained several notations in red ink. Alice used red ink to make notes about pictures only of her most intimate associates. And yes, that's the same Alice Abbot who's called Fat Alice; she shows up again in the story of the Public Arch.

That John Selman was involved, to some extent, in the prostitution that flourished in El Paso in the 1890s there is no doubt at all. The only question is how deeply he was involved. El Paso was one of the Southwest's great Sin Cities—wide-open and proud of it. Over half the police department's budget came from the periodic "roundup" of street prostitutes and the various fines and "license fees" paid by houses to stay open. Betty Morose was a freelancer in a union town when it came to her trade, and as such was not greatly welcomed. Several madams had tried to put her to work in the houses, but she refused. "Muscle," as it's referred to today, was called in to "persuade" her to go to work in a house—and the muscle ran into some *real* muscle. Betty's "Friend" was *un pistolero por verdad*—a man who could have carved, had he been so inclined, more than forty absolutely genuine and unquestionable notches into the butts of his six-shooters. Nobody in his right mind wanted to go up against John Wesley Hardin—at least not from the front.

That left from behind. On the afternoon of August 19, 1895, Wes was in the Acme Saloon in downtown El Paso, shaking dice for drinks with several acquaintances. They had their backs to the door, but there was a bar mirror in front of them, which would have made it possible for them to see anyone approaching from the rear—had they felt any reason to be on the lookout.

Wes won the throw and was about to call for the round at the expense of the loser when Rowdy John, who'd walked quietly up to about ten feet behind Wes, pulled his gun, and fired twice. One bullet struck Wes in the back of the head and exited beside his right eye, the other struck him in the back as he half-turned in falling, came out his chest, and went into his right arm. John Wesley Hardin was dead, shot down from behind.

Some very competent authorities, most notably Leon Metz, will argue that Martin Morose was carrying a pretty fair-sized wad of money the night he went into the Bravo, and he was set up by John Selman, who was supposed to get a quarter of the money taken off the body. Apparently, the other three men—Wes Hardin and lawmen George Scarbrough and Jeff Milton—split the cash among them and left Selman out in the cold. Selman went on the hunt for the other three. He got Hardin from behind but was gotten by George Scarbrough within a few days.

It's a fact that Selman was shot down by Scarbrough—apparently from behind—only a few days after the Hardin killing. Martin Morose's money might have been—and probably was—at least part of the reason Selman killed Wes. I remain firm in the belief, however, that Wes's championing of Betty Morose against "establishment" prostitution in El Paso, in which Selman had a financial interest, likely had just as much to do with it as did the soggy bankroll fished out of the pockets of the late Martin Morose as he floated face-down in the Rio Grande.

Frankly, most of El Paso breathed a sigh of relief when word got out that Wes Hardin was dead. The justice of the peace who rendered the verdict on the body commented, "Had he been shot from in front I would have called it excellent marksmanship. As he was shot from behind, I have to call it excellent judgment." Rowdy John, of course, was not indicted—he said Wes had threatened his son, and that when he saw Wes's eyes in the mirror he "knew he was going for a gun."

Among Hardin's effects was a thick, handwritten manuscript—his autobiography. It was apparently written while he was in prison, and when he was living in Junction he turned up at the office of pioneer printer and publisher Marvin Hunter in Bandera. The young J. Marvin Hunter, who later published the original *Frontier Times*, the first magazine devoted to true stories about early Texas, was in the office when Hardin walked in. He was a little nervous about telling the most famous gunman in Texas that his father couldn't publish the book—Hunter's press capacity was too small to handle a project of that size.

El Paso laid claim to Wes's personal effects, but through the efforts of the Guadalupe County representative in the legislature, they were returned to his children—including the manuscript. The book was illustrated by the later-famous Robert Onderdonk of San Antonio and published in Seguin by Smith & Moore. It was offered at fifty cents per copy. Very few sold. Today it is one of the major Texas collectibles, though it is available in reprint through State House Press in Austin so anyone can read what Wes had to say about himself without taking on a second mortgage.

That's who Wes Hardin was and what he did. Now make up your own mind about him. But in case you decide he was really a bad guy, don't go saying so down in De Witt and Gonzales counties. Wes still has a lot of kinfolk there, and they don't stand for folks bad-mouthing cousin John Wesley.

THE GREAT GUNFIGHT THAT WASN'T

Most of the South had been free of Reconstruction and back under home rule, with most ex-Confederates fully enfranchised, by 1872. The sole exception was Texas. Texas had a constitutionally mandated four-year gubernatorial term, and in 1870—with just about everybody who'd worn grey and butternut still disenfranchised—Edmund J. Davis, a Yankee who'd settled in Corpus Christi in 1848 and a staunch radical republican since before the war, who served from 1861 to 1865 as a Yankee officer and eventually made brigadier general, had been elected.

Davis was not, to say the least, a popular governor. Among other things, he formed the Texas State Police—called the "Davis Police" in Texas—which was less a police agency than the governor's gestapo. There are, to this day, many family Bibles that bear, next to the name of a male member, the words "arrested by the Davis Police and never again seen." Today we have a Department of Public Safety with the Highway Patrol, Division of Weights and Measures, and the Texas Rangers as a Criminal Investigation Division, but there is no organization called the "Texas

State Police" and there isn't ever likely to be again—the legacy of E. J. Davis and the Davis police.

By 1874, the ex-Rebs were firmly in control of the state and the election of Democrat Richard Coke, an ex-Confederate, was a foregone conclusion. Davis, however, didn't want to give up. He appealed to President U. S. Grant to send troops to "save Texas for the Party," but Grant refused. Reconstruction was, Sam Grant decided, at an end, and E. J. Davis was just an embarrassing reminder he'd rather not have around.

Coke and the Democrats swept everything in sight, and Coke called upon the ousted radical republican governor to give over the office like a gentleman. Instead, Davis gathered a small army of local bullyboys—Reconstructionist leftovers and former members of the Texas State Police—and barricaded himself on the second floor of the old capitol building. (If you stand in the middle of Congress Avenue at Eleventh Street, which is not a wise move because of the traffic, and look directly at the south entrance to the current state capitol building, then stretch out your left arm and point to the governor's mansion to the west, you'll be pointing directly across the site of the 1874 capitol building. Though there's a small city park on the site today, the foundation stones of the old capitol are still visible.)

Coke was sworn in at a hotel down Congress Avenue, but Davis still held the capitol, the state seal, and the other appurtenances of office. The Travis Rifles, a local militia company—made up largely of ex-Johnnie Rebs—was on hand to give the proper nineteenth-century military flair to the inauguration, and they were armed with breech-loading .50 caliber rifles. They probably weren't supposed to have cartridge boxes loaded with "forty rounds of ball," but they did.

Governor Coke swore in the entire company as Texas Rangers on the spot and, marching at the head of the formation, moved up Congress to the capitol building. Coke and the Travis Rifles cum

Texas Rangers came in the front door and found the balcony, overlooking the lobby of the building, forted up with overturned furniture and Governor Davis and his bullyboys behind it, apparently looking for a fight.

"Sir," the new governor called, "will you yield as a gentleman, or must we take the capitol by storm? I beg you, sir, let us not have bloodshed here."

"Be damned to you," Davis replied. "We shall never surrender!"

Things were looking a mite sticky, since the Davis folks were armed with Winchesters and six-shooters while the Travis Rifles were armed with one-shooters; but the Travis Rifles were a disciplined militia unit with training in volley fire and were probably more than a match for the men on the balcony. It looked, though, that Texas was about to be short two governors and a lot of fine citizens—as well as a lot of undesirables and riffraff—if anybody made anything like a wrong move.

One of the Davis men, at that point, decided to have a peep over the balcony, and carefully raised his head. As soon as the tall crown of his hat came into clear view, one of the new rangers put a .50 caliber hole in it strictly on his own say-so. There was about thirty seconds of dead silence once the echo of the shot died away and the smoke cloud drifted upward, and then Winchesters and six-shooters began to rain over the balcony. Davis's bullyboys had hoped to bluff the new governor out, but it turned out he was ready to come in a-smokin'—with fifty or sixty well-armed and well-disciplined riflemen to back him up if that was what it took to do the job.

E. J. Davis left the state of Texas under armed guard to prevent anything more lethal than rotten eggs or dead cats from being flung at him and his entourage as he went, and Richard Coke took the governor's chair without further ado. One of Coke's first acts was to re-form the Texas Rangers as both an Indian-fighting militia and a law enforcement agency, and to dispatch a Virginia-born consumptive ex-Presbyterian divinity student named Leander Henry McNelly to the border with orders to "clean it up." During Coke's tenure as governor, Texas's two most notorious gunmen, Bill Longley and Wes Hardin, were brought to justice—Longley being hanged in Giddings and Hardin drawing twenty-five years in the state pen.

Davis eventually sneaked back into the state and lived out his life in obscurity in Corpus Christi. When he died he was buried—as was his right as a former governor—in the Texas State Cemetery in Austin. His family erected a large monument in his memory, which for many years was neglected by the Texas State Cemetery maintenance staff. It attracts few visitors, most preferring to see the Elizabet Ney recumbent marble statue of Confederate General Albert Sidney Johnston, which covers the grave of the man who served the United States, the Texas Republic, the United States again, and died in the service of the Confederacy.

THE BALLAD OF SAM BASS

For reasons that no one has ever been able to explain to my satisfaction, we Americans have an unfortunate tendency to romanticize criminals. We came by it honestly, I suppose—our English ancestors had the same tendency. If they hadn't, the name Robert Locksley, Earl of Huntingdon, might not even be an historical footnote, much less the basis for the Robin Hood legend. We also sing—or we did at one time—songs about our romanticized criminals.

Surely there was a ballad of Robin Hood; but if it's been lost, it's been amply replaced. The ballad of highwayman Dick Turpin and his mare, Black Bess—based not on any actual incident but on a novel written using Turpin as the hero long after he was hanged—proved so popular in the American South that John Hunt Morgan, the Kentucky gentleman who led the Confederate cavalry brigade known as "Morgan's Raiders," named the mare he rode for most of the war after Turpin's fictional mount. Americans continued the tradition with ballads for such obscure entities as Samuel Hall and Thomas Dula (whose ballad was almost lost until a 1960s pop-folk group called the Kingston Trio revived it as "Tom Dooley") and for such well-known figures as Henry McCarty, known as Billy the Kid, and Jesse Woodson James. The tradition continued well into the twentieth century, and there were, in fact, ballads for Clyde Barrow, Pretty Boy Floyd, and John Dillinger.

Somewhere in between lies the Hoosier-born Texas train robber, Sam Bass—the man sometimes called the "Texas Robin Hood." J. Frank Dobie, Texas's premier folklorist, in an essay entitled "The Robinhooding of Sam Bass," insisted that "nobody but just folks can robinhood an outlaw." Here in Texas we've been robinhooding Sam for going on a century and a quarter now, and it doesn't look like we'll quit anytime soon.

That's unfortunate. Jesse James, the "Missouri Robin Hood," seems to have been fairly intelligent. Al Jennings, the "Oklahoma Robin Hood," was a bust as an outlaw but a master of after-the-fact self-promotion. What Joaquín Murieta, the "Robin Hood of El Dorado," was, we don't know for sure and probably never will—but for some reason the feller we Texans picked to robinhood was just dumber'n plow dirt.

"He was born in Indiana, it was his native home,
And at the age of seventeen Sam Bass began to roam."

So begins "The Ballad of Sam Bass," which I must have played a thousand times—at a nickel a play—on the old Wurlitzer juke box in Round Rock's Sam Bass Cafe, in the days when it was in downtown Round Rock just a few steps from the abandoned, tumbledown building that once housed Copprell's Store. I don't know who sang that version, but it wasn't Tex Ritter—though Tex did record it at least once.

Sam was born in Indiana, all right—on a farm near the town of New Albany, just across the Ohio River from Louisville, Kentucky. The name New Albany, Indiana, doesn't ring bells unless you're very well versed in the history of American outlawry, but

New Albany was the home of the Reno brothers, who invented American-style daylight train robbery in 1865 and were lynched in the New Albany jailhouse in 1866 so they'd learn not to misbehave like that any more. Those who recall Elvis Presley's eminently forgettable first movie, *Love Me Tender*, will recall that it was *very* loosely based on the story of the Renos, whom "Hollywood History" identified as "Texas outlaws."

If Sam did leave home "at the age of seventeen"—in 1868—he picked a good time to head south. In the postwar depression, jobs were hard come by in the North, but in the former Confederacy, just about any Yankee could get a government job. Ex-Confederates need not apply, and their fire-eating sons who hadn't quite been old enough for the war—boys like Campbell Longley's son Bill or Preacher Hardin's boy Wes—were often wanted, but not to work. A young man with no tinge of Rebel gray in his background could find work fairly easily.

Sam arrived in Denton, Texas, north and a little west of Dallas, probably sometime in 1869. Shortly afterwards, he went to work for the Denton County Sheriff's Office under Sheriff W. P. "Dad" Egan. From this has arisen the legend that Sam was "a lawman gone wrong"—a former deputy sheriff who understood how the law thought and worked and could outwit it at every turn. All available historical documentation, though, tells us that Sam put in his day's work at the Denton County jail with a broom and a mop—he was the janitor, not a deputy. Though indications are that he did fairly well, financially. According to the ballad:

> Sam used to deal in race stock, one called the Denton Mare.
> He matched her at scrub races and ran her at the fair.

Sam's horse was an excellent one, and Denton Mare bloodlines are highly respected in modern Texas horsebreeding. One legend—unprovable so far as I know, but probably as true as any—insists that she came, eventually, into the possession of Captain Richard

King and, together with a sorrel stud called Red Fox that he bought from a Clay County, Missouri, boy known as Dingus, was part of the founding line of the famous King Ranch Red quarter horses. Of course, the ballad also tells us:

> He always coined the money, he spent it very free—
> He always drank good whiskey wherever he might be.

In 1874, the Reconstruction bubble exploded and virtually every non-Confederate in Texas who held any non-federal public job was out on his ear. In what could have been a major tragedy, but turned into low farce, the radical Reconstructionist governor, Edmund J. Davis, evacuated the old capitol at Tenth Street and Congress Avenue in Austin and left the state under heavy guard to prevent his being assassinated—or worse—before he could get to Yankee territory and safety. Reconstruction—the longest endured by any southern state—was over in Texas. Anyone suspected of having been associated with the Reconstruction government was out of a job. Sam was personally liked in Denton—he was a likable feller—but he'd worked for the Yankees and was Yankee-born himself. When the new Denton County administration, made up entirely of ex-Confederates, took office, there was no room for Sam Bass. His profligate habits with money didn't make life any easier.

For the next couple of years Sam seems to have bummed around the state, possibly working where he could, probably gambling heavily on his fast mare. The ballad tells us:

> First he came to Texas, a cowboy for to be,
> A kinder-hearted feller you seldom ever see.

But if Sam came to Texas with the idea of being a cowboy, it took him a while to get around to it. Historical indications are he first became a "cowboy"—a drover hired to help move a herd north—in 1876, seven years after he first got to the Lone Star State.

We know that Sam was in San Antonio in 1876 because that's where he signed on as a drover with Joel Collins's scrub drive to Kansas. The much disputed photograph on page 109, probably taken at that time, resides in the State Archives of Texas with an *Austin American-Statesman* interview of one Jefferson D. Dillingham, a retired railroad worker who claimed to have witnessed the young outlaw's death in 1878. "People who know" have identified the three figures as, from left to right, Frank Jackson, Sam Bass, and Joel Collins, and Sam Bass, Joel Collins, and unidentified (sometimes tentatively identified as Jim Murphy). Considering that we know for sure Jackson was only seventeen two years after the picture was taken, if the feller on the left is, in fact, Frank Jackson, he raised a whopper of a mustache for a kid of fifteen.

If the description of Sam the Texas Rangers put on the wanted flyers they circulated in 1877 and 1878 can be relied on—"shows his teeth when talking, has very little to say"—the gent in the middle who's showing the pre-Pepsodent grin comes closest to matching, but there's no way to know for sure. The only *other* known picture of Sam was taken before he left home, when he was about fifteen. It shows a clean-shaven schoolboy who looks scared out of his wits the camera's going to bite him. All we can say for sure is, in the picture with three men in it, "Sam Bass is one a them fellers."

In the spring of 1876, probably shortly after the photo was taken, Sam joined up with a cattle-driving outfit in San Antone, becoming a cowboy for probably the first time. The trail boss was Joel Collins of Gonzales, who was known locally—at least according to Frank Bushick's classic story of ol' San Antone, *Wild Old Days*—as "Honest Joe." He was reputed to be the sort of feller who, if he found a dime in the street, would turn it over to the sheriff rather than put it in his pocket. With Joel and Sam were at least four other men and probably several more than that, but the names we know are Tom Nixon, Jim Berry, Billy Heffridge, and Jack Davis. There is reason to believe that Nixon was a Missourian, and some overly enthusiastic "Wild West Of New York" writers have been trying to "prove" he was Jesse James since the 1930s.

Honest Joe might have been honest, but that doesn't mean he was a good trail boss. Apparently the best he could do was a scrub drive—cattle rejected or left behind by the big drives. He seems to have gotten financing from some San Antonio loan sharks, for the story that comes down about his payment agreement holds that the backers wanted their money off the top, and whatever was left—if anything—Collins could split with the hands. There were probably, in fact, no less than a dozen or so cowboys—point man, four to six swing riders, two drag riders, trail boss, *segundo,* and a nighthawk/wrangler, plus a cook and cook's louse–for it took at least that many to move even a small herd any distance.

The herd reached Kansas and was sold—but not for much. We don't know how much Collins got or whether he kept to his reputation and wired home his backers' money before he got into trouble, but there sure doesn't seem to have been enough to pay off the hands. Honest Joe decided to increase his holdings in perhaps the most disastrous way possible—at a faro table in a gambling hall. There might—just possibly—have been a straight game of faro dealt somewhere in the world at least once, but you can bet your Sunday hat it wasn't in a Kansas gambling hall to a Texas cowboy. Collins lost all he had.

When Collins confessed what had happened, he told the men, "Stick with Joe and I'll get you money somehow." Collins and the five named cowboys did stick together, and such history as there is has them climbing on their cow ponies and heading for Dakota Territory.

Sam was dumb, but nobody ever said he was suicidal. For this reason, I tend to doubt the supposed Dakota adventures of Collins, Bass, and company. Just about the time they were getting to Kansas, a vainglorious cavalryman named George Armstrong Custer was setting out from Fort Abraham Lincoln, Dakota Territory, to hunt Indians. On June 26, at a place the Sioux called Greasy Grass, Custer found all the Indians he wanted and then some—the largest single gathering of Plains Indian warriors ever gathered in recorded history. He found 'em on a creek tributary to the Big Horn River in southeastern Montana—a creek called Little Big Horn. For the next year or so, Dakota was a decidedly unhealthy place in which to be a paleface.

Going to Dakota was dumb but that doesn't mean Sam didn't do it. Wherever he and "the boys" went, they didn't do well—Sam later told folks they "stopped stagecoaches for six dollars a time, only sometimes we didn't even get the six dollars." By late August they were thoroughly disgusted, and with the first cold winds of autumn beginning to chill the air, they turned their cow ponies' noses southward.

On September 12, 1876, an eastbound Union Pacific passenger train made a water stop at a wide spot in the road called Big Spring Station, Nebraska. It was just a hop and a step north of the Kansas line and not that much farther from Colorado's eastern border. As the train stopped, six masked men swung aboard the express car—and barely missed committing the biggest train robbery in history: the car's through safe contained $225,000 in cash and negotiable securities.

The outlaws put pistols up the expressman's nose and demanded the combinations to the safes. He lied to them. He was paid to lie to them—all express messengers had combinations to both through and way safes in their cars, but to admit it even under threat of immediate death was to guarantee that—if the messenger survived—he'd never work around a railroad again. The six cowboys roughed him up some, but he stuck to his story, so not being experienced train robbers, they went through the mail feeling for fat, squishy envelopes (a pretty good indication there's money inside), found almost nothing, and started to leave, resigned to just one more stickup where they didn't even get the six dollars. At that point, their luck changed.

There was, on the floor of the car, a stack of small, very heavy wooden boxes. The outlaws demanded to know what was in them. The expressman denied knowing. Somebody—tradition holds it was Sam Bass—reached down and ripped the lid off one. All eyes caught the glint of minted gold. The boxes were a shipment of newly minted double eagles—twenty-dollar gold coins—outbound from the Denver mint to banks for distribution in the coming year. All were dated 1877. Each box contained 500 coins—$10,000 per box, $60,000 in all. The six cowboys had just struck it rich. Any one of the boxes contained, in all likelihood, more cash money than all six had owned in their combined lifetimes.

They rode into the dark, away from Big Spring's water tower, as rich men—if they could keep it. They hung around the area, "getting a line on the posses," for about a week. They hung around, as it turned out, a day or so too long. Somebody got a line on them, and the chase was on.

The group split up, Collins and Heffridge heading for Colorado, Nixon and Berry for Missouri, and Bass and Davis for Texas. On the face of it, Texas was a bad place to be heading. Both the expressman and the townsman who'd spotted them identified them from their clothes, style of spurs, the skirts and rigging on their saddles, and the appearance of their horses, as "Texas cowboys." They'd be expected to head for home.

Collins, Heffridge, Berry, and Nixon were overtaken and killed in less than a week, and $40,000 was recovered, which pretty much eliminates any possibility that Tom Nixon was Jesse James. That left two robbers—and $20,000—still on the loose.

The law, together with elements of the Kansas and Nebraska militia, were looking for a couple of hardcase Texas cowboys. They weren't looking for a couple of preachers headed south in a buggy to "bring the Word to the heathen Texans." Sam and Jack absconded with a couple of Sunday-go-to-meetin' suits and boiled shirts, picked up an unwatched rig and hitched their cow ponies to it, put the money in canvas sacks on the floorboards of the buggy with their dusters over it, and for a time rode along "for protection" with one of the posses hunting them. If the disguise was Sam's idea, it was a good one—but, so far as history indicates, it was the first and last smart thing Sam ever did. If the line in the ballad, "They ran the boys in blue," has any meaning at all, it must come from the Union Pacific pursuit, for the only boys in blue who chased Sam were the Kansas and Nebraska militia.

Sam and Jack arrived in Texas in mid-October of 1876, "All right side up with care," or so says the ballad. At that point, Jack Davis seemingly vanished from the face of the earth—or did he? In the 1920s, western writer Eugene Cunningham, then a war correspondent covering one of Central America's biweekly revolutions, met, in Managua, Nicaragua, an old, well established *estanciero*. The man was an American and didn't deny it, nor did he deny a connection to Texas. He seemed to know a great deal about Sam Bass—up to just after the Union Pacific stickup.

Inquiries revealed he'd been in Nicaragua a long time—about forty years. When he arrived from the States he came equipped with a lot of *gringo* money in its most negotiable form—bright, shiny gold coins. Cunningham forbore to record the man's name—or the one he was using in Managua. After all, forty years is a long time and the Union Pacific robbery was a bloodless one.

Sam arrived in Fort Worth with $10,000 in gold burning holes in his pockets, and promptly proved how dumb he was. It was 1876, and it would still be 1876 for about two and a half more months. Sam's Union Pacific gold was dated 1877, and he and Jack Davis were the only people other than banks and U.S. mints who had any 1877-dated coins.

If Sam had been smart—smart enough, for instance, to have figured out the preacher-suit dodge all by himself—he'd simply have laid low for three or four months before he started spending money.

Instead, he did the equivalent of wearing a sign on the back of his shirt reading, "I ROBBED THE U.P. TRAIN AT BIG SPRING AND STOLE THE 1877 GOLD!" while riding through downtown Fort Worth shooting out the streetlights. He began to spend the newly minted gold in a steady stream in the saloons, gambling halls, and brothels of Fort Worth and Dallas. In less than a week, there was no doubt that a fifth member of the Big Spring gang was in town, and that he was the Indiana kid, Sam Bass, who used to sweep out the jailhouse up in Denton when the carpetbaggers were in power.

Collins, Berry, Nixon, and Heffridge were dead. Davis was gone no one knew where. If Sam Bass claimed to be the mastermind behind the big Union Pacific stickup, no one could contradict him. For the first time in his life, Sam was an important man—the big frog in his own personal puddle, which was the lower end of life in Dallas and Fort Worth. He was—or at least folks *thought* he was, and he did nothing to disabuse them of the notion—the man who'd planned and executed a $60,000 stickup in a time and a place where a man who'd just *seen* $60,000 all at one time was an object of wonder. Sam Bass was the suddenly crowned king of the gambling halls, saloons, and brothels of Fort Worth and Dallas.

Like any good king, Sam distributed largesse to his subjects. In the circles in which he moved, a five-dollar bet was big money. Sam threw double eagles on the table. If a pal got in over his head, Sam bailed him out. If a cutie pleased him, so what?—he had 500 of 'em and what's money for if not to spend and enjoy? Sam's generosity gathered a coterie of admirers, some of whom later became gang members or valuable tipsters and misdirectors of lawmen.

The only trouble with being a bandit-king lies in the fact that sooner or later the money runs low, and to stay a bandit-king you've got to get more money. The only way for a proper bandit-king to get money is to steal it. Sam Bass had never, in his life, planned a train or stagecoach robbery, and he didn't have the faintest idea how to go about it. He'd been in on the robbery of perhaps a dozen or so stagecoaches, mostly unsuccessful, and one train. The train robbery was a fluke, the discovery of the 1877 gold, pure accident. Sam had no inside information on who carried what in the way of money, or where or when it was carried. No way to spot which trains or stages were well-guarded and which weren't. All of which was essential to a successful career as a stickup man.

It appears Sam decided to substitute quantity for quality. Between December of 1876 and June of 1878, Sam and his gang—it ranged from four to twenty-three members—committed an average of one stagecoach or train holdup per month, all in the same general area. If you were to take a modern map of what Dallas and Fort Worth call the "metroplex" and construct a triangle on it, with a baseline running from Mesquite on the east edge of Dallas to Weatherford in Parker County just west of Fort Worth, with the triangle's apex at Denton, it would contain every successful Sam Bass robbery in Texas, save one. That single exception occurred at Allen Station in Collin County, now the town of Allen between Plano and McKinney, just north of Dallas. It's less than five miles outside the Mesquite-to-Denton leg of the triangle.

The robberies were numerous but they weren't particularly lucrative. In the nineteen or so months of Sam Bass gang activity in the Fort Worth-Dallas area, Sam and his gang managed to steal slightly more than $1,500. Figuring Sam's share as an equal split on each successful stickup—there were several "and we didn't even get the six dollars" incidents in there—Sam accumulated a little more than $500. Pay for an ordinary cowboy—not a top hand—was $30 a month "and found" (bed and board) during this period. It doesn't take a calculator to tell you that Sam could have made more money as a cowboy—but if he had, he wouldn't have been "Sam Bass the Great Texas Train Robber" and newly crowned king of the lowlife in Fort Worth.

During this period Sam picked up a number of companions whose names feature in the ballad—"Old Dad" Underwood, Frank Jackson, Seaborn Barnes—who became his closest pal—and Jim Murphy, whose name was once as despised in Texas as Bob Ford's was in Missouri. At least one writer has identified Barnes as "Seaborn Bass," Sam's brother, but research in Indiana tells us Sam had no brothers.

By the late spring of 1878, North Texas was way too hot to hold Sam Bass. The law had gotten uncomfortably close too many times, and was conducting an unprecedented manhunt in the area. An old joke has a ranger addressing a Denton County farmer: "Did you ever, in your entire life so far as you know, lay eyes on Sam Bass? You did? Then you're under arrest as an accomplice!"

In fact, Sam had a lot of "accomplices." His free distribution of double eagles in his flush times helped him, for he apparently did "robinhood" to some extent, slipping money to the poor-but-honest who were up against a wall. Those people were grateful and they showed it. Though the citizens of the area are, for the most part, thoroughly law-and-order-minded today, their ancestors took a perverse delight in waiting until Sam's dust settled on the northbound trail and then pointing pursuers east.

There comes a time in every bandit's career when he realizes that his friends can no longer help him and might even have turned on him. For Sam, that time came in June of 1878, and he had strong suspicions about Jim Murphy of Denton, who'd been the gang's "inside man" since mid-1877. Jim was caught by the law, then mysteriously released. Two tales, from different sources, say Jim either told his pals he broke jail or said, "they didn't have nothin' on me, so they had to let me go." Whichever tale Jim told, ever since Jim came back, things had been going wrong, and everything that went wrong was something Jim knew about ahead of time. It had come time to choose between pulling stakes and riding—or going to jail if you didn't stop a bullet.

> Jim had borrowed Sam's good gold and didn't want to pay,
> So the only shot ol' Jim he saw was to give poor Sam away.

That's what the ballad says. But history says different.

Sam's suspicions were correct—Jim made a deal with the law. He was to deliver Sam and prevent any more stickups. If Sam got away with another robbery, Jim's deal was off and he went to jail with the gang. There were, however, no candidates for a rope—in all the robberies, neither Sam nor any member of the gang had ever killed anyone.

Sam was certainly planning a killing—he wanted Murphy dead, and the quicker the better. When he talked to rangers after Round Rock, Jim related how he'd pleaded for his life, assuring Bass that he'd made no deals and never thought about turning in his pals. He claimed his life was saved by his young cousin, Frank Jackson, who stepped between Murphy and Sam's cocked pistol, saying that if anything went wrong again he'd shoot Jim himself. This is Murphy's version—whether or not it's true is anybody's guess.

In late June, 1878, Sam, Sebe, Frank, and Jim started south. The plan was to hit a small bank somewhere along the road for traveling money—Sam had never robbed a bank and reasoned that the law wouldn't be expecting it—and then make light tracks for the Rio Grande. Murphy didn't expect to survive the stickup—he figured he'd be "caught in the crossfire" or something similar and "accidentally" shot. While we don't know for sure, there's every reason to think that's exactly what Sam had in mind.

The first intended target was a bank in Temple, but Jim objected. Too close to Fort Worth, he insisted—and surprisingly, Sam agreed. Jim's real reason to objecting to Temple had nothing to do with its proximity to Fort Worth. He didn't feel he'd have time to warn the rangers and have them get there to stop it. Since he "knew" Sam was going to kill him, either during the stickup or immediately afterwards, he wanted all the law he could get on hand when the time came. Even if Sam didn't kill him, if the robbery was successful, Jim would go to jail along with everybody else. The prospect of going to prison, having double-crossed both his own gang *and* the rangers, didn't really appeal to Jim.

The boys stopped for a night or two in Waco to sample the town's well-known nightlife. Waco was the home of Baylor University, a staunchly Southern Baptist institution famed for its production of Baptist preachers. That Waco maintained one of the largest quasi-legal red-light districts in Texas—just a stone's throw from the Baylor campus—is less well-known. In all fairness, Waco was also the crossing-point on the Brazos for Kansas-bound trail herds; however, the red-light district remained long after the trail herds were but a memory—finally shut down in 1917 by the U.S. Army, which threatened to put the entire town of Waco off-limits to soldiers unless Waco closed the district. Yet another "badman" of an entirely different sort, William Cowper Brann, would later have much to say on the subject of Waco's strange combination of brothels and Baylor.

While in Waco, by Murphy's recollection, Sam threw a double eagle on a gambling table. "Well, Jim," Murphy later quoted him as saying, "there goes the last of the 1877 gold. It hasn't done me a bit of good, but easy come, easy go—I'll get some more where that came from."

Jim wasn't too interested in either the gambling or the girls. A decision was reached in Waco, and he had to relay it to the rangers without Sam finding out. Since either Sam or Frank was "always watching me," that proved difficult. Eventually, though, he managed to send a frantic wire to Major June Peak of the rangers in

Austin: "We are on our way to rob the bank in Round Rock. For God's sake be there to prevent it."

Saturday, July 20, 1878, like every other Saturday, would be Town Day in Round Rock. Farmers, ranchers, cowboys—just about everybody would be in town to spend what little money they had, and of course the town would turn out to help them spend it. By bank-closing time—five o'clock—the little bank would be bulging at the seams with hard cash. It was a jim-dandy time for a stickup.

The rangers certainly thought so. Early Friday morning, lawmen began to arrive by the drove—rangers from Austin and Waco came in by train (a detachment coming from Mason by horse got in about three hours too late). They were joined by virtually every lawman in Williamson County and volunteers from Travis County. The law was set for a stickup that would occur, they felt sure, on Saturday afternoon. The trap was set and the rangers were determined Sam wouldn't walk out of it.

At about half past four on Friday afternoon, July 19, four men wearing long dusters rode into Round Rock's "New Town" section from the west. One dropped off near a feed store on the western edge of town—Jim Murphy, who told the others he was "going to get some horse feed." It would be a long, hard ride come Saturday, he insisted, and the horses should get a good bait of corn and oats Friday night so they'd be up to it.

The other three—Sam Bass, Seaborn Barnes, and Frank Jackson—rode on into New Town. They tied their horses in front of Copprell's Store, just about in the middle of the New Town business district. As they dismounted, one man's duster opened enough to expose the muzzle-end of a pistol holster.

Henry Grimes, Round Rock's resident deputy sheriff—the town had no city marshal—saw the holster. There was an ordinance in Round Rock that prohibited the carrying of pistols within the city limits, and nobody was going to break the law in Henry

Grimes's bailiwick. He followed the three men into the store. "I believe you're carrying a pistol," he said. "You'll have to give it to me." Grimes's own pistol was still in the holster.

The three outlaws were jumpy anyway. All three whirled, pulling their pistols as they did so. Somebody—later identified by the clerk as Sam—said, "We'll give you both of 'em," and they all let fly. Henry Grimes, Round Rock's overzealous deputy, stands alone as the only man ever killed in connection with any Sam Bass stickup. He was dead before he hit the floor.

All Hell promptly broke loose. Bass, Barnes, and Jackson ran for the door and burst into the street, grabbing for their horses. Rangers and deputies, "assisted" by several local citizens, appeared from everywhere, and they came a-smokin'. Within seconds, the street was the middle of a hailstorm of crisscrossing gunfire. Barnes fell dead almost immediately, shot through the chest. A slug hit Sam in the gunbelt, breaking open two cartridges and carrying fragments of leather, brass cartridge case, and gunpowder into his belly. An instant later, a freak shot passed through the trigger guard of his six-shooter, clipping off his trigger finger. He staggered, holding his belly with his left hand, pressing his mutilated right hand against his side to staunch the bleeding.

Seventeen-year-old Frank Jackson calmly ignored the flying lead, untied his own horse and Sam's, boosted the wounded bandit into the saddle, mounted his own horse, and—holding Sam in the saddle with one hand and guiding both horses with the other—spurred both animals and galloped westward out of town through the gunfire. As they raced by, a five-year-old girl who was swinging on an iron gate in front of her house saw them. Nearly eighty years later when I talked to her, she clearly remembered one of the bandits—Sam Bass, she insisted—yelling at her to get into the house. People were shooting, he said, and they might hit her.

Major June Peak and his officers were expecting the ball to open Saturday, not Friday. The law was caught off guard. One ranger was being shaved in the town barbershop—there were two men inside, one to be shaved, one to watch for back-shooters, which was standard ranger operating procedure. When the shooting started, both rangers bolted for the street, one still with lather on his face and the barber's cape around his neck. As he hit the sidewalk, a slug smashed into one of the posts supporting the shop's wooden awning, spraying his face with splinters. He instantly dropped to his belly and did his shooting from the prone.

Two rangers, Thomas Floyd and Richard Ware, later claimed —or were claimed by others—to have shot Bass. However, a letter dated July 22, written from Round Rock by Ranger John R. Bannister, flatly states: "Dick Ware killed Barnes and Geo. Harrel killed Bass." John A. Lomax's text of the ballad doesn't mention Dick Ware or Harrel, but it takes Tom Floyd to task:

> Oh, Tom's a big six-footer and thinks he's mighty fly,
> But I can tell you his racket—he's a deadbeat on the sly.

There is absolutely no historic certainty about who fired the shot that hit Sam's belly, but John Bannister was in a position to have talked to everyone involved within hours after it happened.

Since the law was caught so unexpectedly, pursuit was organized slowly. Though some parties did fan out to the west, it was well after dark before the pursuit was coordinated—and before a terrified Jim Murphy came out of hiding to add what he could.

Come sunup Saturday, Town Day was forgotten as the whole town turned out for a bandit hunt. Late that afternoon, Sam was found, still alive, sitting propped against a live oak tree west of town.

The most-wanted bandit in Texas was still conscious. He was able to tell his captors that Jackson, the seventeen-year-old who'd rescued him, had wanted to stay with him. The boy insisted the two could make a fight of it, at least. Bass said he told the youngster not to be a damn fool, but to get gone while the getting was good.

Jackson did, and all the ballad has to say of him is: "And Jackson's in the bushes a-tryin' to get away."

The closest hospital was in Austin. Sam couldn't travel that far. He was taken to the old Round Rock schoolhouse, where blankets and pillows were spread on tables to make him as comfortable as possible. He was asked to confess and name his accomplices, but he told the law it was against his principles to "blow on my pals." He lingered throughout Saturday night, and by early Sunday afternoon it was obvious the end was very near. "The world is bobbing around" is usually quoted as Sam's last statement, but according to Bannister's letter—and he was present and heard what Bass said—what Sam actually said was, "This world is but a bubble, troubles wherever you go." A large book had been placed on Sam's chest—as the book rose and fell, his breathing could be monitored. At about 4:20 P.M., just about two minutes after his last statement, the book rose, fell—and didn't rise again. It was Sunday, July 21, 1878—Sam Bass's twenty-seventh birthday.

Young Bannister apparently made a favorable impression on Bass, for his letter to his mother also states: "I have a Relic which he gave me, his Sixshooter Belt & Scabert. The Shot that Killed him passed through the top of the Scabbert & through the Belt." Since Sam was shot in the belly, this says he was packing his shooter slung for a crossdraw under his duster that day.

Jim Murphy, the traitor, was released and went home to Denton.

He was not warmly welcomed. Within a year there had been so many threats on his life that he asked the Denton County sheriff for permission to sleep in the jail as a precaution against being murdered in his bed.

Jim suffered from chronic eye trouble, which he treated with an eyedrop containing belladonna—a deadly poison. Within two years of Sam's death, Jim was found dead in the cell where he slept. The official version insists that some of the eyedrops trickled into his mouth and killed him—but the fact that he put the eye-drops in while lying flat on his back seems to be what doctors call a "contraindication." According to J. M. Thorne of Fort Worth, who went to school with Murphy as a boy, someone slipped a more dangerous drug into Murphy's eye medicine and "he died a raving maniac." Official records, though, show that he died of belladonna poisoning.

There is a legend—nothing more—that says a water glass that was beside Jim's bed when he was found dead had mysteriously disappeared by the time the doctor arrived to render the final verdict. Since Jim was definitely poisoned with belladonna, it's just possible the doctor might have been able to find traces of the poison in the water glass had he the chance to examine it. The ballad says nothing of the manner of Jim's death, but it does indicate that it was written after he died.

> He sold out Sam and Barnes and left their friends to mourn.
> Oh, what a scorching Jim will get when Gabriel blows his horn!
> Perhaps he's got to heaven, there's none of us can say,
> But if I am right in my surmise, he's gone the other way.

But what of Frank Jackson, the youngster who became as close to a hero as an outlaw can be that hot July afternoon? Did he "vanish from the face of the earth" as Jack Davis was alleged to have done? As late as the 1960s, true wild west-type magazines published in New York were fond of saying "and the Texas Rangers still maintain an open file on the Sam Bass gang—Jackson has never been caught." We know that the search for him was extensive. A newspaper article in Winnipeg, Manitoba, Canada, from the summer of 1879, records the presence of "two Texas officers" in the area, "searching for the renowned bandits, Jackson and Underwood." The only Jackson and Underwood the rangers ever hunted that thoroughly were Frank Jackson and Dad Underwood of the Sam Bass gang.

Frank Jackson was "seen" by "those who knew" in places as widely separated as Canada and Brazil. As late as the 1980s, another of those New York-published true wild west magazines carried a long article, purporting to describe the post-Sam Bass career of the "desperate Texas outlaw," Frank Jackson, which stated that the file remains open in the Texas Department of Public Safety.

Well, the file isn't still open and hasn't been for quite a while. It was quietly but firmly closed in 1937. The hand that closed it was that of Texas Ranger Captain Frank Hamer.

Along about 1920, the rangers began to get tentative contacts from "an old bandit" who lived in New Mexico and wanted to "get square with the law" before he died. One of those who was involved in arranging contact, somewhat later, was the famous western writer Eugene Manlove Rhodes. The "old bandit," as it turned out, was a longtime, highly respected New Mexico resident, a rancher and businessman with a large spread and a large family. Though the name he was using in New Mexico never surfaces in the file, he had once been known in Texas as Frank Jackson.

For about fifteen years Texas lawmen urged the old man to come back and clear his name—he was, after all, considered almost a hero for his fearless rescue of Bass from the hailstorm of hot lead in downtown Round Rock. He resisted all efforts.

Perhaps it was the man they sent to talk to him. Had he spoken to affable Jim Gillette, one-time ranger sergeant, former sheriff of both El Paso and Brewster Counties, and one of the Mason County rangers who arrived in Round Rock about three hours too late for the show, or to well-liked, jolly Bill Sterling, who became the last ranger adjutant general of Texas, the old man might have agreed. Instead, the man sent to talk to him was Frank Hamer. There has never been a more dedicated, honest, efficient lawman than Frank Hamer—and never one more frightening to look at. Captain Frank, for those who never saw him, was what female romantic novelists might call "strangely handsome"—tall, smooth-faced, and with a peculiar rounded face that might have looked jolly on someone else. The Cap'n's eyes spoiled the effect. They were blue—and cold as North Pole ice. Those who looked him in the eye—and when I was a boy, I was one—can tell you. Frank Hamer could look completely through about six grown men and near four feet into solid granite on the other side.

The old New Mexico rancher never came back to Texas to clear his name. When Hamer closed the file in 1937, Jackson had been dead for some time. When a member of the Jackson family contacted me a while back to see if I had any information on where Frank might have gone after Round Rock or who his descendants might be, I had to tell the lady exactly what I've set down here and no more—because that's all I, or anyone else now living, knows for sure. Frank Hamer, said one female reporter, was "about as talkative as an oyster."

The ballad tells us:

> Sam met his fate at Round Rock, July the twenty-first.
> They pierced poor Sam with rifle balls and emptied out his
> purse.
> Poor Sam, he is a corpse, and six feet under clay . . . .

Well, the date's pretty close to right, anyway. He died on the twenty-first, though he was shot on the nineteenth. Few rifles were fired that day—the law had been caught as much by surprise as Sam, and for the most part all they had handy were six-shooters. As for rifling his purse—Sam was broke, having dumped his last double eagle at a gambling table in Waco, in spite of the ten thousand and one tales of "Sam Bass's buried treasure" that abound in Williamson County. But Sam, he *is* a corpse, and six feet under clay—or under Round Rock caliche, anyway.

They buried Sam in the Round Rock graveyard, over in a corner to keep him away from the law-abiding folks, and they buried Sebe Barnes beside him. Sam's sisters, up in Indiana, sent money for a tombstone—one of those old Cleopatra's Needle sorts—and on it was inscribed:

SAMUEL BASS
July 21, 1851
July 21, 1878
A BRAVE MAN REPOSES IN DEATH HERE
WHY WAS HE NOT TRUE?

Somebody put up a stone for Sebe and inscribed it HE WAS RIGHT BOWER TO SAM BASS. Over the years, both stones were chipped away to stumps by souvenir hunters.

A good many years ago, when I last visited Sam's grave, I'd have had trouble finding it save for the crude signs reading "Sam Bass" that pointed the way. The Johnson grass was four feet high around it, but Sam's plot was cleared. The only marker was a small "Texas Red" granite stone reading SAM BASS 1851-1878. I looked to my left—Sam's right—and saw nothing but weeds.

"Lookin' for somebody?" the groundskeeper asked.

"Seaborn Barnes," I said. "He was Sam's best friend, and he was killed right in front of Copprell's Store. He was buried on Sam's right, and his stone said, 'He was right bower to Sam Bass.'" "You sure about that?" he asked. "I been in Round Rock all my life an' I reckon I heard that story about a million times, but I never heard of anybody named Seaborn Barnes."

To say "*sic transit gloria mundi*" at this point would be rubbing salt in it.

An auspiciously placed X beneath the State Archives copy of this much disputed photo indicates that Sam Bass is the middle figure. The photo seems to have been taken in San Antonio in the spring of 1876, but that's not certain either. According to "those who knew," the men are, from left to right, Sam Bass, Joel Collins, and Jim Murphy; or Frank Jackson, Sam Bass, and Unknown. As to which, at this late date pick one. You might have a 50 percent chance of being right. Photo courtesy Texas State Archives, Austin, Texas.

THE MURDER OF BEN THOMPSON

Ben Thompson was born in 1843, and that's about all you can say for sure about that. He might have been born in Yorkshire, England—there were at least five boy babies named "Benjamin Thompson" born in Yorkshire in 1843—he might have been born in Nova Scotia, Canada, and he might have been born in Lockhart, Texas. It was in Texas, Kansas, and Colorado—but mostly in Texas—that he came to fame. Let's make no mistake about it—Ben Thompson was a badman. He was, at one time or another, a successful cattleman, a business owner, and city marshal of Austin, Texas. He was also a gambler, a hired gunman, a killer, and a drunk-and-dangerous menace to anybody who got in his way. One more thing: along with possibly Clay Allison but darn few others, he was one of the very few "Old West" gunmen who was fast—really fast—on the draw. Fast draw—the stuff you see in the movies and the sort of thing you saw on television in the western era of the 1950s and 1960s—was the invention of one man. His name was Dee Woolem, and he was a fast-draw showman on the fair circuit. He invented the fast draw because he invented the holster you could fast draw with. His holster was steel, covered with leather, and from it you could jerk a six-shooter with speed unheard of in the nineteenth century. Dee—along with showmen and trickshooter-trainers like Rodd Redwing and Joe Bowman—created the fast draw.

Yes, there were some pretty swift fellers before Dee and Rodd and Joe. Tom Threepersons was one of them, the legendary Cherokee lawman from Oklahoma. Most of 'em, though, were twentieth-century folks, and most of 'em were lawmen. The legends of fast draw in the nineteenth century were, for the most part, the creations of pulp magazine writers of the 1920s and 1930s, men and women who often had never been west of the Hudson River and never fired a gun of any kind in their lives. They wrote about it, and the movies, which turned much of the pulp writers' output into Poverty Row westerns, made it "so" by judicious use of film-speed variations and cutaway shots.

There were exceptions. Clay Allison of Abilene, who styled himself a "shootist" and insisted that he never killed a man who didn't need killing, was one. Ben Thompson was certainly another. After that, the list grows short and uncertain.

Thompson and his partner, Phillip Coe, first went into business with the Senate Saloon and Variety Theater in Austin, on Congress Avenue, just south of the old capitol building. It featured drinks and hurdy-gurdy gals—some of whom no doubt did more than dance for the patrons, and kicked back a portion of their earnings to the proprietors—and was well-patronized by officials of the state's government. Later they moved to Abilene, Kansas, where they opened a saloon called the Bull's Head. The sign featured a full-figured—and anatomically correct—painting of a bull, which offended a number of people. The boys got into an argument with the city law over it—a feller known as Duckbill from his big nose. His last name was Hickok. Ned Buntline changed it to Wild Bill for the dime novels.

Thompson and Coe had a large cactus added to the painting to conceal the objectionable anatomy, but Hickok remained angry with them. Using the fact that Coe shot a mad dog in the street without first calling the law, therefore being guilty of the crimes of firing a gun in the city limits and carrying a pistol contrary to city ordinance, he shot Phil in the back with a derringer pistol. Ben was out of town at the time. By the time he returned, his property had been seized and Hickok had gunmen waiting to ambush him if he tried to take revenge for the killing of Coe. Ben knew when the cards had been stacked, and he'd been gambling long enough not to bet into the other feller's game. Over the years it became obvious that Ben Thompson was two people. When sober, he was a responsible and upstanding citizen, a husband and father, who ran his business and paid his taxes with the best of them. When drunk, he was a holy terror with a six-gun in each hand, and woe betide the fool who set him off. The tales of Thompson's shooting sprees in Austin alone would fill several books, and there's little reason to doubt the Austin police were deathly afraid of him.

On one occasion, Thompson entered a gambling hall in Austin, and—apparently for no more reason than to see the balls fly—put two slugs in the keno goose. (Keno is similar to bingo but uses a four-by-four rather than a five-by-five board. The goose is the long-necked bottle or cage used to dispense the numbered balls in either keno or bingo.) Calls were sent out to the police to arrest him. The *Austin Statesman* had this to say on the pursuit:

> Ben bought sixteen copies of the *Statesman* containing an account of his shooting the Keno Goose, and went down to the International depot to take the train for Kansas. The police heard that he was at the depot and hurried with all dispatch high on hill in rear of the capitol to look for him, and continued the search until the train was gone. On Monday morning the police force will present the *Statesman* reporter with a leather medal for his faithful

and impartial account of their Herculean efforts to arrest Ben Thompson.

The International & Great Northern depot in Austin was almost on the north bank of the Colorado, near where the present Amtrak depot is located. The "hill in rear of the capitol" is College Hill, where the University of Texas tower building is now located—and, at the time, that was about as far north in Austin as you could go and still be in the city limits, and pretty close to as far from the I&GN depot as you could get. The "leather medal" referred to is probably a whack upside the head with a lead-loaded leather sap.

Ben actually ran for City Marshal in Austin, and records of his first run are clear. Captain Edward Creary, the incumbent—who ran as an independent greenbacker—garnered 1,174 votes to Thompson's 744. The republican candidate, Burns, got 75 votes. According to Thompson's close friend and later biographer, Austin attorney W. H. Walton, Ben took the defeat in good grace and left Austin for two years, returning in time to run in the next election. What Walton reveals is that the next time Ben ran for city marshal, he ran unopposed. Legend has it he came back to Austin on the fight, and when Creary announced that he would oppose Thompson once again, Ben shot him. The wound wasn't fatal, but it definitely discouraged Creary, who withdrew his candidacy. Nobody else filed. Ben became Austin's city marshal and chief of police, more or less by default.

There's not much question Ben played favorites as chief of police—virtually every city police department in Texas in the nineteenth century (and much of the early twentieth century) was corrupt to some degree. One thing was certain, though—you might pay off the Austin police, but you didn't back 'em down. Ben Thompson backed water for nobody.

When the gambling halls of Austin began to grow old, Ben was known to travel to San Antonio to tempt chance. In San Antonio, facing on what is now Alamo Plaza, was a saloon, gambling house, and theater called the Vaudeville Variety Theater. It was owned by a one-armed Confederate veteran named Jack Harris. W. H. Walton spares no adjectives in heaping calumny on the head of Harris and upon his business, describing him as "the owner of a lost and disowned name" and "king of the 'guttersnipe' and 'ward politician' world," while he described the Vaudeville as "a vile place where robbery at gambling, craziness from whiskey, women's prostitution, and the wreck and ruin of manly youth is a nightly if not a daily occurrence." In fact, Jack Harris and Ben Thompson were two peas in a pod—save for the fact that Jack seldom drank—and the Vaudeville had a lot in common with saloons Ben owned in Austin and Kansas.

Jack Harris had a faro dealer named Joe Foster, and—as I've mentioned before—there might once have been a straight game of faro dealt, but if it was it has yet to be identified as to time and place. Foster probably was dealing a crooked game of faro when Ben Thompson lost everything but his shirt.

You can beat the house at faro, even if the deck is stacked, but you have to know how. Ben knew how. He hocked his personal jewelry—according to Walton, several thousand dollars worth (gamblers, in particular, wore lots of fancy jewelry; it was getaway or burial money as well as flash)—and went back to the game. He then began to play recklessly and unsystematically, bucking the game limit every time he bet.

Stacking the faro deck is effective only when the dealer can predict with fair accuracy what cards the players are going to bet on. When a player really plunges and bets unpredictably, he has as much chance of winning as a faro player ever has, because the deck can't be stacked to anticipate the play.

Thompson won back all the money he'd previously lost and most of the value of his jewelry, and then demanded the return of his sparklers. They were returned to him, leaving him "light"—owing the bank—about $300. He then tried to quit the game, and Foster demanded payment of the remainder of his debt.

Thompson immediately flew into a rage. He pulled his six-gun and jammed it up Foster's nose, accused the dealer of cheating—which he probably was—and then told the entire house just exactly how Foster was stacking the faro deck.

Jack Harris, who wasn't in the house when Ben made his play, felt obligated to defend his dealer. He stated that Thompson, not Foster, had cheated, had robbed the game, and was a tinhorn. Those were fighting words and Harris knew it. Walton insists that Harris had gunmen out looking for Ben, but that seems unlikely since Jack was the sort of feller who packed his own loads, and there were very few people in Texas who were foolish enough to go after Ben Thompson, regardless of how much money was offered. At any rate, the next time Ben was in San Antone, he met Jack and said he'd heard tell Jack was on the hunt for him. Jack said no, he wasn't hunting Ben—he was waiting for him in the Vaudeville, and if the Austin gambler set his foot through the door he'd get cut off at the pockets with a shotgun.

Rumors flew. In a situation like that, they always did. Gossip had it that Harris had hired "dozens" of gunmen to ambush Ben with rifles or shotguns, had promised them virtual fortunes for proof of Thompson's death, and had boasted that he could guarantee a "speedy trial and acquittal" for anyone charged with murdering Ben Thompson in the streets of San Antonio. Some of the talk may actually have been true, but not much was. One thing we do know: Harris, who had never been much of a pistol man, provided himself with a double-barreled ten-gauge shotgun. Since he was one armed, there were questions as to whether or not he could use it. "I can hit a bird on the wing," he said. "I reckon I can hit a man standing."

As it turned out, Jack never got to find out. Ben stepped into the Vaudeville and began making fighting talk, and Jack came downstairs with his shotgun. As soon as Ben saw him he said, "Jack, what are you going to do with that gun?"

"Shoot you!" Jack said, swinging the gun to level.

When a man's coming down on you with a shotgun, one-armed man or not, you don't have much time to do whatever you're going to do. Ben didn't need much. He drew and fired three times, two shots hitting and disabling Harris before Jack could get the shotgun level. That's fast gunhandling in anybody's book. Jack Harris lived about three hours.

Ben turned himself into the San Antonio law and was tried for the murder of Jack Harris. He resigned his job as Austin's city marshal, of course—he sorta had to, being under indictment for cold-blooded murder. He was defended by four different Austin law firms at the same time, one of which was Walton & Hill.

Thompson was eventually acquitted on the charge of murder—it was, after all, about as fair a fight as fights got. Harris was armed with a shotgun to Ben's six-shooter, the men were facing one another, and there was no doubt in either one's mind that there was a shooting about to take place. The fact that Ben deliberately provoked the fight was balanced by the fact that the entire town of San Antonio knew Jack Harris had said, "I'll kill Ben Thompson." Nearly a year later Ben got on the train for San Antonio once again. He was drunk—as he usually was when he went to San Antonio. On the train he met John King Fisher, Jr., of Uvalde, who went by King Fisher, to distinguish him from his father, John King Fisher, Sr., who went by John.

King Fisher and Ben Thompson were not close friends. They were at best acquaintances, though King—who was no slouch with a six-gun himself—certainly respected Ben's prowess with a shootin' iron, even if he respected nothing else about him. King had been a budding badman in his younger days but had managed to turn his life around to some extent. Still, when he met the drunken Thompson on the train, he agreed to go with Ben for a run at the saloons and gambling houses of San Antonio.

At about 8:00 P.M., March 10, 1884, the train arrived in San Antonio. Thompson and Fisher hit a couple of saloons and drank a bit, then went to Turner Hall, a "legitimate" theater, to see the tearjerker melodrama *East Lynne.* At about 11:00 P.M. the final curtain fell, and Thompson and Fisher made their way to the Vaudeville Variety Theater.

Joe Foster, the faro dealer Ben accused of cheating, and W. H. Sims, Jack Harris's old partner, were running the place. At about 1:00 A.M. on the eleventh, Thompson and Fisher met with Sims, and Thompson—even more obnoxiously drunk than usual—called for Joe Foster to come out. Foster came downstairs and Thompson asked to shake hands with him. Foster refused.

What happened next is a matter of the "official story" versus evidence. The story is that Thompson tried to pull his gun, that a private policeman named Coy grabbed him around the arms to prevent it, that Thompson shot Coy in the leg, and that a "general melee" erupted, with Foster, Sims, Coy, Thompson, and Fisher all shooting at once. In the scrape, Thompson and Fisher were killed.

The physical evidence says there were at least twenty-two shots fired, because nine of them hit Thompson and thirteen hit Fisher. We don't have an autopsy report on Fisher's body, but when Thompson's remains were returned to Austin, they were autopsied by the noted Austin surgeon, Dr. Goodall Wooten.

Thompson, Fisher, and Coy were all armed with .45 caliber Colt revolvers. What Foster and Sims were carrying is unknown, but at least one source says they were packing smaller caliber guns—Foster a double-action Colt .38 and Sims a Smith & Wesson .32. In the body of Ben Thompson, Dr. Wooten found nine slugs—none of which came from a .45 Colt. All nine were the distinctive flat-based, flat-nosed, 200-grain slugs from the .44 Winchester or .44-40 cartridge—which, in Texas, meant they came out of rifles or carbines, not six-shooters. In addition, every slug in the body entered from above and behind and ranged downward through the body.

Conclusion? Jack Harris's old friends set up an ambush, Ben walked into it and got blown away. King Fisher happened to be in the line of fire. The "official story" is pure bull.

THE DEVIL'S DISCIPLE OF WACO

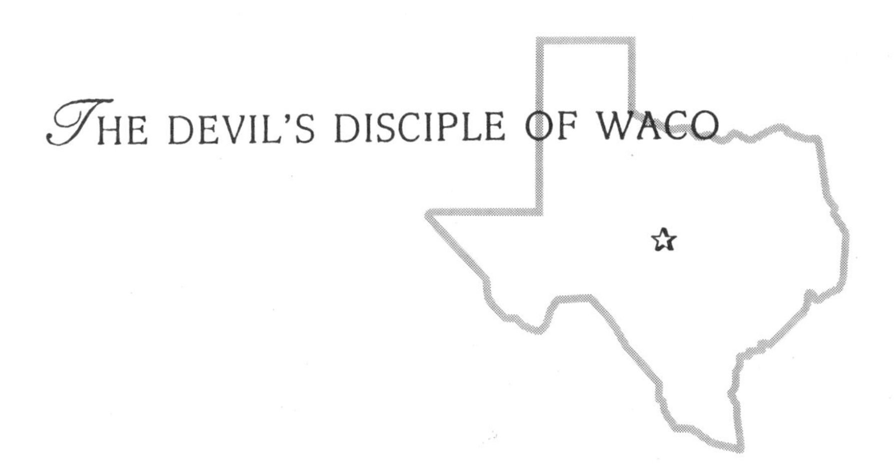

The most successful muckraking newspaperman in history lived—and died—in Waco, Texas. He was so successful that he not only persuaded the students of Baylor University to try to lynch him, he managed to get himself assassinated in the middle of downtown Waco. His name was William Cowper Brann, and even today certain citizens of Waco turn purple in the face and begin to sputter over those five syllables.

Brann's list of occupations before he turned Waco on its ear reads like the résumé of a man nobody would want to hire. He started work at thirteen as a bellboy in a hotel in Illinois, his native state. By the time he turned twenty-one, he had been a drummer for a job printer, a housepainter, a printer's devil on a newspaper, a fireman for the MKT railroad, a brakeman on the I&GN, a pretty fair pitcher for a semi-pro baseball team, and road manager of a traveling opera company. He then embarked on the career of peripatetic newspaperman, working for the *Saint Louis Globe-Democrat*, the *Galveston Evening Tribune*, the *Galveston News*, and the *Houston Post*. While in Houston, he suffered the first great tragedy of his life—the death of his thirteen-year-old daughter Inez. The girl took an entire bottle of morphine pills (at that time available over-the-counter at any drugstore) after an argument with her parents. Her suicide note read, in part, "I don't want to live. I could never be as good as you want me to. I was born for a rowdy and you would be ashamed of me."

Shortly thereafter, Brann moved to Austin, where he bought the assets of a small, faltering newspaper and established what he called the *Austin Iconoclast.* It was a newspaper from which Brann couldn't get fired—he owned it—and one in which he could freely express his opinions. He did so, but most of Austin wasn't interested. The paper lasted about fifteen months, in 1891 and 1892, retitled the *Texas Iconoclast* for the last few issues. When it failed, the assets were bought for $250 by an Austin bank teller named William Sidney Porter, who lightened the tone and renamed it the *Rolling Stone.*

After the failure of the first *Iconoclast,* Brann returned for a time to Saint Louis to work on the *Saint Louis Post-Dispatch* as a reporter. In November of 1892 he came to San Antonio as editor of the *San Antonio Express.* He'd barely been there two months when a San Antonio lawyer named W. H. Brooker made statements about two *Express* employees which Brann considered slanderous. He let fly with an editorial in the *Express* which raked Brooker from stem to stern. Brooker, who had local political connections, either went himself or had some of his friends go to the owner of the *Express,* who demanded Brann publish an apology. Brann refused—so the owner wrote the apology and signed Brann's name to it.

Brann, infuriated, went to the *San Antonio Light* and offered to tell all about the apology. At the *Light* office he came face-to-face with Brooker himself, who threatened to blow Brann's brains out. If he thought he might intimidate the editor, he was sadly mistaken—Brann went immediately to a gunshop and bought a pistol and holster, which he began to wear in plain view. Brooker thought about it a while, then withdrew the threat, but the damage was done. In March of 1894, the *Express* informed Brann that his services were no longer required.

For most of the rest of the year, Brann made a bare living for himself, his wife, and his two surviving children by working the popular but not overly well-paying lecture circuit. Then, in November, he was offered a job as an editorial writer on the *Waco Daily News*.

Waco was a strange town in 1894. There were four church-supported colleges there: the Methodist Waco Female Academy; the Catholic Academy of the Sacred Heart; Paul Quinn College, operated by the African Methodist Episcopal Church; and Waco's major claim to fame, Baylor University, operated by the Southern Baptist Church. There were over sixty churches, most of them Baptist.

Besides being a center of church-sponsored education, Waco was a thriving business town. In the 1890s, Waco regularly handled the marketing of over 100,000 bales of cotton a year; wool mills, cottonseed mills, planing mills for East Texas timber, and flour mills employed over 500 people. The discovery of a hot artesian well in 1889 made Waco a health spa, and hundreds of tourists flocked to "take the waters." In 1894, it was the sixth-largest city in Texas—population 25,000—and was closing in on number five.

In that same year, Waco boasted more than eighty saloons, and was one of only two cities in the United States that maintained a legal prostitution district. While other cities would adopt the plan later—San Antonio, El Paso, and New Orleans being three—at the time only Waco, Texas, and Omaha, Nebraska, had reservations set aside by city ordinance in which prostitution existed on quasi-legal footing. This fact was not lost on William Cowper Brann.

If there was anything Brann hated above all else, it was hypocrisy —and he'd landed right in the middle of perhaps the single most hypocritical town in Texas, if not the entire United States. In February of 1895, Brann began a new publication with an old title. The first issue of Brann's new *Iconoclast* hit the streets.

In that first issue, Brann's statement of the guiding philosophy of the *Iconoclast* was mildly worded but contained the potential for high explosive. "The *Iconoclast* makes war upon no religion of whatever name or origin that has fostered virtue or added aught to the happiness of the human race," he wrote. "It is simply an independent American journal, exercising its constitutional prerogative to say what seemeth unto it best, without asking any man's permission." It didn't take long for folks to find out that those mild words concealed some heavy artillery.

T. DeWitt Talmadge was a Baptist minister who was both an evangelist and a newspaper columnist, syndicated in more than 3,500 newspapers. Today, he would probably be a television evangelist, but in those days he traveled as a revivalist. Brann's previous editorials in other papers had prompted Talmadge to devote an entire newspaper column to condemning Brann as the "Apostle of the Devil." For one reason or another, Talmadge and the publisher of the *Tyler Telegram* got crossways, and the *Telegram* blasted Talmadge in an editorial. For reasons not clear, the *Telegram* shortly withdrew the remarks in an apologetic editorial. This infuriated Brann, who rolled out the *Iconoclast*'s cannons and opened fire.

"The *Tyler Telegram* humbly apologizes for having called that wide-lipped blatherskite, T. DeWitt Talmadge, 'a religious faker.' Next thing we know our Tyler contemporary will apologize for having inadvertently hazarded the statement that water is wet. When a daily newspaper tells the truth, even by accident, it should stick to it instead of crawling on its belly in the dust to humbly ask pardon of the Devil. The *Iconoclast* will pay any man $10 who will demonstrate that T. DeWitt Talmadge ever originated an idea, good, bad, or indifferent. He is simply a monstrous bag of fetid wind. The man who can find intellectual food in Talmadge's sermons could acquire a case of delirium tremens by drinking the froth out of a pop bottle."

Waco blinked, shook its collective head, blinked again, and reread. Something with teeth and claws had landed in the middle of Waco and of Texas journalism, and neither would ever be the same again.

The *Iconoclast* and its editor-publisher were inseparable. It was really no more and no less than an extension of Brann's own ego, which he allowed the public to examine for a dime a copy or a dollar a year. The public—at least outside Waco—loved it. It was the first American-published magazine to exceed 100,000 circulation in its first year of publication, and for a very long time the only Texas-published magazine ever to get 100,000 readers. By the time Brann died, the monthly print run regularly topped 120,000 and the subscription list went from Europe to Hawaii. Yet it was a mightily unprepossessing thing—usually printed tabloid style in two columns, without illustrations, and in small type. It used neither blasting headlines nor spicy pictures. It seldom exceeded sixteen pages. An advertisement from Brann's first "Annual" described it well—"An Intellectual Cocktail. Brann's *Iconoclast*. The only American magazine that ever secured 100,000 readers in a single year. It Strikes To Kill."

Indeed it did. And since William Cowper Brann wrote it all and was solely responsible for everything that appeared in it, if you loved it or hated it, you loved or hated Brann. There seems to have been no middle ground.

Brann himself, although a deeply religious man, was a freethinker on religious grounds. He was something of a philosopher of the Ambrose Bierce/H. L. Mencken school, a scathing critic of hypocrisy wherever found, and an amazingly well-read—and apparently almost completely self-educated—man. In his essay entitled "The Buck Negro" in the February 1895 issue of the *Iconoclast* (which a Ku Klux Klan member once used in an attempt to recruit me), Brann also expressed himself as a terrifyingly intense racist:

> It were better that a thousand "good negroes"—if so many there be—should suffer death or banishment than that one good white woman should be debauched. . . . The rights of the white man are paramount, and if we do not maintain them at any cost we deserve only dishonor. During the slavery régime the negro kept his place like any other beast of the field . . . but when his shackles were stricken off and he was accorded political equality with his old-time master he became presumptuous, insolent—actually imagined that the foolish attempt of fanatics to humanize him had been successful—that a law of nature had been repealed by an act of Congress! . . . The negro will remain right where he is, wear the cast-off clothes of the white man, steal his fowls, black his boots, rape his daughters, while the syphilitic "yaller gal" corrupts his sons. Yes, the negro will stay, stay until he is faded out by fornication—until he is absorbed by the stronger race, as it has absorbed many a foul thing heretofore.

But above all, Brann was a phenomenally talented writer who could dip a pen in the most corrosive of acids. A man with a biting wit. His favorite targets were Baptists.

In the second issue of the *Iconoclast,* Brann fired both barrels at the *Baptist Standard,* published in Waco and the guiding light for Texas's many Southern Baptists. "There are many things of which I would speak to you," he wrote, "but what lies heaviest on my heart is the fact that most, if not all of the religious contemporaries of the *Iconoclast* are in the habit of ladling out saving grace with one hand while raking in the shekels with the other for flaming advertisements of syphilitic nostrums, 'lost manhood' restorers and kindred quack remedies for diseases with which the faithful are supposed to be unfamiliar." Quack medicine ads were an extremely reliable source of revenue for nearly all publications of the day, but the *Iconoclast* didn't carry them—possibly because it had never been approached to carry them. At any rate, that the *Baptist Standard* carried not merely quack medicine ads—a lot of them—but quack medicine ads for diseases and disabilities which came only from the sort of life that the *Standard* itself, and every Baptist minister in the country decried, was powder for Brann's guns.

When the American Protective Association, an anti-Catholic, anti-Jew secret society which began in Clinton, Iowa, in the early 1890s, sent one of its spokesmen, a former Roman Catholic priest named Joseph Slattery, to speak in Waco, Brann primed the community ahead of time. Renaming the A. P. A. the "Aggregation of Pusillanimous Asses" and referring to Slattery and the organization as the "Apes," Brann wrote: "It is safe to say that should an apostate Protestant prefer the same sweeping charges against the clergy and the female members of their flocks that Slattery prefers against priests and nuns, no power between the two oceans could prevent him being torn to pieces and his foul carcass fed to the buzzards."

Slattery, upon arriving in Waco, didn't neglect Brann, calling him an "agent of Popery" and the "Apostle of the Devil." Brann, in an interview with a local newspaper, had no kind words. "Slattery is not up in the art of peeling the cuticle off an opponent. The pathetic is his great lay. He can't skin for shucks."

Yet Brann was at his best not in specifically aimed shots but when he fired a shotgun at a generalization. When he was called a heretic, he replied, "An heretic, my dear sir, is a fellow who disagrees with you regarding something which neither of you know anything about." About atheists he said, "An atheist once solemnly assured me that he couldn't possibly believe anything which he couldn't prove; but when I asked him what led him to take such a lively interest in the welfare of his wife's children, he became almost as angry as a Calvinist whose confession of faith has been called into question."

Brann, of course, was constantly being called a disciple of the Devil—which he denied. He did, however, "confess to a sneaking respect for Satan, for he is preeminently a success in his chosen profession. He sat into the game with a total cash capital of one snake; now he's got half the globe grabbed and an option on the other half." A self-educated man, he valued education but detested schools. "If it be a waste of lather to shave an ass, what must it be to educate an idiot? Neither the public nor any other school system has produced one really great man. Those who occupy the dais-throne among the immortals contended single-handed with the darkness of ignorance and the devil of dogmatism."

It is reported—by Brann, of course—that after one of his many speeches in which he lambasted fakery in general and in as many specifics as he could, he was approached by a doctor who commented that Brann had not included the medical profession in his remarks. "The power of language hath its limits," the speaker replied.

Brann also found time and energy to criticize everything from literature to society reporting. Of James Whitcomb Riley, the Hoosier poet whose "bucolic style" was welcomed by some as a refreshing change from the overly romantic European poetry, Brann wrote, "James Whitcomb Riley, the poetical ass with the three-story name, which he invariably inflicts upon the public in full, has broken out again." Yet to Lord Byron, the poetic ideal of the other side of the poesy coin, he was no kinder: "Perhaps of all Byron's poems Don Juan is the most read—an apt illustration of the Shakespearean axiom that the evil that men do lives after them." And when it came to satirizing the society columns, he left nobody unscathed: "Her ample figure was attired in a glove-fitting plum-colored bikeing suit of Belfast corduroy, trimmed with sable fur, with bellyband of untanned leather fastened with a massive buckle made in an adjacent blacksmith shop. A diamond scarf-pin in the form of a crupper loomed up like the headlight of a trolley car, while her left thumb supported a massive ring of beaten gold as large as a cuspidor." While Brann was having fun at the expense of everybody he could think of and making—for the day—bundles of money at it, something was going on on the Baylor campus that would bring Brann to his finest hour—and then kill him and take three more lives in the process.

In 1892, a thirteen-year-old girl, the orphaned daughter of a Brazilian Baptist preacher, was brought to Waco to be schooled and then returned to Brazil as a missionary of the Baptist General Convention of Texas. She was placed in the house of Dr. Rufus C. Burleson, who was at once an ordained minister and president of Baylor University. In 1895, at the age of sixteen, Antonia Teixeira, the Brazilian girl, was unmistakably pregnant. To make matters really bad, she named Steen Morris, the brother of Dr. Burleson's son-in-law, Reverend Silas Morris, as the father of the child.

If ever, in all of history, a situation tailor-made for exploitation by a muckraker had ever arisen, this was it. It had it all: a beautiful and at least allegedly virtuous girl, high religious muckety-mucks, and dirty work within the sound of churchbells. William Cowper Brann loved it. He sailed the *Iconoclast* straight into the battle with all guns blazing.

On the statement of Antonia Teixeira, H. S. "Steen" Morris was arrested and lodged in the McLennan County jailhouse. According to the girl, in early November of 1894, Morris forced her to drink a "whitish, sweet-tasting liquor," which rendered her semiconscious and unable to resist him, after which he "threw me to the ground and took liberties with my person." She said that after the first assault she told Mrs. Burleson that Morris had been "bothering" her, but gave no particulars. Later in the month, she said, he accosted her again, but was prevented from completing his intended purpose by the approach of "someone." This time, the girl claimed, she told Mrs. Burleson the particulars, but Morris denied assaulting her and the Burlesons refused to believe her statements. Then, in the last few days of November, she was again assaulted by Morris, and the result was the pregnancy.

Morris was interviewed by the *Waco News* in his jail cell, and, of course, denied everything. A rumor was circulating that Morris had previously assaulted a female employee of the Burlesons, a woman named Maggie Bettinger. Maggie's parents refused to allow the *News* to interview her, but stated that Maggie had, in fact, been the object of improper advances while employed in the Burleson home. The man who made the advances was not Steen Morris, they insisted, but a young man named Jones, whom they could not or would not further identify. The *News* then interviewed Dr. Burleson, who made perhaps the worst mistake he could have made under the circumstances. Instead of denying outright that Morris raped the girl, he disparaged the sixteen-year-old's character. He claimed that, ever since she came from Brazil, he and his wife had been hard put to tolerate her. She was a thief, he insisted, and "crazy after boys," and what had happened to her was her own fault.

On June 17, 1895, Antonia was delivered of a premature baby girl weighing but three pounds. The child died early the following year—but the trouble didn't.

With the July issue of the *Iconoclast,* Brann entered the fray. In a blast over 30,000 words long, he attacked Baylor University, Dr. Burleson, and the entire Baptist denomination. Burleson, in his statement, said that the family "prayed over and cried over" the girl, and Brann asked, "Are prayers and tears the only safeguards thrown around fourteen-year-old girls at Baylor?" After a comparison with Catholic convent schools—deliberately calculated, of course, to infuriate Baptists—he went on to say, "No matter how 'crazy after boys' a girl in short dresses may be, she is not permitted to go headlong to the Devil." He concluded his diatribe by stating that, to his certain knowledge, "Antonia is not the first young girl to be sent from Baylor in disgrace—that she is not the first to complain of criminal assault within its sanctified walls." He ended by comparing Baylor to Sextus Tarquinius, one of the great villains of ancient Rome.

The following month, a pamphlet appeared, authored by Dr. Burleson. It was four pages long, and set forth Burleson's and Baylor's position, which was much as Burleson had outlined in his statements to the press. It was, of course, far too little, far too late—and it certainly didn't have Brann's 100,000+ circulation. Waco's, Baylor's, and the Texas Baptist General Convention's dirty laundry had been washed in public for most of the English-speaking world to see, and there was no way to reply effectively.

Brann, of course, continued the assault. In the August issue of the *Iconoclast* there was a second blast, which Brann ended by saying, "Of course she may get justice, but it's a 100-1 shot."

Morris, in the meantime, was released on his own recognizance and went home to his new-since-January wife—a point Brann didn't neglect to point out to his readers. In October he wrote: "The *Iconoclast* did not find fault with Baylor for the child's misfortune," which was not quite true, but he did truthfully say that "it did criticize Dr. Burleson for trying to shield that institution by branding as a wilful bawd the fatherless little foreigner committed to its care. It called attention to the fact that, instead of striving to bring to justice the lecherous scoundrel who dared invade the sacred precincts of Baylor and debauch a child, Dr. Burleson employed all his energy and influence to protect the man accused of the crime"—all of which was completely true, but was the sort of thing the Texas Baptist General Convention didn't care to have announced to the world.

In March of 1896, the child died, and was buried in an unmarked grave in Waco. In the *Iconoclast,* Brann proposed to pay for a monument to the grave, to be inscribed: "Sacred to the memory of the infant daughter of the 14-year-old ward of the Baptist

Church, and an unknown member of the Baylor University Stud." That, of course, added fuel to the fire. When, in June, Morris's trial ended in a hung jury—seven to five for acquittal—he predicted that "somebody" would try to get the girl out of the country before the trial could be reconvened.

That, unfortunately for those who wanted the matter hushed and forgotten, is exactly what happened. Antonia swore an affidavit before a local justice of the peace exonerating Morris, and left the United States for Brazil the same day. Brann didn't let it go without comment. "By some means [the affidavit] was secured. The Lord may have sent it in response to prayer. Possibly Antonia concluded that, before leaving Texas, she would give it to Captain Blair (one of Morris's attorneys) as a keepsake. When Captain Blair asks the court to dismiss the case on the strength of this affidavit, let him be required to state why the drawer of the remarkable document purchased Antonia's ticket home, and who furnished the funds. Of course, her long conference with Steen Morris and his attorneys on the day before her departure may have been merely a social visit. If the currency question was discussed at all, it may have been from a purely theoretical standpoint."

Having won the day, Brann was not content to retire. He continued to assail the Baptists in the *Iconoclast,* and by 1897, the Baptists had had enough of Mr. Brann. Anonymous letters flooded his office, and one, from Nacogdoches, told him that his distributor in that town had been forced to drop the *Iconoclast* "under penalty of expulsion from the church." He published the letter—and an extensive reply in which he charged that the Baptist Church, "which boasts that it was the first to establish liberty of conscience and freedom of speech in this country . . . has been striving desperately for a hundred years to banish the last vestige of individuality and transform this nation into a pharisaical theocracy with some prurient hypocrite as its hierarch." When Baylor reopened its doors for the fall 1897 term with a record enrollment, he charged that Texas Baptists "believe it better that their daughters should be exposed to its historic dangers and their sons condemned to grow up in ignorance than that this manufactory of ministers and Magdalenes should be permitted to perish."

The edition containing the above hit the newsstands on October 1, 1897. That night, two of Baylor's largest male social societies —which served the same purpose at Baylor as Greek-letter fraternities at other colleges—-the Philomathesians and the Erisophesians, held a joint meeting. The purpose of the meeting was to plan the abduction, tar-and-feathering, and murder of William Cowper Brann by hanging him from a tree on the Baylor campus. A subcommittee of three, two from the Philomathesians and one from the Erisophesians, was appointed to do the actual kidnapping. On the evening of Saturday, October 2, three masked men, all armed with pistols, burst into Brann's home, abducted him at gunpoint, and loaded him into a waiting hack driven by a fourth.

Brann was driven at breakneck speed from his home to a point directly in front of Baylor University's main building, where a knot of students was already congregated. He was tightly bound and led to the steps of the building, where the students began to beat him with their fists, and then with sticks and rocks. Cuts opened on his head, and he was partially blinded by his own blood. A cry went up for the tar and feathers, which had been hidden under a bridge. Someone, apparently wanting to interfere but not daring to do so publicly, had removed them and hidden them elsewhere. Brann was dragged to a tree and a rope was thrown over a limb. At that point, two Baylor professors, John Tanner and a man named Brooks, interfered. The students, prevented from hanging Brann, made a dash for the school's armory to get rifles to shoot him, but found the entrance blocked by yet another professor. The plan to kill Brann hadn't succeeded, but the students weren't through. They cut the rope and shoved a paper and pencil in his hand, saying, "Sign this or you'll be killed right here." He signed his last name, and as he finished someone hit him on the head from behind, stunning him. He was bundled into the hack that brought him, but before he could gather up the reins someone whipped the horse and it raced away down the street, the semiconscious Brann holding on for dear life.

Less than a week later, Brann was again assaulted—this time by a student named George Scarbrough and his father, John. While George held Brann against a wall with a pistol, his father caned the editor, breaking his right wrist.

The November issue of the *Iconoclast* exposed the whole story of the assaults to the world in a lead article entitled "Revolvers, Ropes, and Religion." Once again Waco, Baylor, and the Texas Baptists were held up to the scorn of Brann's immense readership.

Though it would seem that the entirety of Waco hated William Cowper Brann's guts, that isn't quite true. He had a powerful ally in the person of Judge George Bruce "Big Sandy" Gerald, a Confederate veteran and one-time frontier Indian fighter. Judge Gerald wrote a spirited and fire-eating letter in defense of Brann, which he hand-delivered to the offices of the *Waco Times-Herald.* He informed the editor, J. W. Harris, that if it was not published he wanted the letter returned. Harris refused to publish the letter, but apparently showed it to several people. Judge Gerald confronted him about it and a fistfight ensued, with the Judge coming off second best.

This made Judge Gerald mad, and Judge Gerald was a very bad man to have mad at you. He had printed a handbill, which he circulated throughout McLennan County, branding Harris "a liar, a coward, and a cur." That there was going to be a killing over it there seemed to be no doubt—the only doubt was who and how many would die.

On the afternoon of November 19, 1897, Judge Gerald met J. W. and his brother, W. A., at the corner of North Fourth and Austin in downtown Waco, and the six-shooters commenced to pop. Exactly who fired first is a matter for debate, but when the smoke cleared, J. W. Harris was dead with a slug through his heart and W. A. was dead with several holes in him, the last one fired into his neck from a range so short that the gun flash set fire to his shirt collar. Judge Gerald collected a non-fatal hole in his crippled arm and had a button on the back of his coat smashed by a bullet. The score stood two to nothing on the shooting range, in favor of Brann's side of the question.

Brann, of course, was not content to let the dead rest in peace. He continued to assail Baylor University and Baptists in general in the *Iconoclast* all through 1897 and into 1898. Since the assault on him, though, he'd made one change. He now carried a long-barreled .45 Colt on his person everywhere he went. He was urged by both friends and foes to leave Waco but refused, saying he might someday leave of his own accord but he would not be driven out. He wrote in the *Iconoclast* that he was lining up some new writers, and "should the editor chance to swallow too much water the next time he is baptised, they can be depended upon to keep the flag of the *Iconoclast* afloat, at least until the red-headed heir-apparent learns to write with one hand and shoot with the other." In the same issue he wrote a tribute to Dr. Rufus Burleson, who was under fire from the Baptist General Convention and looked to be about to lose the presidency of Baylor. Characterizing Burleson as a man with "more brains, more good morals, and more manhood" than those who were looking to replace him, he concluded by saying, "Shake, Doctor; Baylor has treated you a damned sight worse than it has treated me." Whether or not Dr. Burleson appreciated what was, all in all, a magnanimous tribute from a man he'd once called a "limb of Satan," no one knows, but it wouldn't be amiss to think that few others in the Texas Baptist General Convention did.

Brann's good friend William H. Ward urged him to take a "vacation" in the spring of 1898. It would be a working vacation for

Brann (who would today be called a "workaholic" and was never "on vacation")—an extended lecture tour around Texas, with the first lecture to be given in San Antonio. Ward was to manage the tour, and was staying at The Oaks, Brann's beautiful home in Waco. The two friends were together in downtown Waco on the afternoon of April 1, 1898. As they walked down Fourth Street a shot cracked in the afternoon stillness, and Brann lurched forward. He staggered, then whirled, pulling his gun as he did so. He saw a large man aiming a pistol at him, and fired at the man, who went to his knees at the shot. Ward lunged at the man and grabbed the pistol just as a second shot was fired. The slug tore through Ward's hand and went wild. Brann emptied his pistol at the man.

As soon as the shooting stopped, two Waco police officers, Sam Hall and a man named Durie, arrested Brann. Though he was severely wounded—the first shot hit him "right where his suspenders crossed"—he was marched almost four blocks to the Waco police station, where he lay on a hard bench without medical attention for almost three hours.

The assassin was Thomas E. Davis, a substantial and prosperous citizen of Waco. Although many theories have been advanced for why he chose, apparently on the spur of the moment, to shoot Brann, no explanation has ever come forth—possibly because Brann, wounded as he was, shot Davis four times. Davis died at 2:30 P.M. the next day.

Brann was taken to his home where, at 1:55 A.M. on April 2, he died in the arms of his wife. He was buried on Sunday, April 3, at Waco's Oakwood Cemetery. The Reverend Frank Page, rector of St. Paul Episcopal Church and a long-time friend of Brann's, conducted the funeral.

Waco, though, wasn't content to let Brann rest in peace. His grave was marked with an elaborate obelisk tombstone, surmounted with a stone representation of a Lamp of Truth, and bearing a low-relief profile of William Cowper Brann. It was paid for by a number of Brann's friends.

Brann's grave is still in Oakwood Cemetery, still marked by the obelisk—but the portrait is marred. Shortly after it was erected, one of Brann's many enemies approached it under cover of darkness and shot the stone profile of the *Iconoclast*'s editor in the temple. William Cowper Brann, without doubt, would have loved to write a vitriolic essay about the incident.

Brann's *Iconoclast* has had its imitators—in Texas and elsewhere—over the years, but none has ever come even close to the original, possibly because none of those who attempted to imitate Brann had his combination of erudition and writing talent. His magazine is considered a publishing phenomenon, and he is widely quoted even today. He was truly an image-breaker, but offered nothing to replace the images he broke. Perhaps the truest statement ever made about Brann and the *Iconoclast* was this one: "If men cannot live on bread alone, still less can they do so on disinfectants."

THE PECULIAR INCIDENT OF THE PUBLIC ARCH

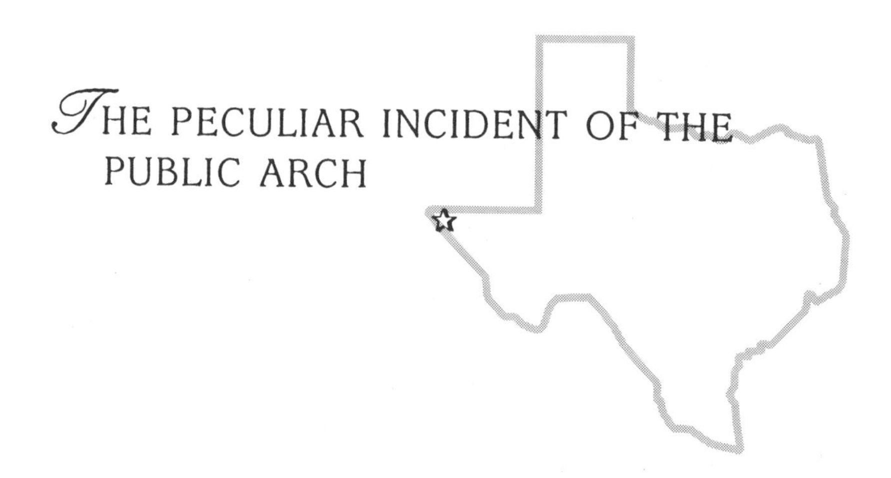

Texas outlaw legends are in proportion to the size of the state. That is to say—they're BIG. Over the years, Texas has been home to many a badman—and bad woman. In time, notoriety often fades to obscurity. But not every tale is lost. Some are duly recorded. Others are passed down by word of mouth. And occasionally, tales are preserved for posterity quite by accident.

This is the tale of three such women that might have been lost if it hadn't been for a mistake of proportions more mythic than the story itself. A mistake launched by a fabled creature every writer knows well. I call him Typo the Gremlin.

Typo and I are old, warm enemies. That's not to say we hate each other specifically, but he's out to do me all the dirt he can by scrambling my type, and he knows that if he does it and sticks around I'll mash him like a bug. There are dents in the wall of my writing room where I've might-near gotten him from time to time, but he's fast on his feet. He has to be—he's been around a long, long time, and everybody who's ever written anything has tried to kill him at one time or another.

I got Typo's life story from him a while back, right after I went from a typewriter to a word processor, and he was lamenting the fact that electronic type would soon make him obsolete and he would have to retire to the Old Gremlin's Home. We commiserated—at the time, western writing wasn't selling all that well, either.

Typo began life as an ordinary or garden-variety rafter-dwelling gremlin way back in the tenth or eleventh century, in Europe. When he was only a few hundred years old—only a juvenile gremlin—he happened to be resident in the shop of a feller named Johannes Gutenberg, and when Gutenberg invented movable type, Typo realized he'd found his life's work. Gutenberg was printing Bibles, and it wasn't long before somebody turned his back at the wrong moment. The page being set was from Exodus, and contained the Ten Commandments. Typo dropped quietly from the rafters to the type and carefully removed the negative implication from the commandment about adultery.

This caused, after the Bible was printed, some excitement—as you might imagine. Today that particular Bible is known as the "Devil's Bible," but Typo resents that most strongly. The Devil works in an entirely different way from gremlins. The two, according to Typo, aren't even related. Not even remotely.

I asked Typo about his greatest triumph. At first he talked about a minor triumph or two, including the famous "bride" headline in the old *Lubbock Avalanche*, back in the 1940s. It seems Lubbock had been having some severe rains, and after a week a bridge just outside town was washed out. The headline was intended to read "Bridge Crumbles After Seven Days Pounding." Typo took the "g" out of "bridge." Finally he made up his mind. It took place, he said, in Texas, out in El Paso, on April 18, 1886. It took me some time to run down the particulars, but this is what happened.

What is now South Mesa Street in El Paso used to be called South Utah Street, and when it was, it was the center of El Paso's long-lived, sometimes-legal red-light district. The queen of the district was a woman known as Alice Abbott, better known as Fat Alice. A certain El Paso editor once suggested that if P. T. Barnum was looking for a mate for his celebrated elephant, Jumbo, to replace the deceased and lamented Jumio, he need look no further than a certain address on El Paso's South Utah Street. Fat Alice was about six-feet tall and weighed somewhat better than 300 pounds.

Across the street from Fat Alice's place there was a house run by a woman called Little Etta. Her real name, in as far as women in her profession used real names, was Etta Clark. Little Etta stood about five-feet tall and might have weighed about a hundred pounds soaking wet with both skirt pockets full of buckshot and fishing sinkers.

The bone of contention, in this situation, was a woman called Bessie Colvin. Bessie was a small woman—about five-two or thereabouts—and her main claim to fame seems to have been a figure that could best be described as Dolly Partonesque.

For whatever reasons—there are several stories; you pick and choose as to which one to believe—Bessie decided to leave her employment with Fat Alice and take her chances with Little Etta. Fat Alice objected for several reasons, two of which seem to be that Bessie's figure was a major drawing card and she'd invested a bundle in fancy clothes for the girl—which wouldn't fit any of the other, less well-endowed girls at the house.

The situation came to a head on the evening of April 18—a date that used to be familiar to all schoolchildren who had to memorize poems:

> 'Twas the eighteenth of April in Seventy-five.
> Hardly a man is now alive who remembers that famous day and year.

One hundred and eleven years later, and a long way to the southwest, April 18 became famous for something besides Paul

Revere spending a night in a redcoat jailhouse while Billy Dawes made the ride Paul became famous for.

Bessie decided to quit Alice, went to Etta, and asked for a job. Etta agreed to give her a place, and Bessie went back to get her clothes. Alice caught her and the fight was on.

Alice was big and heavy—and slow. Bessie was fast on her feet. She got away and ran across the street, pursued by the behemoth. Bessie locked herself in Etta's house and when Alice pounded on the door, Etta opened it and said, "She doesn't want to see you," which was about as effective as saying "Stop that!" to King Kong. Alice charged through the door and grabbed Bessie by the wrist. Etta commenced to whack Alice with the gas lighter she'd been using to turn on and light the gas fixtures in her establishment, and wound up getting knocked across a hallway and into her own bedroom by Alice's ham-sized fist.

Outside, Bessie again broke away from Alice and ran back into the house, where Etta had recovered herself and was standing in the door, a nickel-plated, bone-handled Iver Johnson Bulldog .44 in her hand. When Alice turned around to pursue Bessie once more, Etta told her to stop. She didn't, and Etta let fly.

The slug hit her—well, there's an old joke about a prosecutor who was questioning a witness to an affray. "Was the victim shot in the fracas?" he asked.

"Nossir," the witness replied, "she was shot 'bout halfway 'twixt the bellybutton and the fracas."

Let's describe the location as an inch and a half above and an inch to the right of the "fracas." Not ordinarily a fatal wound, but certainly a painful one. The doctor who treated Fat Alice gave her a fifty-fifty chance of survival, but that was more due to the sanitary conditions he knew prevailed in Alice's house than to the nature of the wound. Etta surrendered herself to the El Paso police immediately, was charged with attempted murder, and posted a $2,000 cash bond. When the full particulars became known, it took a jury fifteen minutes to acquit her.

The news of the shooting was immediately relayed to the *El Paso Herald*, which—like all El Paso papers—tended to report the scandals of the reservation whenever they became news. The location of the bullet hole, however, was a problem to describe. It was finally decided to describe the wound as being in the "pubic arch."

Enter the ever-watchful Typo the Gremlin, who, like other notorious characters, had moved West in search of new territory. Typo was lurking in the rafters. As soon as the typesetter's back was turned, Typo dropped to the newly set page form, separated the *b* and the *i* in *pubic,* and inserted an *l,* creating perhaps the most unintentionally accurate and descriptive typographical error in the history of newspapering.

Alice took offense at the description, decided it was deliberate—it was, after all, the *Herald* that suggested Alice as a replacement for Jumbo's deceased mate—and announced she was going to blow a hole "a horse could walk through" in *Herald* editor Frank Brady. It is recorded that *very* shortly thereafter, Brady took an editing job in Albuquerque, New Mexico, and never returned to El Paso.

Alice Abbott died April 7, 1896, in El Paso. Etta Clark died in Atlanta, Georgia, at the home of her sister Eva Mercier—a one-time madam who'd gotten out of the game—on October 25, 1908. What happened to Bessie Colvin, no one knows. The story of the "Public Arch," though, has entered the folklore of writing and newspapering throughout the Southwest and the United States.

The West isn't as wild as it once was, but Typo's still around. Waiting. These days he's working with a cousin of his. A guy named Glitch.

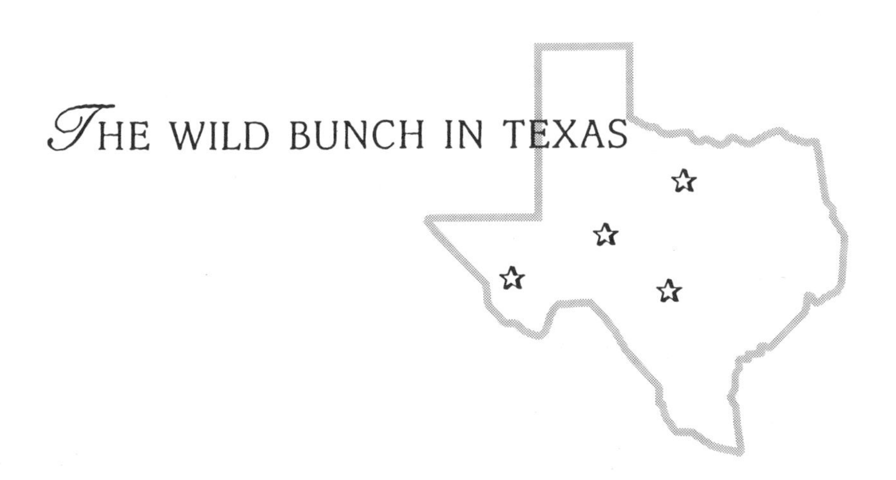

THE WILD BUNCH IN TEXAS

Almost anyone who's ever watched a western movie on TV is familiar with two names—Butch Cassidy and the Sundance Kid. The Paul Newman-Robert Redford movie of that title, together with the "prequel," as Hollywood has come to call sequels set before the time of the original movies, *Butch and Sundance—The Early Years,* have painted an altogether false picture of the careers of Robert Leroy Parker, alias Butch Cassidy, and Harry Longabaugh, alias the Sundance Kid, and their gang.

In fact, Butch Cassidy and the Sundance Kid were involved with two gangs of outlaws, to some extent. One, called the Wild Bunch, was primarily a gang of rustlers, and it was the real Butch Cassidy-Sundance Kid gang. The other, known as the Hole-in-the-Wall gang, from its hideout at a place called Hole-in-the-Wall near present-day Jackson, Wyoming, was led by a man called Flat-Nosed George Curry. The Hole-in-the-Wall gang robbed trains and banks. Its members included not merely Flat-Nosed George and his two nephews, Lonny and Harvey Logan—who sometimes went by the last name Curry (Harvey Logan was known much better as "Kid Curry")—but three Texas boys: William R. Carver, today called Will Carver, though he was usually called Bill when he was alive; Benjamin A. Kilpatrick, called Blackie Kilpatrick or the Tall Texan; and O. C. Hanks—Camilla Hanks—better known as Deaf Charlie. All three of these men were killed and are buried in Texas.

The two gangs, the Wild Bunch and the Hole-in-the-Wall gang, were acquainted and occasionally celebrated together. Once in a while, when the Hole-in-the-Wall bunch didn't have enough men to handle a job, members of the Wild Bunch would join in. Over the years, though, pulp fiction, the movies, and the "all-fact" Wild West magazines have so thoroughly muddled the story that most folks think Butch Cassidy and the Sundance Kid were the heads of a gang known either as the Wild Bunch or the Hole-in-the-Wall gang.

One of the few crimes in which both gangs participated was the robbery of a Winnemucca, Nevada, bank in 1900. The take seems to have been substantial—the bank, of course, tried to minimize it, but rumors of as much as $37,000 in gold have been circulated.

What we do know is that the group split up following the robbery. At least six of them—Parker, Longabaugh, Carver, Kilpatrick, Harvey Logan, and Hanks—came to Texas. Everybody but Hanks went to Fort Worth, where they had their picture made—probably the best-known "outlaw picture" in American history. Deaf Charlie went to San Antone.

Hanks was a native of De Witt County, and his father, Wyatt Hanks (the family name seems originally to have been Hahnke), farmed there. Deaf Charlie visited his folks, had a custom-tailored suit made while in Cuero, and then went up to San Antone for to see the elephant. He got into a scrape in a bawdy house on San Saba Street and guns were pulled. A man who was, in 1900, if not the only then certainly one of the few regular-force black police officers in San Antonio was wounded, as were two "special officers"—the early twentieth-century equivalent of what is known today as a "rent-a-cop." Deaf Charlie had three holes in him. One of 'em made the other two not worth patching.

There wasn't any question in the minds of the San Antonio P.D. that they'd just downed a well-wanted badman, but they didn't know who he was. Deaf Charlie wasn't carrying any identification.

A close examination of the clothes the deceased was wearing revealed a tailor's label in the suit coat—it wasn't a store-bought suit, it was custom-made, and it had been custom-made in Cuero, Texas. Working on the assumption that nobody in his right mind would have a suit custom-tailored in Cuero, Texas, unless he had some connection to Cuero and De Witt County, the San Antonio police contacted the De Witt County sheriff. A deputy was sent to San Antonio by train, and when they rolled the sheet back from the face of the dead man, he identified him as "Old Man Wyatt Hanks's boy Camilla—the one they call Deaf Charlie." From all indications, Camilla Hanks's grieving family returned the remains to De Witt County, and that's where Deaf Charlie came to rest—at least, he's not listed in the potter's field books of San Antonio or Bexar County.

We left Butch Cassidy, the Sundance Kid, Kid Curry, the Tall Texan, and Bill Carver in Fort Worth. Etta Place, whom the movies portrayed as a "schoolmarm who fell in love with a boyish-looking bandit," was with them, as was a woman called Della Rose, whose real name was Laura Bullion. Pinkerton files are less kind to Etta Place than was Hollywood—they list her as a "prostitute and confidence-game worker." Laura Bullion, alias Della Rose, they list as "consort of criminals"—what Hollywood called, in movies set in a slightly later era, a gun moll.

What happened to Butch and Sundance we know—or at least we think we know. They—together with Etta Place—boarded a British steamer called *Honorius* in New York in early 1901 and sailed to South America. There—or so the story goes—Butch and Sundance were shot to kitty litter by the Bolivian army about 1906.

Butch Cassidy's late sister is one who'd argue the truth of that. According to her, Butch came home to Utah to visit his kinfolk in 1921, and she had a nice long talk with him. By her account, he looked and acted mighty lively for a feller who'd been dead since 1906. There are historical indications that Butch Cassidy—or somebody who looked and acted almighty like him and knew a lot about him—was managing a ranch in Sonora, Mexico, as late as the late 1920s. There's even a photograph of a feller who mightily resembles Butch Cassidy, which is known to have been taken on that ranch about 1923.

An historian also claims he has all sorts of records proving that Harry Longabaugh, the Sundance Kid, died in Oregon in 1956. In an interesting connection, the last time the Pinkertons recorded the whereabouts of Etta Place she was in Oregon—about 1921, just about the time Butch supposedly came home to Utah to visit his kin before settling in Mexico.

While Butch and Sundance went north, the other three fellers in that picture—Bill Carver, Ben Kilpatrick, and Kid Curry—went south. Specifically, they went to a place called Planche Spring farm, about seven miles north of Eden, Texas, in Concho County. Planche Spring farm was the property of the Malloy Land and Cattle Company of Concho County, and the quarter-section that made up the farm was leased to one Daniel Boone Kilpatrick, also known as Boone or D. B. He was Ben's oldest brother.

The quarter-section immediately to the north was leased by a man named Oliver G. Thornton. Thornton was an ex-schoolteacher, married to the then-schoolteacher Mary "Mamie" Steen. They'd been married slightly less than a year.

Now, the fact some badmen stayed at the Kilpatrick place was pretty much an open secret in Concho County, but since the badmen hadn't made a local nuisance of themselves, everybody let them alone. For reasons unknown, Ollie Thornton decided to sneak over to the Kilpatrick place and have a look at the badmen. He was armed—with a single-shot .22 caliber rifle, which was and is a dumb thing to go badman-huntin' with.

None of the stories about why Ollie went to the Kilpatrick place make much sense. One says he went over to talk to Boone about some hogs that got in his garden and packed the rifle to back it up. One says he went to try to blackmail the outlaws in exchange for not telling the law where they were (the law already knew). And one says he tried to arrest them for the rewards on them, intending to disarm three men—two of whom were known as gunmen—with his .22.

Why ever he went, he didn't come home. Somebody shot Ollie square in the gizzard, right next to the hog pen—and that's when the trouble started at Planche Spring.

Immediately after the shooting of Ollie Thornton, several folks made gaping holes in the wind. They were Ben Kilpatrick, his slightly older brother George, Etta Kilpatrick (the mother of the brood), and sisters Ola and Alice. Boone had been gone a while—he was at a sheep camp he had on some leased land to the southwest. By the time Mamie found Ollie's body and got to the law in Paint Rock, the only people left at the farm were Ed Kilpatrick and the two smallest Kilpatrick boys, Felix and Will.

George and a man called Bob McDonald—at least, that's the name he was using in Concho County—headed southwest, eventually ending up near Sonora in Sutton County. McDonald was actually William R. Carver, who'd been a well-known—and very well liked—cowboy in Sutton County several years before. Bill was known as a loner—a shy and retiring sort of feller who was much more at home with a horse and some wide-open spaces than with a crowd of people. He'd worked as a cowboy most of his life, and several years before was briefly married to a girl named Viana Byler. She died in childbirth—two days short of her eighteenth birthday.

Bill Carver apparently continued to work as a cowboy for several years after his wife's death, but sometime around 1895 he drew his time. He made a statement to his friends that has been quoted in various forms, but the gist of it was, "The next time you see me I'll be wearing diamonds or a pine box."

Nobody seems to know exactly where he went immediately after quitting, but one rumor has him owning part-interest, for a time, in a saloon and gambling house in San Angelo. Most folks who knew Carver doubted this, as do most historians who know anything about his character. If the story's true, the other part-interest belonged to a man named Sam Ketchum—remember that name.

In early 1896, a gang of outlaws began to ravage New Mexico and Arizona. They were led by a man named Tom "Black Jack" Ketchum. In late August of 1896, Black Jack Ketchum's gang stuck up the bank at Nogales, Arizona. One of the participants in the robbery was named as George Franks, alias Bill Carver. Before 1896 ended, the Ketchum gang added two more stickups to their total.

The Ketchum brothers—Tom, Sam, and Berry—owned a ranch near Sonora. Berry Ketchum was a well-respected rancher and breeder of fine horses—racing stock. One of the things every lawman who ever chased the Ketchums commented on was their horses—they were some of the fastest and best ever seen, and they regularly outran everything the New Mexico and Arizona lawmen had.

In September of 1898, the gang held up the Colorado & Southern train near Folsom, New Mexico. The train's conductor was a man named Frank Harrington. That's another name to remember. This was the last job of Black Jack Ketchum's gang—Tom split off to go it alone, leaving Bill and Sam with the gang.

Several more robberies followed, with Bill Carver getting better and better known to lawmen with each one. In July of 1899, Bill, Sam, and the boys made another try at the Colorado & Southern, just about in the same place as the first one. This time they got off with a reported $50,000. The conductor was Frank Harrington—again. This time the law got on the trail quickly and cornered the gang in Turkey Canyon, northwest of Cimarron, New Mexico. There was a terrific shoot-out and the outlaws got away, but Sam Ketchum was mortally wounded. He was taken to a ranch by Carver, and he died in the custody of the New Mexico law on July 24, 1899.

When the gang got back home to Texas and began to lament the loss of Sam, Black Jack said, "I can rob that train all by myself." He tried it on August 16, 1899—same train, same place. Also same conductor—Frank Harrington, who by this time was thoroughly tired of being robbed. Under his blue frock coat he'd stashed a sawed-off ten-gauge shotgun loaded with blue whistlers—twelve double-aught buckshot to the barrel.

When Tom said, "Stick 'em up," Conductor Harrington let that shotgun do his talking. The Colorado & Southern chugged away, leaving Tom "Black Jack" Ketchum bleeding and near death on the roadbed, most of one arm blown off. Lawmen returned to the spot and found him, still alive. He was hospitalized and by a miracle survived—so the law could hang him, which it did, bright and early on the morning of April 26, 1901. (Well, it tried, anyway. Tom died by the rope—but not by hanging. His head was yanked off.) This left Bill Carver the well-known only survivor of the notorious Ketchum gang. He was a *very* well-known survivor. On August 29, 1900, he was identified as one of four men who robbed the Union Pacific train near Tipton,

Wyoming. Two of the other three also were identified—Butch Cassidy and Harvey Logan. On September 19, 1900, the usually dapper Carver was identified as "dressed like a bum" during the holdup of the Winnemucca bank. He also had a distinctive odor, and when one of the ladies who happened to be in the bank when it was robbed complained of it, Carver said, "I'm sorry 'bout it, ma'am, but I can't help it—that skunk shot first."

In November of that year, he, Cassidy, Sundance, Harvey Logan, and Kilpatrick had the famous group picture made in Fort Worth. As were many pictures of the day, it was put on display in the window of the photographer's studio. It was spotted by an operative of Pinkerton's National Detective Agency, who recognized one of the men immediately—not Butch Cassidy nor the Sundance Kid, nor even the notorious Kid Curry, but Bill Carver, which gives some idea of the relative notoriety of the men when they were active.

Carver went with Ben and another man who used the name Charles Walker to the Planche Spring farm, probably in time for Christmas in 1900. Sometime toward evening on March 27, 1901, somebody made a fatal hole in Ollie Thornton, and the boys had to leave. There are those who will tell you that Bill Carver and George Kilpatrick were spotted heading southwest toward Sonora about noon on the twenty-sixth, the day before the killing, and this may be true. What seems to be most true is that, despite what happened later, Bill Carver didn't shoot Thornton. Charles Walker did. And the physical description of Charles Walker fits Harvey Logan exactly.

At about 9:00 P.M. on April 2, 1901, a local man named Boosie Sharp reported to his brother, Sutton County Deputy Sheriff Henry Sharp, that he thought he'd seen some of the suspects in the Thornton murder in the vicinity of Ogden's Store in downtown Sonora. Henry contacted his boss, Sheriff Elijah S. "Lige"

Briant, who gathered Deputy J. L. Davis and Constable W. D. Thomason and went to see about it.

Briant and his officers stepped into the store and ordered two men bending over the feed sacks to put their hands up. What happened next we don't know for sure—one report says the taller of the two men made a fumbling grab at a .41 on his belt, while another says the shorter one made a first-rate snatch at a .45 but couldn't beat the drop. Whatever happened, the officers opened up, firing twenty to twenty-four shots at the two, who never managed to return the fire.

Both men were seriously wounded, the shorter of the two—Bill Carver—mortally. Shortly before midnight on April 2, 1901, Bill Carver died in the Sutton County courthouse. His inventoried belongings were two revolvers, a pocketknife, a silver pocket-compass, a gold watch, a small photograph of a girl (later identified as Laura Bullion, the niece of his late wife, who "looked just like her aunt") and a thin gold wedding band "sized for a woman's hand." Oh, yes—and a half-carat man's diamond ring. Bill got 'em both—diamonds and a pine box.

Carver was buried in a pauper's grave in the Sonora cemetery. Some months after his burial, a headstone mysteriously appeared. It's a small stone, only about knee-high, with a singular inscription: April 2, 1901. Who put it there—and why Bill's name isn't on it—no one knows for sure. When George and Bill Carver went southwest, Ben and Charles Walker—Kid Curry—went north. There are rumors that they were in Sonora the night Bill was killed, but something cut the phone line north of Paint Rock on the night Thornton was killed, and it wasn't the wind.

We've got a pretty good idea where they went after that, too, because an express car on the Great Northern Railroad coughed up a wad of unsigned paper banknotes so big neither the express company, the railroad, nor the banks have ever admitted how much was taken. The stop was made not far from Wagner, Montana, and the Wagner Stickup is one of the legends of train robbing.

We know two of the people who were there—Kid Curry and Ben Kilpatrick. We know the Kid was there because he later got into a scrap in a Knoxville, Tennessee, pool hall and put non-fatal holes in two Knoxville policemen—which indicates he must have been having an off day, because Kid Curry never felt that charitable—and was later overpowered and arrested in Jefferson City, Missouri. He was identified by the engineer and fireman of the Great Northern express train as the leader of the stickup men at Wagner.

We also know Ben was there, because he and Laura, using the aliases James A. Allen and Della Rose, were living the high life in Saint Louis on Wagner banknotes when the Saint Louis police and the Pinks swooped down and snatched them up. Ben drew ten years in the supposedly escape-proof Ohio State Penitentiary. It accepted federal prisoners then, and both Al Jennings and William Sidney Porter—O. Henry—did their time there. Laura drew five years in a women's prison in Massachusetts for being an accessory to train robbery and a general nuisance besides.

Laura served her five years and apparently went to Mertzon, Texas, which was her home. Ben served nine years of his sentence, was called into the warden's office, given his cigar and five-dollar bill, told he was a free man—and was then introduced to a Texas Ranger who was holding rendition papers on him, together with a warrant charging him with murdering Oliver G. Thornton by "shooting him with a gun." The Tall Texan came home in chains and was locked up in the Runnels County Jail at Ballinger, "there being no jail in Concho County to hold said prisoner." (For the record, Concho County still doesn't have a jail.)

Benjamin A. Kilpatrick was tried in Thirty-fifth District Court. He was acquitted—the only eyewitnesses to the murder were his brothers, his sisters, and his mother, and they wouldn't testify against him.

In the meantime, the tribe had scattered, with Boone and Felix moving to a sheep ranch south of Sheffield, near the Pecos/Terrell County line. When a young lady asked the handsome ex-outlaw what he planned to do, he said, "Well, ma'am—I reckon I'm gonna go down to Sheffield with my brothers, get me some sheep, and sit on the side of a hill and watch the world go by." As it turned out, that wasn't quite what the Tall Texan had in mind. Ben came home broke, to all appearances. Shortly after he got home, at distances of two- and three-days' ride to the south and east, several small banks were robbed by a tall, lone bandit who knew exactly what he was doing. The bandit was never caught. Within three months of his arrival in Sheffield in his cheap prison-release suit, cloth cap, and prison-made shoes, Ben was sporting fancy handmade boots, a fifty-dollar Stetson, and tailor-made clothes. Draw your own conclusions.

By mid-February of 1912, it was pretty clear to anyone who cared to get curious that something peculiar was going on down at the Kilpatrick place. Several people were spotted coming and going, and most of them avoided being recognized. One of them was a hatchet-faced, grizzled old-timer some folks thought they recognized as an ex-railroader who went by the nickname Old Beck. At one time or another he'd also gone by the names Ed Walsh, Ed Welsh, Ed Beck, Ed Becker, and Nick Grider. You'll also find him called Ole Beck, Ole Becker, Ole Oldbeck, and Ole Hobek in references.

Several occurrences in late February and early March of 1912 had later significance. A man named Hub Noelke was herding horses with Berry Ketchum when Berry's hat blew off and was lost on the range. Noelke had both a woolen scarf and a woolen tie-on cap with earflaps, so he wrapped the scarf around his head and gave the cap to Berry. A youngster named Walter Fulcher found tracks of some of Ketchum's racehorses pointing southwest toward the Rio Grande. Whoever was riding them was making a definite effort not to be seen by anyone who happened to be traveling the road from Sheffield to Dryden.

Late on the afternoon of March 12, 1912, a boy named Erwin Grigsby was playing under the Southern Pacific water tower at Dryden, Texas and saw two men—a tall, handsome, youngish man and a grizzled, hatchet-faced, older feller. He thought they were hoboes. After talking to them a while, he thought they were pretty nice folks.

Promptly at midnight on March 12, Galveston, Harrisburg, and San Antonio Number Nine rolled into Dryden for a water stop. As the train started to pull out, a tall, dark-haired man swung aboard the engine. He jabbed a Winchester model 1910 semiautomatic carbine into the engineer's ribs and said, "You just do like you're told and nobody'll get hurt. Take her to the first iron bridge, and stop on the bridge." The first iron bridge was a steel-supported trestle that crossed the southernmost arm of Sanderson Canyon, about fourteen miles to the northwest.

The train was stopped on the trestle and the second outlaw, who'd apparently boarded the train between the baggage car and the first coach, expertly uncoupled the coaches. The train was pulled forward about a half-mile to Baxter's Curve, where the last major train robbery attempt in Texas history—and the last major criminal act of any member of the old Wild Bunch/Hole-in-the-Wall gang—began.

Once the train was stopped, the outlaws marched the engineer and fireman to the door of the express car and told Wells Fargo's messenger, David Andrew Trousdale, to open up and throw out his gun or they'd start shooting the train crew one by one. Trousdale threw out his gun.

The taller bandit entered the express car and immediately threw out two sacks of registered mail. He then went through the rest of the mail, feeling the envelopes for the squishy feel that indicates there's money inside. He found two, and took thirty-seven dollars from them. Eventually he made a fatal mistake—he turned his back on Trousdale, who caught him three times on the back of the head with an iron-banded wooden maul used to crack ice. Trousdale then took the bandit's rifle and put a bullet through the other bandit's head. Galveston, Harrisburg, and San Antonio Number Nine arrived at Sanderson five hours late—but unrobbed.

The dead outlaws were photographed and buried. Hub Noelke saw the cloth cap the tall one—Ben Kilpatrick—was wearing and recognized it. It was the one he'd loaned Berry Ketchum a few weeks earlier. The horses found tied alongside the tracks the next day wore Ketchum's brand. Berry indignantly denied any involvement—the horses were stolen, he said.

The graves of Ben Kilpatrick and Ole Hobek, train robbers, were finally marked by the Terrell County Historical Society in 1985. They stand in the northeast corner of the Sanderson Cemetery.

After Ben's death, Laura Bullion dropped out of sight. Only recently has the Bullion family revealed that she went to Tennessee and spent the rest of her life wearing widow's black. She used the name "Mrs. Freda Lincoln, widow of the late Maurice Lincoln," and supported herself by doing fancy needlework and alterations for clothing and department stores in Memphis, Tennessee, until her death in 1961. Her tombstone in Memphis, only recently set, reads:

FREDA BULLION LINCOLN
LAURA BULLION
THE THORNY ROSE
1875-1961

According to local rumor, Wagner-stickup banknotes were still circulating in Sheffield as late as 1922.

GREGORIO CORTEZ

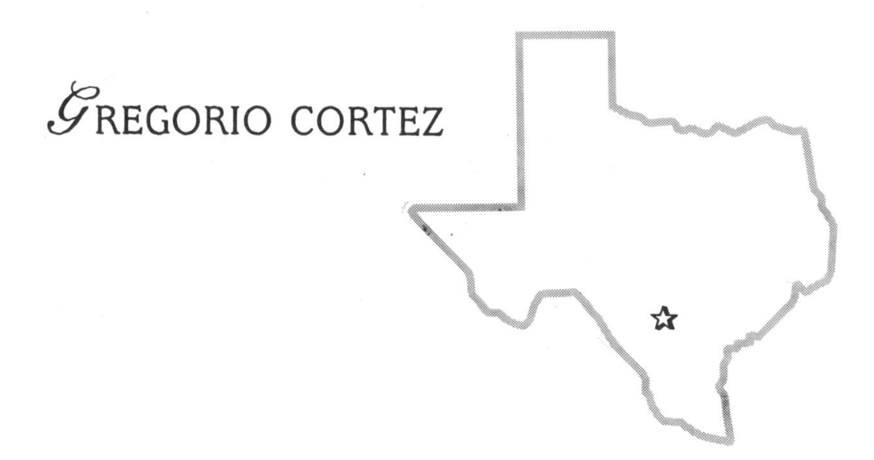

If you mention the name Gregorio Cortez, from the Hispanic citizens of South Texas you will get a smile. From the Anglos, unless they're very old or very well versed in the area's more obscure history, you'll get mostly blank stares. Gregorio Cortez? Hey, we know about Hernán Cortez, the conquistador, but who's Gregorio Cortez?

Gregorio Cortez is probably the most lied-about man in Texas history, not even excluding Davy Crockett and Pecos Bill. The Mexicans lie about his greatness, those gringos who know about him, about his villainy. Somewhere in between is some truth.

His real name was Gregorio Cortez y Lira, and his parents were Román Cortez y Garza and Rosalía Lira y Cortinas. He was born, by best evidence, just south of the Rio Grande, on a ranch between Matamoros and Reynosa, on or about June 22, 1875. He was the next to the last of eight children. His parents were not wealthy.

Like many Mexican citizens, before and since, the Cortez family crossed the Rio Grande in search of a better life. By 1887, the family was living at Manor, Texas, just east of Austin in Travis

County. By 1889, Gregorio, then fourteen, moved to Karnes County with his elder brother, Romaldo. He and Romaldo worked as *vaqueros*, farm workers, and common laborers from then until 1900.

There are probably 10,000 descriptions of Gregorio, but the most accurate one is on the commitment warrant that placed him in the Texas State Prison in Huntsville. It recorded his height as five-feet, nine-inches, his weight as 144 pounds, his hair as black and wavy, his eyes as brown, and his complexion as "medium dark." In other words, he was by no means remarkably prepossessing in appearance. It is said that he was startlingly handsome, and this may be true—for in addition to his wife Leonor Díaz, whom he married in 1890 when he was fifteen, he seems to have had at least three and possibly as many as seven mistresses/girlfriends scattered around South Texas by 1901.

By that year, Gregorio and Leonor had four children—Mariana, then ten; Valeriano, eight; Severo, six; and Crispín, three. The family lived on rented land on the W. A. Thulemeyer ranch about ten miles west of Kenedy. Gregorio's older brother Romaldo and his wife also rented land on the Thulemeyer ranch and lived about a mile from Gregorio's family. Romaldo and his wife had no children. From all indications, they were law-abiding, hard-working people who gave nobody any trouble.

In June of 1901, Sheriff Brack Morris of Karnes County received word from the sheriff's office in Atascosa County to be on the lookout for a horse thief who was described as "a medium-sized Mexican with a big, red, broad-brimmed Mexican hat." Allegedly, this thief had stolen a sorrel mare, and had been tracked to Karnes County where the trail was lost.

A man named Andrés Villarreal had a recently acquired sorrel mare. In questioning him, the sheriff found that he had acquired the mare in a trade for a horse from Gregorio Cortez. It is alleged by Cortez's biographer, Dr. Américo Paredes, that Cortez had acquired the mare legally, but no proof of the legal acquisition is offered. At least two other accounts insist that Cortez, much later, claimed he had found the mare as a stray, and one says he admitted stealing the mare—but not from Atascosa County.

Karnes County Deputy Sheriff Boone Schoate spoke Spanish, after a fashion. He, Deputy John Trimmel, and Sheriff Morris went out to talk to Gregorio Cortez about the mare, but apparently to do no more than talk to him. The sheriff had no warrant on Cortez, and he, Trimmel, and Schoate went to Cortez's house in a buggy—certainly not a possible pursuit vehicle should the man try and run away. Schoate was not even armed, which would indicate that the officers certainly were not expecting any trouble.

As the buggy approached the house, at a distance of about a half-mile, it came to a gate where there were some pens. At this point, Trimmel—the only man armed other than the sheriff—got out of the buggy, probably to look at any horses that were there.

When the buggy arrived at the house, Leonor was sitting on the floor of the porch with Gregorio's head in her lap. Romaldo was sitting on the front steps. Gregorio was armed, and as he saw the buggy approach, he slid the pistol around in his waistband until it was about over his hip pocket, out of sight. Whether he did this because he didn't want to make the sheriff nervous or so he would have an advantage in the event trouble started remains moot. At any rate, he did not get up. Instead, he told his brother to go see what the men in the buggy wanted. In a moment the brother returned and said, "*Te quieren,*" which means, literally, "They want you," but is also an idiomatic way of saying, "They want to talk to you." Schoate understood this to mean that Romaldo had said to his brother the equivalent of, "They've come to get you."

Gregorio got up and came almost, but not quite, to the fence. At this point Schoate asked, in Spanish, if Gregorio had traded *un caballo*—a horse—to Andrés Villarreal. In English, "horse" is a generic term—it can mean stallion, gelding, or mare. If an

English-speaker asks another English-speaker, "Did you trade a horse to Joe Blow?" the gender of the animal is ignored.

In Spanish *un caballo* means "a male horse." "No," Cortez answered—and he was telling no more than the simple truth, for he had not traded *un caballo* to Andrés Villarreal. He had traded *una yegua*—a mare.

At that point, everything promptly went to hell in a handbasket. The sheriff got out and told Schoate to tell Romaldo and Gregorio that he had come to arrest them. Gregorio said, "*A mi no me arreste por nada,*" which means "You can't arrest me for nothing." However, what Schoate and Morris understood him to say was "*A mi no me arreste por nadie,*" which can be understood to mean something very like, "Like hell you're gonna arrest me, *gringo!*"

Exactly what happened next is agreed on by everyone. Romaldo Cortez rushed at the sheriff. The sheriff, apparently taken off guard, grabbed his gun and shot at Romaldo, hitting him in the mouth. The bullet passed through his mouth, knocked out several jaw teeth, and embedded itself in his shoulder. The sheriff then snapped a shot at Gregorio, which missed. Gregorio returned the fire and did not miss. Whether or not Gregorio was in the act of going for the gun he had stuck in his waistband behind him before the sheriff pulled his gun is still arguable.

Gregorio's first shot hit Sheriff Morris in the chest. Morris tried to return the fire and did get off at least two, and perhaps three more shots, but they all went wild. Cortez then shot the sheriff a second time, causing the man to stagger back and fall next to the gate. Cortez then walked up to the prostrate man and shot him a third time.

Boone Schoate was completely unarmed. Like a sensible man, he took to the mesquites. About a quarter-mile down the road he met Deputy Trimmel, who was headed in the direction of the gunfire. All Trimmel had was a six-shooter, and he wasn't too enthusiastic about going up against two or possibly more armed men, especially since the terrified Schoate—whose brother, Crockett Schoate, had in fact been murdered by the Sutton gang during the Taylor-Sutton feud—was babbling about a "gang of horse thieves." The two officers headed for Kenedy and reinforcements.

Gregorio picked up his brother, washed his face, and instructed his son Valeriano to gather the family's horses. Out of the *remuda* he picked a sorrel mare for himself and another animal for Romaldo and saddled both. Then he unhitched the sheriff's team from the buggy, hitched it to his own wagon, loaded his wife, his brother's wife, and the children in the wagon, and told them to go to Kenedy, to the house of a friend. Ten-year-old Mariana was instructed to tell any *gringos* who asked that the family came from a ranch nearer town than Thulemeyer's place.

In the meantime, Schoate and Trimmel reached help, Schoate still babbling about the strong gang of Mexican horse thieves. Posses set out in all directions from Kenedy—looking not for two men, one badly wounded, but for a gang of unknown size.

Unbeknownst to anyone, Sheriff Morris was not yet dead. After everything was over but before the posses arrived, he staggered into the brush and died, 200 yards from the house.

The *corrida,* or ballad, of Gregorio Cortez makes much of his gallant *yegua trigueña*—his little brown mare—but not many people are aware that he started his monumental flight from Kenedy not merely afoot, but wearing a pair of pointed-toe, low-quarter dress shoes. In addition, he went—at least at first—not south toward the border, but north. He left his brother with his family in Kenedy and, while eventually in excess of 300 rangers, sheriffs, deputies, and ordinary citizens were scouring the landscape between Karnes County and the Rio Grande looking for a desperate bandit at the head of a gang of horse thieves that had by now grown to mythical proportions, the object of the search, a lone Mexican man of generally unprepossessing appearance, was hiking north in his Sunday-go-to-meeting shoes. It is likely he was headed toward Manor, where he still had relatives.

About a day and a half after he left Kenedy—Paredes gives the time at thirty-four hours—Gregorio arrived at the home of Martín Robledo, a close friend, who lived on the Schnabel ranch outside Belmont. It was a magnificent feat of hiking—the straight-line distance is about sixty-five miles, and what with the natural lay of the land and the necessity to seek crossing spots on creeks and rivers, Gregorio probably walked nearly ninety miles in shoes not intended for more than dress-up and dancing.

Gonzales County Sheriff Robert M. Glover was a close friend of Brack Morris. He knew Cortez had friends in Gonzales County, and he resorted to brutal means to find out who they were and where Gregorio might be hiding if he came there. Once he had the name of Martín Robledo, he gathered a posse of eight and headed for the Robledo house. There is rumor that the posse stopped in Ottine and tanked up on some liquid courage—which is entirely possible, but it's never been proved. Subsequent events seem to indicate that the posse wasn't acting like it had all its oars in the water.

What actually seems to have happened was that at the first shots, Martín Robledo and his oldest son, Bonifacio, along with a visitor named Martín Sandoval, took to the brush. Gregorio, who was resting his sore feet, traded shots with the sheriff and killed him, then headed for the brush barefoot—and promptly ran through a patch of sticker burrs. He stopped, swept the burrs from his feet, tore his vest in half, tied the halves over his feet, then took to the brush himself.

What happened at the Robledo house after Cortez left is hardly anything to be proud of. From the posse's own reports, they seem to have been chasing one another around barns and trees, mistaking each other for *banditos*. In one of these chases, Deputy Henry Schnabel, who owned the ranch on which the Robledos lived, had half his face blown off. In fact, the only Mexicans on the place—

Refugia Robledo, Martín's wife, his sons Tomás, sixteen, and Encarnación, thirteen, and a boy named Ramón Rodríguez, about twelve, who was staying with the Robledos—were unarmed. Although the posse reported finding ten Winchesters and a "lard bucket full of cartridges" at the Robledo house, all anyone ever produced was one Winchester and an old single-barreled shotgun. According to a report in the *San Antonio Express*, young Encarnación Robledo was "questioned" about the possible whereabouts of Cortez and the others. To quote the report precisely, "He was hung up to a tree until his tongue protruded and life was nearly extinct, but he steadfastly refused to reveal any of the secrets of the gang." Encarnación was thirteen and he didn't know any "secrets," because there wasn't any "gang."

After the shooting stopped and the posse left, taking their dead and prisoners—the Robledo family and the Rodríguez boy—Gregorio went back to the house, got his shoes, and started south for the Guadalupe. He walked about ten miles to the house of Cerefino Flores. There he gave Sheriff Morris's gun—the only weapon he had—to Flores in exchange for another pistol. Flores hid the pistol and gave Cortez a sorrel mare and a saddle. For this he got the same treatment Encarnación Robledo got and was later sent to prison for two years.

The posses were hot on Cortez's heels as he left Flores's place, so he doubled back and recrossed his own trail dozens of times between the Guadalupe and the San Antonio. He left the Flores house early on the morning of Saturday, June 15, three days after shooting Sheriff Morris, and by noon Sunday the mare was showing signs of playing out. Just as he crossed the Cibolo near Stockdale a posse spotted him, and there ensued a six-hour chase at a flat-out gallop. He finally eluded the posse about 6:00 P.M. and ran into a thicket, where he pulled the saddle and bridle off the sorrel. The horse dropped dead almost immediately.

That night, Gregorio found the *yegua trigueña* of legend—the little brown mare—in a pasture near where his sorrel died. She was little, too—barely thirteen hands high. He caught and saddled her, and together they headed for the Rio Grande.

That little brown mare was later described as "the best-bottomed horse in Texas," which might not be an exaggeration. It's only about 100 miles from Floresville to Cotulla, where Cortez was to lose his brown mare, but with his cutbacks and false trails he must have ridden the little horse at least 300 and possibly 400 miles in the next three days. He and his *yegua trigueña* were spotted dozens of times, and one posse killed six horses trying to catch the pair.

Even the best horse will play out eventually, and near Cotulla the brown mare took a wire cut on her hind leg and began to limp. Reluctantly, Gregorio Cortez abandoned her, and she was soon found by a posse. The word went out that Gregorio Cortez was cornered.

He wasn't. He simply walked away—all the way to El Sauz, less than thirty miles from the Rio Grande. At one point he came on a bridge across the Nueces that was heavily guarded. He walked down to the river, took his clothes off, took a bath, picked up his clothes, swam across, and sat and rested a while, while the possemen guarding the bridge nervously fingered their triggers and paid him no mind whatever.

In the meantime, a reward of $1,000 had been posted for Gregorio Cortez. When he arrived at the sheep camp of Abrán de la Garza, almost to the Rio Grande, Jesús Gonzalez, known in legend as *El Teco,* recognized him. Shortly afterward *El Teco* contacted Texas Ranger Captain J. H. Rogers and told the ranger he could lead him to Gregorio Cortez. That was exactly what he did, and Gregorio was taken without a shot being fired.

Gregorio Cortez was tried, at one time or another, for the murders of Sheriff Brack Morris of Karnes County, Sheriff Robert M. Glover of Gonzales County, and Deputy Sheriff Henry Schnabel of Gonzales County. He was convicted on all three counts, all three were overturned on appeal, and he was eventually retried and acquitted of murder in the shootings of Morris and Glover. Enough question was finally raised about the shooting of Schnabel that he was not retried on that charge—but no one else was ever tried for it, either. He was eventually convicted of manslaughter in the death of Sheriff Morris and of horse theft, and sentenced to fifty years at Huntsville. *El Teco* didn't get his thousand dollars —it was split up among several people, and he eventually got about $200 of it. He was also completely ostracized by his own people and had to leave the border country for good.

Cortez never ceased to insist that he was innocent of any crime and had fired on Sheriff Morris only in defense of his own life and that of his brother. As he wrote to the governor of Texas, seeking pardon, "Deep regret I have always felt for the sad occurrence, but repentance I have never felt, for I could not bring myself to the hypocritical state as to so plead to gain an end that was my just due."

While in jail awaiting trial and in prison, Gregorio began to have problems he really didn't need. Somewhere between five and nine women, most of them carrying children of various ages, began to come out of the woodwork and accuse him of being lover and father. How much was true and how much was publicity-grab is hard to say, but there was enough smoke to convince Leonor there was fire someplace. She divorced him. He remarried while in prison, but the record is unclear on what became of that wife.

Secretary of State F. C. Weinert of Seguin apparently never believed Gregorio was guilty, and in June of 1912 he managed to secure a pardon for the man. It was, however, a conditional pardon—he could never return to South Texas. He settled in Anson, north of Abilene.

In 1916, Gregorio died in Anson, probably of a heart attack. He was attended at death by wife number three—or four, the details are blurred—a girl in her mid-teens.

THE UNFORTUNATE CIRCUMSTANCES SURROUNDING THE MORAL PICTURE FILM COMPANY ✩

El Paso is a town unique in Texas. It is not the original El Paso—the original El Paso del Norte is the town we now know as Juárez. Present-day Juárez was El Paso del Norte until 1866, when—in the aftermath of the downfall of Maximilian Von Hapsburg, the erstwhile Maximiliano I of Mexico—a pure-blood Indian named Benito Juárez became president of Mexico. It then renamed itself La Villa de Benito Juárez, and the little American town of Franklin, Texas, north of the river, renamed itself El Paso to perpetuate the name that had been in the area since the 1500s. El Paso is also farther from the capital of Texas than it is from the capitals of New Mexico, Arizona, Colorado, and Wyoming.

For most of its history, El Paso has been a town apart from the rest of Texas, so far removed from Texas "proper"—that is, the area east of present I-35—that it has been almost a state unto itself. It is, in fact, the only "large city"—over 250,000 population—anywhere west of a line drawn from Fort Worth through San Antonio to Corpus Christi, which takes in considerably more than one-half of the physical area of Texas.

In addition to being a long way from the rest of Texas, for many years El Paso was isolated by geographical features—like the Davis-Guadalupe mountain range and a pretty fair chunk of the Chihuahuan desert—from the rest of the state's population. It took over a week by stagecoach, and almost a month by mule wagon, to travel from San Antonio to El Paso in the 1860s and early 1870s, and arrival was a matter of pure luck and whether or not you outsmarted, outshot, or outran first the Comanches, then the Apaches. You could not cross Texas by rail from east to west until 1881, the year after the last Indian fight in the state. (And you couldn't cross it from north to south by rail until 1920 or thereabouts; even then you could only travel from Borger to Brownsville—from Borger to the Oklahoma line was by horse or Model T Ford.)

Given El Paso's isolation, its proximity to the border, the frontier territories of Arizona and New Mexico (which didn't become states until 1912), and its generally independent frame of mind, it's not unusual that it should have developed some "unique" institutions. One of those institutions was South Utah Street.

South Utah Street—they changed the name of it later to South Mesa—wasn't truly unique. It was the "reservation"—the quasi-legal red-light district, where prostitution was condoned but not necessarily encouraged. A lot of Texas cities had similar districts: both Dallas and Fort Worth, Houston, Galveston, Austin's East Pecan Street—later East Sixth Street—Corpus Christi's Sam Rankin Street, and, of course, San Antonio. Even Waco, at the same time it was home to what was at the time the world's largest institution for the production of Baptist ministers, was also home to one of Texas's widest-open red-light districts. So what was so bloomin' special about El Paso's?

Well, to begin with it was probably the oldest "reservation" in Texas. We know that Sarah Borginnis, known as the "Great Western," a woman of truly notable proportions—she was blonde, stood somewhat over six feet tall, and weighed better than two hundred pounds—was operating a "hotel" that was probably a brothel in Franklin as early as 1849. In addition, it was the scene of the great embarrassment of the Moral Picture Film Company.

We don't know much about the Moral Picture Film Company. We know it came out of New York, it was sponsored by several churches and church groups, and it had as its purpose the making of motion picture films that depicted the evils abroad in the world—which, of course, all morally upright people had to be aware of so they could be agin 'em. Sometime in 1910, the officials of the Moral Picture Film Company decided to make a three-reel film—about thirty-six minutes, which was a pretty long film for 1910—depicting the evils of "white slavery." The plot of the film was the downfall of two innocent immigrant girls who arrive at Ellis Island, are seduced, and are eventually forced into prostitution.

For reasons unknown, the Moral Picture Film Company decided to film the red-light district scenes in, of all places, El Paso. From a perfectly reasonable point of view, there was no better place to film it—in the South and Southwest, El Paso was second only to New Orleans in reputation as a wide-open town, and while Storyville has gotten more publicity recently, South Utah Street was just as famous in its day.

Unfortunately for the Moral Picture Film Company, El Paso had just undergone one of its periodic convulsions of morality, and the reformers were looking over the police department's shoulder.

In September of 1910, the entire cast and crew of the moralism epic moved, bag and baggage, to El Paso, to shoot the final scenes of the degradation of the two heroines. The location manager, a man named London, applied to the chief of police for permission to film on location in El Paso's actual red-light district.

The chief, who was having problems of his own—being beset on the one hand by merchants who were losing their shirts because trade attracted to El Paso by the wide-open brothel district was going elsewhere, and on the other by the local moralism crusaders who temporarily had the upper hand and were making the most of it—felt he didn't need any further aggravation. He said, "Not just no, but Hell no!"

The forces of moral uplift were not to be denied. The Moral Picture Film Company found a building on South Santa Fe Street, only a few blocks from the actual red-light district, which had the appearance of a typical crib-line deep in the lowest sections of the reservation. The building was leased, some cosmetic changes were made, extras were hired, and filming began.

Three days later, somebody told the cops, "Hey, them moom-pitcher folks is makin' a moom pitcher down on Santy Fee Street, and them gals in it ain't got much clo'se on a-tall." A pair of detectives were dispatched to investigate.

The investigation revealed that the Moral Picture Film Company had done its work well. "It looks just like the Line," a newspaper quoted one of the detectives as saying. The actresses portraying the prostitutes were dressed accordingly, and were posing in the doorways of their movie-set "cribs" exactly as the girls deep on South Utah and South El Paso Streets did.

The chief filed a complaint in Corporation Court, charging the moralists with "corrupting the morals of youth," and the law in its infinite majesty went out to pinch the lot of them—only to discover that the pseudo-soiled doves and their entourage had flown the coop. A frantic search discovered the Moral Picture Film Company, all properly attired and moral once more, at the train station waiting for the Rock Island to take it back to New York.

The whole shootin' match was arrested and dragged downtown, where the managers immediately pled guilty to avoid missing the train. El Paso's city coffers were deemed in need of being fuller by the sum of $100 for every member of the cast and crew. The company promptly paid up and scooted for the Rock Island tracks.

Unfortunately, we don't know what the name of the film was or who was in it, and it seems doubtful that any print has survived.

The tale of the Yankee moralists who got fined for corrupting the morals of youth in one of the most wide-open cities in North America, though, is part and parcel of the legends of El Paso.

THE BADMAN NOBODY KNOWS

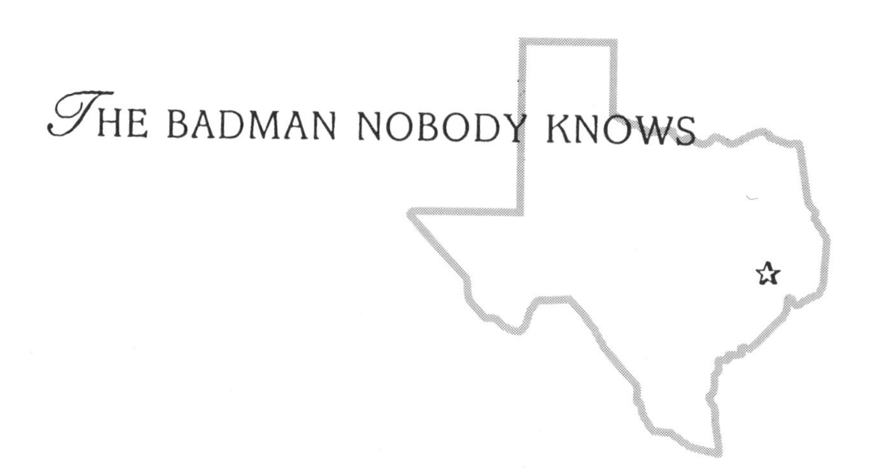

If you were to go on the hunt for a badman's badman—a real hard case who was, in fact, as deadly as Jack Palance looked in *Shane*—you wouldn't have to go any farther than San Augustine County, Texas, over in the red dirt and piney woods. There, in the 1890s, you'd find a young, rather handsome, but small and partly crippled man named Lycurgus C. Border.

You never heard of Curg Border? Doesn't surprise me in the least. Not many people have outside San Augustine County, and not many people have heard of the Wall-Broocks-Border feud, which brought Curg to his brief prominence as a man-killer.

Lycurgus C. Border was one of the sons of George Border, a first-generation resident (his father, William, was born in Lincolnshire, England, famed for "Lincoln Green" and its most famous wearer, one Robert Locksley, known as Robin o' the Hood) who married into the long-time resident Broocks family of San Augustine County. Curg, at about five-five or five-six, maybe 130 pounds, had been thoroughly bullied as a boy because of his size. Some of the bullies, in particular, were the Wall brothers: George

Washington, Pez (Lopez), Ney, Brune, and Eugene Beauharnais Wall.

Curg Border grew up fast and he grew up tough. Because he could seldom if ever win a fight with his fists, he learned to win fights with his gun—and it was a hard lesson. In one of his first shooting scrapes, he was wounded in the knee and spent the rest of his life wearing an iron brace on his leg so he could walk. The other feller, as it turned out, didn't need to walk any more after the fight. Curg Border may not have been a fast gun in the sense that Ben Thompson or Clay Allison were, but he was plenty fast for the red-dirt country of East Texas, and since that's where he was, that's what counted.

There was another side to Curg Border. Ladies who had known him insisted that he was handsome and a perfect gentleman at all times, and that before he was wounded, he was an ideal dance partner. Other folks insist that he was generous to a fault—Curg would give you the shirt off his back, they insisted, if he thought you needed it worse than he did. The only thing I ever heard that anyone—other than the Walls and their kin—held against Curg Border was his lifelong friendship with Archibald "Arch" Price. You see, Arch Price was a black man, and in those days, in deep East Texas, white men didn't have close friendships with black men.

The election of 1894 caused a lot of upset in Texas. It was the first election in which William Jennings Bryan's Populist Party really came to prominence, and in San Augustine County the biggest boosters of the Populists were the Walls. The Borders and the Broocks were dyed-in-the-wool, Jeff Davis southern democrats, who reckoned the new Populists no better than radical republicans, and not quite as smart. George Washington Wall, the oldest of the Wall boys, was elected sheriff of San Augustine County that fall, and the stage was set for trouble.

There are two stories about how Curg Border ran afoul of the new law. One was that he was levying a "tax" on local cotton farmers, in the form of "pay me or something bad—like maybe a fire—could happen to your cotton." The other was that he was hired by a local storekeeper named Lynch to collect overdue debts, and he and Arch Price used unpleasantly persuasive methods to collect overdue debts from the black folks who worked for Buck Wall. As to which is true, at this late date, pick one. It's as likely to be right as the one you don't pick. Whatever was going on, there were shots exchanged between Curg and Arch on the one side, and a couple of the Wall boys on the other—without much damage to either side—and the county realized that it had the beginnings, at least, of a feud between the Border-Broocks clan and the Wall family.

Feuds are peculiar things. They simmer for years, sometimes with a killing or two along the way, sometimes with a lot of noise and little else, and then they suddenly explode. The Wall-Border feud simmered for six years. Then, in early 1900, Sheriff George Wall arrested Curg Border and locked him up. The exact charge is unclear, but at least some sources say that George refused to allow Curg to make bail "so he can't run off," which was a mortal insult. Six weeks later, in April, Curg caught George without anybody to help him, and when the smoke cleared, San Augustine County was short one sheriff.

This didn't set well with the Walls, and on June 2, 1900, Eugene Wall met Ben Broocks, Curg's first cousin, on the courthouse square and put four holes in him, tying the score. Curg was gone at the time, so Eugene strutted the town, defying the Broocks and Border kin to do anything about the killing. The newly appointed sheriff, Noel G. Roberts, Eugene's nephew, made no attempt to arrest the killer, and when he did finally tell his uncle "you're under arrest," it was at Buck's farm, where Eugene was allowed to remain on his word not to run off.

Two days later, Curg, two of Ben's surviving brothers, and a brother-in-law jumped the sheriff, his brother Sid, and their uncle Felix, in the courthouse. Sid was the local superintendent of schools and Felix was a notary public. When the smoke cleared, Sid and Felix were dead and Noel weighed several ounces more than he did before the shooting started.

This divided the county right down the middle—Uncle Buck Wall was reported to have 200 men at his farm, ready to swoop down and clean Broockses and Borders out of San Augustine County, and the Broockses and the Borders were similarly prepared. Somebody yelled to Austin, and into town came the redoubtable Captain Bill MacDonald of the Texas Rangers.

Bill MacDonald was known as "the biggest mouth in the rangers," and the fact that he did talk a lot led some folks to think he was all talk. The survivors didn't make that mistake again—but there weren't a lot of survivors.

With MacDonald in charge, things slowed down considerable. Eugene and Brune Wall were tried for the murder of Ben Broocks. Two of the Broocks boys were tried for the shooting of the Roberts clan, and Curg Border was tried for shooting George Wall. Everybody was acquitted, which was the way it was done then. The rangers went home.

Very shortly afterwards, somebody bushwhacked Pez Wall, and not long after that, they got Eugene. Curg Border was suspected, but there was no proof. Brune Wall took the hint and went to Oklahoma, where old Buck shortly joined him. The feud, for all practical purposes, was over. Some still insist that the trigger finger that pulled on the Walls was black—Arch Price, doing for his friend what Curg couldn't do for himself because he was so closely watched.

Curg Border ran for and was elected sheriff of San Augustine County. He served less than a year when his bond was withdrawn—all police officers had to be bonded—and he was forced to resign.

Sneed Nobles, distantly related to the Walls, was appointed in his place. Curg tried to face him down—and died.

And Arch Price? Well, we know what happened to him, but we don't know why. He apparently got in an argument with Curg's sister. What was said, nobody knows—Miss Olivia Border never elaborated on it. Whatever it was, Arch backed away from her and reached for his gun—and she gave him two loads of blue whistlers right where his vest made the vee. The last of the San Augustine gunslingers was dead, and with Arch Price died a lot of secrets—including the identity of the murderer of the last two Walls. San Augustine County is quieter these days, but I wouldn't want to go taking sides in a discussion of Curg Border. Curg's still got a lot of kin there.

WHEN SANTA CLAUS ROBBED THE BANK

On December 24, 1927, Santa Claus and three helpers robbed the First National Bank of Cisco, Texas. Santa Claus—or the man in the Santa Claus suit and mask—was Marshall Ratliff, a twenty-four-year-old ne'er-do-well who'd been in and out of trouble for most of his life. He wore the Santa suit and mask because he was well known in Cisco and expected he would be recognized without a disguise. The disguise he chose led to much more attention than he wanted or expected, and gave Texas the story of the Santa Claus Bank Robbery.

With Ratliff were Robert Hill, Louis Davis, and Henry Helms, all jobless and—with the exception of Hill—all with prior criminal records. All were West Texas natives, but none as well-known as Ratliff.

In the late 1920s, bank robbery was a major criminal industry. So many banks were robbed that the Texas Bankers Association offered a reward for robbers. The reward was $5,000—a substantial sum for the time. The reward was offered for dead bank robbers. There was no mention of a reward for live ones.

If the Bankers Association expected the reward to discourage bank robbers, they were disappointed. It didn't. What it did do was to cause unscrupulous "private detectives," working with equally unscrupulous local police officers, to stage nighttime "bank robberies"—actually burglaries—and to ambush and murder the would-be robbers for the reward. Texas state law, then and now, did not permit the use of deadly force in the apprehension of business-house burglars unless the burglars themselves were armed and threatened the persons attempting to apprehend them, or unless the burglars had completed the burglary and were fleeing with the proceeds. In every case save one in which "bank robbers" were killed and the persons killing them applied for the reward, the robbers were shot outside the bank in the nighttime and the bank had not been entered. In one case, though the robbers were equipped with an acetylene cutting torch, ostensibly to be used to enter the bank and the vault, the torch had no cutting tips and was useless. The one exception was the Santa Claus stickup at Cisco on Christmas Eve, 1927.

The time chosen for the robbery was noon on Christmas Eve—one of the busiest times the bank had. The getaway car—stolen, of course—was a 1926 Buick four-door sedan. The robbers forgot to check the gas gauge. When they drove into Cisco, the gas tank was nearly empty, and they neglected to fill it before the stickup.

It started fairly smoothly. All four men—including the bogus Santa Claus—made it into the bank and started the routine of a stickup. At that point, a little six-year-old girl who'd been promised "one last wish" if she saw Santa on Christmas Eve, dragged her mother into the bank. The mother instantly realized what was happening, burst out the bank's back door, and began to scream, "They're robbing the bank!"

Unfortunately for the robbers, they didn't realize the alarm had been given. They continued to work, putting $12,200 in cash and nearly $150,000 in negotiable papers in a potato sack. In the meantime, about two-thirds of Cisco showed up, all packing guns and ready to collect five thousand dollars per dead bank robber. Somebody inside the bank fired a shot—nobody knows who to this day—and then Bob Hill fired four shots into the ceiling "to let 'em know we're armed."

The reaction was swift, unexpected, and devastating. Over a hundred shots poured into the bank building from all directions. No one in the bank—robber, employee, or customer—was hit, but one customer later recalled one of the robbers saying, "It must be the police!" and the man in the Santa suit saying, "It must be every damn body in town!" Marshall Ratliff wasn't far from wrong.

In the shoot-out that followed, both Louis Davis and Cisco Chief of Police G. E. "Bit" Bedford were mortally wounded, while over a dozen citizens took major to minor bullet wounds—some few from the bandits, no doubt more from the reckless shooting of their neighbors. Though all four men made it to their car, the big blue Buick sedan ran out of gas only a few miles out of town.

The robbers made an attempt to commandeer a passing car, but the driver simply removed the ignition keys and threw them into a nearby field. Since the pursuit was closing in on them rapidly, the three surviving robbers—Ratliff, Hill, and Helms—were forced to abandon their loot and flee on foot.

For the next eight days, a massive manhunt, involving over a hundred lawmen and citizens and utilizing an airplane for the first time, covered the country south and west of Wichita Falls. In the manhunt, the fugitives were spotted several times and both Helms and Ratliff were wounded in exchanges with officers or other members of the posse. When they were finally captured, Helms was almost dead and Ratliff was given only a fifty-fifty chance to live to stand trial.

Louis Davis died of his wounds, but no reward was ever paid for him as a "dead bank robber." Robert Hill pled guilty to armed robbery and received a sentence of ninety-nine years in the Texas state penitentiary. Both Marshall Ratliff and Henry Helms were tried and found guilty of bank robbery and the murder of Chief Bedford. Both were sentenced to what Texas felons in the 1920s called a "ride on Ol' Sparky"—death by electrocution.

Before Helms's and Ratliff's dates of execution came up, a smart lawyer discovered a hole in the law. It wasn't even in their cases; it was in the case of one Harry Leahy, who was tried and convicted of murder and sentenced to die. An obscure law stated that, even if a criminal was legally sane when he committed his crime and legally sane when tried and convicted, if he subsequently became insane, he could not be executed until—and if—he regained his sanity. As soon as the case became known, virtually every inhabitant of Texas's death row "went crazy."

That some of them already were insane there can be no doubt. That many more—indeed, most—"done a crazy" to stave off a ride on Old Sparky, the state's electric chair, is equally obvious. Both Helms and Ratliff tried it. Unfortunately for Leahy, the man who started it all, as he is reported by witnesses to have said to Henry Helms, "I just couldn't act the part. They finally got to me. I couldn't keep going." Harry Leahy was executed.

Helms said in reply, "Well, watch me put it over." Henry Helms gave it a good try, but he couldn't "put it over" either. On September 6, 1929, he was executed—right on schedule.

Marshall Ratliff was either a much better actor than Helms or he did manage to drive himself to some sort of insanity. Opinions are divided to this day. He did, however, manage to convince at least some people that he was insane—too insane to die. His mother filed a petition for a sanity hearing in Walker County, far from where the crime was committed. Eastland County, concerned that Ratliff might escape punishment for the murder of the well-loved lawman, issued a bench warrant for Ratliff on charges of having robbed a citizen of Cisco when he tried to take her car after the getaway Buick ran out of gas. It removed Ratliff from Walker County and brought him to the jail in Eastland.

Ratliff returned to Eastland County on October 24, 1929. He remained in jail there—to all appearances hopelessly and helplessly insane—until the night of November 18 when he left his cell—which carelessly had been left unlocked—got a .38 revolver out of the sheriff's desk drawer, and murdered jailer Thomas Jones in an escape attempt. When subdued, he relapsed into his insanity—whether fact or pose we will never know.

That was enough for Eastland County. On the night of November 19, Marshall Ratliff was dragged from the Eastland County jail by a mob and hanged to a guy wire between two light poles on the Eastland County courthouse lawn. Afterwards, someone recovered the rope used to hang him, coiled it, and built a frame for it. The morbidly curious can see it in the courthouse museum in Baird, west of Eastland, labeled "Marshall Ratliff's Last Necktie."

Was Marshall Ratliff in fact insane? That's been debated for more than sixty years. A. C. Greene, in *The Santa Claus Bank Robbery,* makes a good—though fictionalized—case for insanity. One thing West Texas agrees on, though—legally insane or not, he was plumb crazy to try to rob the Cisco bank on Christmas Eve while dressed up like Santa Claus.

THE REAL STORY OF BONNIE AND CLYDE

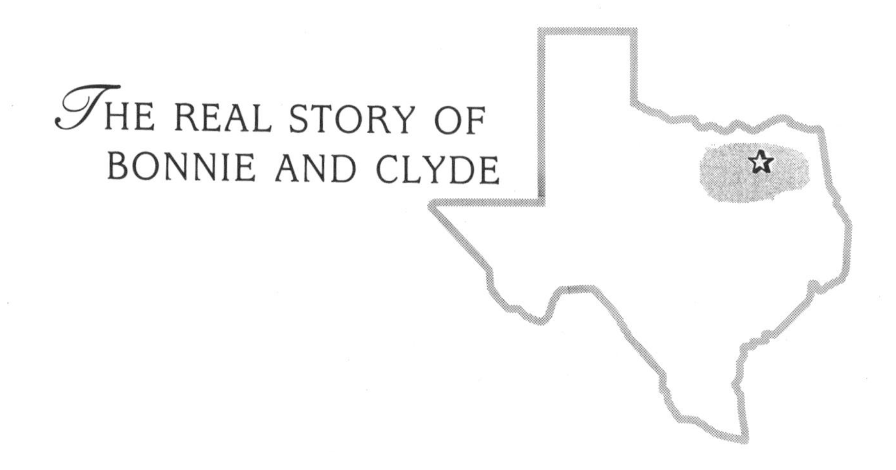

A little more than twenty years ago I picked up, on a paperback book rack, a book entitled—as I recall it anyway—*Bonnie and Clyde: A Love Story*. It was the novelization of the screenplay for the movie *Bonnie and Clyde*, starring Warren Beatty and Faye Dunaway. On the first page I found something that caused me to put the book back on the rack without ever reading it, and to avoid, for a long time, at least, watching the movie.

Bonnie Parker, speaking to a young man, asked him if he knew what kind of car she and Clyde were driving. "Sure," the young man said. "It's an eight-cylinder Chevrolet coupe."

"No," Bonnie replied, "It's a *stolen* eight-cylinder Chevrolet coupe."

Now, leaving out the fact that Clyde never drove anything but a Ford V-8, according to the records of General Motors, the first eight-cylinder engines went into production Chevrolet automobiles in July of 1954, when the 1955 models began manufacture. There has long been a rumor among car enthusiasts that in late 1948, two 1949-model Chevrolet convertibles were experimentally equipped with Pontiac straight-eight engines, and one of them was inadvertently sold and never recovered, but GM has never confirmed this. Even if the earlier date is accurate, Bonnie Parker and Clyde Barrow had been in their graves for fourteen years when the first eight-cylinder Chevrolet hit the streets, and if it isn't accurate, they'd been dead for twenty years when somebody finally made an "eight-cylinder Chevrolet coupe."

What the rest of the novel was like, I don't know—I never read it. I did finally see *Bonnie and Clyde,* and I can say that it bore about as much relation to reality as something written by someone who'd mention an eight-cylinder Chevrolet coupe in 1932 could be expected to.

The true story of Clyde Barrow and Bonnie Parker has been told only twice. Shortly after Barrow and Parker were killed, Captain Frank Hamer, the former Texas Ranger who tracked them down and killed them, gave a long interview to his close friend and poker-playing companion, Dr. Walter Prescott Webb of Austin. Dr. Webb was then engaged in writing the complete history of the Texas Ranger service, and to make the story timely, he added Hamer's interview to it. Hamer never again talked to anyone about the case, either in public or—so far as is known—in private. At the time he talked to Webb, several participants in the case were still alive, and it is likely, had Hamer told Webb some names and had Webb published them, that some killings would have resulted.

Francis Augustus Hamer died in Austin on July 10, 1955. Some thirteen years later, John H. Jenkins, a Fellow of the Texas Historical Society and an accomplished writer, and H. Gordon Frost, an El Paso schoolteacher and past president of the El Paso Historical Society, who would later become president of the American Society of Arms Collectors and a Director of the National Rifle Association, were allowed access to Hamer's private files to write a book called *I'm Frank Hamer—The Life of a Texas Peace Officer.* In that, making use of Hamer's own files as well as an immediate copy of the notes Webb made during his two-day interview with Hamer on the subject of Bonnie and Clyde, they were able to add details missing from Webb's version.

A third book, *Assignment Huntsville: Memoirs of a Texas Prison Official* by Colonel Lee Simmons, who was the director of the Texas State Prison System at the time Clyde Barrow and Raymond Hamilton were at large, contains any number of details concerning how Colonel Simmons decided to have Barrow and Parker captured or killed. It also supplies dates and names inside the prison.

What follows is taken from Webb's book, *I'm Frank Hamer,* and *Assignment Huntsville*—the only historically accurate versions of Barrow and Parker's career and demise—and from some research I've done on the subject over the years. It's not intended to be the "whole story of Bonnie and Clyde"—for that you'll have to read Webb or *I'm Frank Hamer.* It will, though, put to rest a good many falsehoods circulated about Bonnie and Clyde over the years—probably the least important of which has been the creation of eight-cylinder Chevrolets by Hollywood twenty years before there were any Chevy eights.

Clyde Champion Barrow was born at Teleco, Texas, on March 24, 1909. His father was a perpetual hired hand on farms and ranches, and only his mother could read or write. Clyde was one of eight children. He did not begin school until he was ten years old, and over the next six years he attended intermittently. He was assigned to the fifth grade when he finally dropped out altogether. In 1924, he and a small group of boys began to make a business of small-time burglary, shoplifting, small-time "smash the window, grab, and run" robberies, and occasional car theft in the Dallas area. In 1926, when he was seventeen, he was first arrested for car theft in Waco, Texas. Many years later, a retired Waco police officer, who was there when Barrow was brought in, recalled him for me.

> Clyde Barrow was the damndest crybaby I ever saw. We got him for stealing a car. He hadn't stolen it yet, but he was sure trying, and the owner spotted him and called the police. It was a Buick roadster he was trying to steal—a red one. You could have spotted it ten miles off, but he was so dumb he was trying to steal the only red Buick roadster in all of McLennan County.
>
> Anyway, we walked up on him real quiet and stuck a gun in his ribs, and when he turned around and saw badges he commenced to bawl. I never saw the like of it from somebody who should have at least tried to act like a man. He bawled like a two-year-old. He cried and begged us not to arrest him and not to take him to jail, but of course we did. He spent two days in the Waco jailhouse and I don't think he quit bawling the whole time. There was never a prisoner I was more glad to get rid of. All that bawling and whining and "I-ain't-never-gonna-do-it-no-moreing" flat got on my nerves.

Clyde stood five-feet, seven-inches in height, weighed between 120 and 130 pounds, had wavy, dark blonde hair, which he usually dyed black or dark brown, and eyes of that indeterminate color called hazel. He had a thin face and large ears, and was often described as "rat-faced." According to Hamer, Barrow drank very little and did not use any form of narcotics. He chain-smoked Bull Durham roll-your-owns, and an occasional cigar when he felt the occasion warranted it.

Bonnie Parker was born at Rowena, Texas, on October 1, 1910. She was one of three children. According to some accounts, she was an excellent student and graduated from high school with honors. There may be reason to doubt this, considering that when she was seventeen she eloped with a twenty-eight-year-old career criminal who was a fugitive under indictment for bank robbery and murder. In "honor" of her marriage, she had entwined hearts pierced by an arrow and inscribed "Bonnie" and "Roy" tattooed on the inside of her upper right thigh.

Bonnie was recalled to me by high school acquaintances as "real loud and vulgar. She had a really foul mouth." Bonnie stood four feet, ten inches tall and weighed between eighty and ninety pounds. Her natural hair color was best described as "dishwater blonde" and her eyes were brown. She liked the color red and dyed her hair almost carrot-red, which she attempted to match by wearing red dresses, red shoes, and red hats.

In 1928, when she was eighteen, Bonnie's erstwhile husband was sentenced to life imprisonment at Huntsville, and Parker supported herself by working as a waitress. According to some old Dallas policemen, she also worked as a part-time streetwalker, but though she was well-known, "We had bigger fish to fry than some ugly little half-pint gal with dyed red hair, so as long as she didn't roll her johns we let her alone."

In January of 1930, Raymond Hamilton, who had been dating Bonnie though she was still legally married, introduced her to Clyde Barrow. Barrow and Parker were immediately attracted to each other.

In February, Clyde, who was under indictment for burglary and auto theft, was captured and placed in jail in a small town near Dallas. In early March, Bonnie visited him. She had a .32 caliber automatic pistol taped to the inside of her thigh. This time, Clyde stayed out of jail about ten days, but he was recaptured, and on April 21, 1930, he was sent to Huntsville to serve a ten-year sentence.

Clyde actually stayed in prison only two years. His older brother Buck—an escapee—gave himself up and reentered prison in what his wife Blanche later described as "an attempt to get his life right." The Barrow family worked feverishly to get Clyde a pardon, but in late January of 1932 he became despondent—at least according to his sister Nell—and had another convict chop off his toe. Clyde was pardoned and released February 2, 1932.

Almost as soon as he got out, Clyde found Bonnie and they began their two-year crime spree. Clyde's style was hit-and-run—hit a store, a filling station, or a small bank for what you could grab immediately, then hit the road hard and fast. He partnered with Ray Hamilton, and on March 22, 1932, they attempted a bank robbery at Kaufman. Something went wrong and Bonnie was caught and jailed.

On April 28, 1932, Clyde and an unknown, light-haired woman drove up to the Bucher Grocery, a combination filling station and grocery store on the outskirts of Hillsboro. The place was owned by J. W. Bucher and his wife, Martha. Clyde went in, carrying a package under his arm. The package contained some pocketknives, and after some bargaining, Bucher bought them for a small sum, which allowed Clyde to see where the store's safe was.

Shortly before midnight, April 30, Clyde and the as-yet-unidentified woman returned to the Bucher store. Clyde banged on the door, and when Bucher opened a window he identified himself as the "boy who sold you the knives the other day" and demanded Bucher sell him some guitar strings. After some argument, Bucher agreed to come down.

Once inside, Clyde selected a package of guitar strings—a fifty-cent purchase—and handed over a twenty-dollar bill. Since this would require change, Bucher had to open the safe, but since he'd left his glasses beside his bed upstairs, he had to call his wife to come open the safe for him. As soon as the safe was opened, both Barrow and the woman pulled guns. Bucher lunged for Barrow's gun, and Barrow shot him through the head. The pair then fled, leaving the money behind. Martha Bucher identified Clyde Champion Barrow as her husband's murderer from a police photo. This is usually considered the first Bonnie and Clyde murder, but Bonnie wasn't there. She didn't get out of jail in Kaufman until June 17.

When Bonnie came home to her mother she swore she was through with Clyde Barrow, but by the end of June she, Clyde, and Raymond Hamilton were sharing a rented house in Wichita Falls.

On August 5, 1932, at a dance near Atoka, Oklahoma, Barrow and Hamilton got into a fight. A deputy sheriff named E. C. Moore went to break up the fight, and a "small, light-haired, foul-mouthed woman" with Barrow slapped him, attempted to kick him in the groin, and cursed him. When he tried to arrest her for assault she ran to Barrow's car. A moment later there was a shot and Moore was dead, hit almost squarely between the eyes. The county sheriff came to his deputy's aid and was shot in the chest. He died four days later.

Clyde ditched the car and stole another one. By this time he had begun to specialize in Ford V-8 sedans. The car, brand new in 1932, was light, roomy, rugged, extremely maneuverable, suited to back roads, and violently fast. More important, a Ford could be fixed almost anywhere; they were becoming more and more common almost by the hour, and if one had to be abandoned, there was almost sure to be another, ready to be stolen, somewhere in the next block.

Part of the reason Clyde preferred Ford V-8s may have lain in the fact that they were extremely easy to steal. While the steering wheel could be locked by turning it all the way to one side or the other when the ignition was turned off, very few people actually did that. This left the steering unlocked unless the thief accidentally locked it before the lock could be disabled, something which could be done in minutes with a pair of pliers. The back of the ignition switch was wide open, with all wiring exposed. The application of a short length of wire, a half-dollar coin, or even the crumpled tinfoil from a cigarette package to the back of the switch would "hot-wire" the car, and the tinfoil could be applied from the driver's seat. In 1933, in one of his many acts of bravado, Clyde sent a semiliterate letter to Henry Ford, praising the Ford V-8 sedan as the finest getaway car ever built.

After the Atoka killing, Clyde and Ray dropped Bonnie at her mother's, ditched the car and stole another, and then robbed the

Neuhoff Packing Company in Fort Worth. The next morning they were back for Bonnie and headed north for Oklahoma.

Parker and Barrow, minus Hamilton, surfaced in New Mexico in mid-August. They'd gone to visit an aunt of Bonnie's, and in the process kidnapped a local law enforcement officer and drove him around for almost an entire day before dropping him off—unhurt. The incident made headlines, crowding such characters as Pretty Boy Floyd, Machine Gun Kelly, and John Dillinger off the front pages.

Almost immediately afterwards they took off for Michigan, this time in company with Hamilton. The object—at least the stated object—was to visit Hamilton's father. The three staged several small bank robberies, but bank jobs weren't Clyde's style. Ray was the bank robber; Clyde preferred the faster, flashier—and usually deadlier—grocery store or filling station stickup. The group split up yet again, and very shortly afterward a woman turned Hamilton in. He was returned to Texas, indicted on something in excess of twelve counts of armed robbery and murder, tried, and sentenced to 263 years at Huntsville.

On October 11, Barrow and Parker entered the Hall Grocery at Sherman, owned by a retired cowboy named Howard Hall. Bonnie picked up some bread and a can of salmon, and Clyde handed the clerk a five-dollar bill. As the clerk opened the cash drawer, both Bonnie and Clyde pulled pistols. Clyde reached for the money, but Hall was standing near the cash drawer, so he rammed his pistol barrel into Hall's belly. The old man grunted and staggered back. Barrow laughed and said, "Did that hurt, you old sonofabitch? This'll hurt a lot worse." Then he shot Howard Hall twice in the chest. He and Bonnie selected some groceries, got a sack, put the food in it, cleaned out the cash drawer, and drove away in their current Ford.

On December 5, in Temple, Doyle Johnson was reading the evening paper in his living room when he heard his new Ford V-8 sedan start. He ran out and saw his car pull away from the curb with a man at the wheel, followed by another Ford V-8 sedan driven by a woman witnesses described as "so little she could barely see over the steering wheel."

Johnson ran from his house. The woman fired at him but missed, and he jumped on the running board of his own car, reached through the window, and grabbed the small, rat-faced driver by the neck. The driver put a pistol to Johnson's head and fired. As soon as Johnson's body stopped rolling the woman stopped the car she was driving, jumped out, ran to the other car, got in with the car thief, and the two drove away at high speed. Witnesses identified the man and woman from police photographs as Clyde Barrow and Bonnie Parker.

On January 6, 1933, Clyde went to the home of his aunt, Lillie McBride, in Dallas. Officers had been warned that he was in town and would try to visit Mrs. McBride. Deputy Sheriff Malcolm "Mal" Davis was in the shrubbery, while a half-dozen other lawmen waited in the house. Mrs. McBride was not at home.

Barrow drove up, got out of his car, and started for the house. Something must have warned him that all was not as it seemed to be, and he pulled his pistol.

Davis stepped out of the bushes and ordered Barrow to throw up his hands. "Not for you or any other John Law," Clyde yelled, emptying his automatic pistol at Davis. Two slugs struck the officer, who fell dead on the spot. Clyde then ran back to the car, where Bonnie was in the driver's seat. Clyde jumped on the running board and held on as Bonnie screeched away, her foot pressing the accelerator to the floorboard. Witnesses said she was so far down in the seat only the top of her head showed over the window.

Following the murder of Dallas County Deputy Sheriff Malcolm Davis, Bonnie and Clyde once more hit the road. For several weeks they were not heard from, but—in southern Missouri—a National Guard armory was burglarized. It was the Depression, and riots were not uncommon in large towns. The Guard, being the official state militia as well as part of the army, was the governor's army in the event of civil strife. Unlike today, when essential parts of Guard weapons are stored in a bank or city vault rather than in the armory, Guard units kept weapons and ammunition in the armory. Stolen in the burglary were a number of .30 caliber Browning automatic rifles and a large number of Colt .45 caliber automatic pistols.

The Brownings, in particular, were serious ordnance. The BAR was, in fact, a light machine gun. It weighed about twenty pounds, carried an integral bipod for precision shooting, and loaded a twenty-round magazine filled with .30 caliber U.S. Army cartridges—which, today, are called .30-06s. It could be fired semiautomatically or fully automatically, and the ordinary metal-jacketed bullet it used would penetrate a twelve-inch creosoted pine post and both sides of a military steel helmet on the other side of it. No automobile of the day provided cover behind which one could hide from a BAR.

In March of 1933, people in South Joplin, Missouri, began to complain to local police about a very noisy foursome occupying a small, rented, stone bungalow. They drank heavily—in particular a small woman with dyed red hair, who often drank herself into immobility and had to be carried inside by her male companion. Someone got nosier than anyone else and sneaked a peek into the bungalow's garage. There were dozens of license plates, from Missouri and other states, lying on the floor. The neighbors noticed that the two women seldom left the house, though the men would often be gone for several days, usually returning just at dawn.

Two Missouri highway patrolmen examined the premises and decided something was definitely going on. They contacted the local law and, together with three local officers, returned to make a full investigation. It was just about dusk, April 13, 1933, when the officers approached the house.

Joplin Constable J. W. Harryman was in the lead. When he got within ten feet of the garage door, he was shotgunned without warning. Detective Harry McGinnis of the Joplin P.D. jumped out of his car and ran to help Harryman. As he did, a small, light-haired woman leaned out of an upstairs window and yelled, "Pour it in 'em, Clyde! We're comin' right down—keep 'em out of the garage!" Clyde Barrow opened an almost steady fire from the garage door, wounding McGinnis.

The other three officers—a Joplin detective named McGrath and two Highway Patrolmen named Kahler and Grammer—took cover and returned the fire, and Grammer headed up the street to find a telephone to call for reinforcements. Inside the house the officers could see the women running up and down the stairs with suitcases. Someone was warming up the car, and the officers could hear the men swearing at the women and urging them to hurry. Then, quite calmly in spite of the hail of gunfire, Clyde Barrow walked out of the garage and kicked the body of Constable Harryman off the driveway. A few seconds later, a Ford V-8 sedan emerged at high speed, machine guns and pistols firing from all four windows.

The reinforcements arrived too late. Both Harryman and McGinnis were dead and McGrath was wounded. Inside the bungalow, officers found a poem, apparently authored by Bonnie Parker, entitled "Suicide Sal." A newspaperman found—and did not turn over to officers—a roll of exposed box-camera film. When it was developed, it proved to have twelve "family photos" of Bonnie and Clyde on it. Most were fairly innocuous "boyfriend and girlfriend" pictures showing Clyde and Bonnie embracing, Clyde holding Bonnie on his arm, Bonnie posed in front of a Ford coupe, and Clyde and Bonnie kissing. In others, though, the pair posed with firearms, and in one—destined to leave the greatest impression on the public—Bonnie posed with her left foot on the front bumper of the Ford, a huge revolver in her right hand, and a large cigar in her teeth. Bonnie was definitely a smoker—she chain-smoked Camels—but she spent the rest of her short life denying that the cigar was anything but a prank. Nevertheless, the image of "Bonnie Parker, Clyde Barrow's cigar-smoking gun moll," has entered popular legend and is probably indelible by now. The photographs were distributed widely, and used on wanted posters in Texas, Oklahoma, Missouri, and Arkansas.

Again the pair dropped out of sight, to resurface near Wellington, Texas, on June 11. Clyde, driving—as usual—with his foot in the carburetor, missed a detour sign and the car went over a low bluff into the Salt Fork of the Red River. Several people came to the aid of the pair, and Bonnie—who was both badly injured in the crash and burned in the subsequent fire—shot the woman who nursed her in the hand. Someone escaped and brought two local officers, but Clyde captured and disarmed them, leaving both men stripped to their underwear, handcuffed together around a tree, and tied around their throats with barbed wire, near Erick, Oklahoma. It was almost two days before the two officers, both suffering from exposure and exhaustion, were found.

Twelve days later, the gang robbed a grocery store in Fayetteville, Arkansas. Their getaway was reported, and town marshal H. D. Humphrey of Alma, who saw the tan Ford come tearing through his town, yelled at the driver to stop. Bonnie leaned out of the window and calmly shot Humphrey through the head. The man was unarmed and nowhere near a car in which he could have given chase.

Five days afterward, in Platte City, Missouri, local police surrounded a tourist court where the Barrow gang was reported to be holed up. The gang fled in their usual hail of machine-gun and shotgun fire, but Buck Barrow was hit and mortally wounded. A few miles down the road there was another shoot-out, in which both Buck and his wife Blanche were captured. Bonnie and Clyde, though severely wounded, escaped. Buck Barrow died within hours. Blanche later told officers that she and Buck had only been traveling with Bonnie and Clyde to persuade Clyde to give himself up. She was not widely believed. Bonnie and Clyde dropped out of sight for most of the rest of the year.

On January 16, 1934, Texas State Prison System guards Major Crowson and Clem Bosman led a work party of convicts out to the cotton fields along the Trinity. Joseph Palmer, one of the convicts, lagged behind slightly and, when the guards' backs were to him, reached behind a log. From there he retrieved a .45 caliber automatic pistol. He promptly yelled, "This is a break! Don't you guards make a move or we'll let you have it!" Raymond Hamilton, Henry Methvin, Joe Palmer, W. H. Bybee, and one other prisoner began to back away, and Hamilton retrieved yet another pistol from behind the log. A light-colored Ford coupe pulled up on the highway fronting the cotton field—and suddenly and without warning the occupants of the Ford and the two armed convicts began shooting at the guards, both of whom had their hands in the air. Crowson was killed, Bosman severely wounded. Clyde Barrow and Raymond Hamilton later came almost to blows over who was to get credit for killing Crowson.

Hamilton, Methvin, and Palmer were the major plotters. Their outside contact was James Mullin, alias Jimmie Lamont, who had recently been released from Huntsville's Eastham unit. He went from Eastham upon release to Dallas, where he contacted Floyd Hamilton, Raymond's brother. Floyd contacted Clyde Barrow, who provided the guns and the getaway car. (In the mid-1960s, three Browning automatic rifles, identified by serial numbers as having been stolen from the National Guard Armory in Missouri at the same time as one known to have been in Clyde's possession, were dug up by an earthmover less than 100 yards from where Hamilton and Palmer made their break.)

Colonel Lee Simmons, head of the Texas State Prison System, decided enough was enough. He determined to see to it that Clyde

Barrow and Bonnie Parker were put out of business—once and for all. He had in mind the perfect man for the job.

In his autobiography, *Assignment Huntsville,* Simmons wrote that he lay awake nights working on a plan to capture or kill those responsible for the murder of his guard. When he had the plan worked out, he realized that it rested on some very shaky ground. Not only did he have to get the approval of the prison system board, but of the governor, and that presented a problem. The nominal governor of Texas, in 1934, was Mrs. Miriam Amanda Wallace "Maw" Ferguson. (There's an old southern tradition that if your initials spell a pronounceable word, that word is your "lucky" name; the newspapers later called her "Ma," and as an extension of that, called her husband "Pa.") The actual governor was her husband, James E. Ferguson, who had been impeached and convicted for corruption in office—the only Texas governor ever impeached—and prohibited by law from ever holding elective office again. The Fergusons' administrations—all of them—were marked by extreme corruption, and virtually every competent law enforcement officer in the state resigned rather than turn a blind eye to the criminal activities "protected" by the Fergusons when Maw came to office for the final time.

Simmons got authorization for the creation of a new position—Special Investigator for the Texas State Prison System. The prison system's governing board asked Simmons who would be appointed—appointments, under Ferguson administrations, were strictly political—and he replied that he had not yet made up his mind, but when he did he intended that as few people as possible should know.

In fact, Simmons had long since made up his mind as to who would be appointed to chase down Barrow and Parker. The problem lay in getting gubernatorial approval, since his choice—former Texas Ranger Captain Francis Augustus "Frank" Hamer—had tangled with the Fergusons on numerous occasions in the past.

Before he even approached Hamer, the Fergusons had to be agreeable to his working on a state salary.

The Fergusons, it turned out, had already assigned some rangers—political appointees and mostly incompetent, a situation which characterized almost the entire ranger force any time the Fergusons were in office—and offered a $1,000 reward, dead or alive, for Clyde. Simmons, like most good peace officers, had little but contempt for "Ferguson rangers," and he was fully aware that even the enticement of $1,000 in the depths of the Depression was unlikely to inspire someone to try to take Clyde Barrow any way but in the back.

Simmons broached the subject directly. He needed a special investigator, and he needed the best there was. The best man was Frank Hamer. Did the governor(s) have any objection?

"Frank is all right with us," Governor Maw said. "We don't hold anything against him."

Simmons then told the governor(s): "I might have to put somebody on the ground"—a promise of clemency or even pardon in exchange for information. This was a touchy subject—much of the Ferguson money and political power came from the sale and judicious granting of pardons. Governor Jim said, "Go ahead. I told you we would do anything you want to assist you."

Simmons turned to Governor Maw—the legal governor. "Is that all right with you, Governor?" he asked.

"Yes, that's all right with me," she said, leaving Lee Simmons with just one major hurdle left.

Frank Hamer was in private life. He was employed as Chief of Security by an oil company in Houston, at a salary of $6,600 a year—a virtual fortune in Depression-era Texas. He was fifty years old—an age at which most men begin to think of retirement. If he took employment with the state he would lose his oil company job and might have little prospect of getting it back; he would take a cut of over $5,000 in annual salary; and if he were killed on the job, his family would collect only a small insurance policy from the state. He would also be working for, at least indirectly, a man he despised—James E. Ferguson.

Simmons told Hamer that his name had been mentioned only once—to the Fergusons. He then said, "I will put you completely in charge of the investigation and back you to the limit."

"How long do you think it will take to do the job?" Hamer asked, and Simmons knew what was behind the question. If a time-limit was set, he would refuse the job—he knew, as did Simmons, that no one could begin to guess how long it might take to develop the contacts necessary to make the final move on Barrow and Parker.

"That's something no man can guess," Simmons reports he said. "It might be six months, it might be longer. Probably it will take you thirty days to get your feet on the ground before you start to work. No matter how long it takes, I'll back you to the limit."

"Well, Lee, if that's how you feel about it, I'll take the job," Hamer answered.

The interview took place at Hamer's home on Riverside Drive in south Austin, sometime around the first of February, 1934. Hamer went to Houston, wound up his business there and resigned his $550 per month job, picked up a few specialized tools—including a custom-made twenty-round magazine for his .35 caliber Remington semiautomatic rifle—and put his affairs in order. At about 10:00 A.M. on February 10, he climbed into a black 1934 Ford V-8 four-door sedan and took up the trail. At that point, Clyde Barrow and Bonnie Parker had exactly 102 days to live. On July 4-5, 1934, Hamer gave a long interview to his long-time friend and poker-playing partner, Walter Prescott Webb. In it he described the process of tracking down a wanted criminal.

Using criminal sources of information—available to him because Hamer was well known for never having betrayed a confidence, even from a criminal—he determined that Barrow had a "home range"—a circle from Dallas to Joplin, Missouri, to northern Louisiana. He learned that Barrow was an absolute master of back roads, and that he and Bonnie had vowed never to be taken alive.

He learned that Clyde maintained hideouts and contacts in Texas, Missouri, and Louisiana, but not in Oklahoma or Arkansas. He reasoned that, since the pair were not "hot" in Louisiana, never having killed anyone there, they would be holing up in Louisiana rather than in Texas or Missouri. By the time the chase was over, Hamer knew the size and pattern of many of Bonnie's dresses, the size of underwear Clyde wore, the brands of tobacco both habitually smoked, the brand of whiskey Bonnie preferred, and—in at least one case—he determined that Clyde slept on the right side of the bed and Bonnie on the left side.

Hamer also learned that there were a number of officers in Louisiana who, for one reason or another, could not be trusted. Clyde's hideout was in a parish in which the sheriff was untrustworthy. In Hamer's own words, ". . . it was arranged to have Barrow's hideout moved into a parish where the officers were more reliable. In a comparatively short time the hideout was established in Bienville Parish at a place well-known to me." Exactly how Hamer accomplished this is still unknown—and one would probably live much longer if one didn't try and find out, even at this late date.

Hamer visited the camp several times, carefully examining the signs left by Barrow and Parker. An ambush was arranged at the camp, and would probably have resulted in taking the pair a month earlier and possibly alive. Unfortunately, the day before the ambush was to be sprung, Louisiana State Police and FBI agents raided several places in Ruston, Louisiana, only a few miles from Clyde's hideout. The raid was completely unrelated to Hamer's work, but it panicked Clyde and he quit the area for nearly a month. When he returned, he changed the location of his hideout. Hamer's plans had to be re-laid.

Like most well-known fugitives, Bonnie and Clyde were "seen" all over the United States. Reports of Barrow-Parker sightings came in from points as widely separated as southern California, the Pacific Northwest, New York, and Florida. Apparently, Bonnie and Clyde did some extensive traveling, for Hamer found evidence that they had—seemingly on impulse—driven to South Carolina to visit a cigarette factory.

Law enforcement officers, in the light of rumors that the pair might pop up anywhere, were jumpy—and understandably so, given their reputations for shooting policemen with little or no provocation. Late in 1933, a United States Army Air Corps second lieutenant, recently graduated from flight training in San Antonio and en route to his first assignment at Langley Field, Virginia, spent almost two hours handcuffed in a Tennessee Highway Patrol car. He found it difficult to convince skeptical Tennessee policemen that just because a man in his early twenties was driving a new Ford V-8 coupe with Texas plates on it across Tennessee at night and had a military-issue .45 automatic in the glove compartment and his deer rifle and bird gun behind the seat, it did not necessarily mean that he was either Pretty Boy Floyd or Clyde Barrow—or was associated with them.

Sometime in late February or early March of 1934, twenty-one-year-old Fred Eckhardt of Austin, a finance company collector who played bush league professional baseball on the side and raced automobiles for a hobby, was driving home from Temple. In those days, the Texas baseball season started as soon as the spectators wouldn't freeze to death in the bleachers and ended when they would. Basketball—"bounceball," it was derisively called—was considered a "sissy" sport in Texas. Texans watched or played football from September through December and baseball any other time the weather was dry and warm enough. Fred had played a doubleheader and gotten paid about twenty dollars; together with some other money, he had about sixty dollars on him. This was no dark secret.

Eckhardt was driving a 1930 Model A Ford coupe that had been modified for racing—an early hot rod. It had underslung axles, four-wheel brakes, wide balloon tires, a water pump, fuel pump, and oil pump, an overhead-valve racing cylinder head, a distributor rather than a timing gear, and a Holley carburetor specifically built for four-cylinder Ford race cars.

It also had a special modification of Eckhardt's own—the intake manifold had been drilled and tapped, and a petcock inserted. A rod ran from the petcock to the dash of the Model A. When the rod was turned the petcock opened, supplying a sudden rush of extra air to the manifold. It was, in effect, a primitive supercharger. That petcock was Eckhardt's secret weapon on the racetrack, enabling his four-cylinder Model A to hold its own with, and even outrun, V-8s.

About two miles south of Temple, Eckhardt noticed a light-colored Ford V-8 sedan coming up behind him at a high rate of speed. Being a cautious highway driver, he moved to the right to allow the speeder to pass. The sedan pulled alongside him, then swerved to the right to force him into the ditch.

Eckhardt had been driving in dirt-track races since he was fourteen. He slammed on his four-wheel brakes, causing the sedan, equipped with rear-wheel brakes only, to shoot by him. He then steered to the left and accelerated past the V-8. The driver of the sedan accelerated to catch him, and Eckhardt opened his primitive supercharger, jumping the Model A's speed nearly twenty miles per hour, as though it had a rocket booster.

The chase, at speeds of eighty to ninety miles per hour, continued until the cars reached the north city limit of Belton, where the driver of the V-8 broke it off. Eckhardt observed that the sedan was driven by a man, and that a girl or very small woman occupied the right front seat. With whom my father played ninety miles per hour bumper tag between Temple and Belton on that cold winter night in 1934 he could never say for sure, but he felt he had good reason to believe he'd either outrun or out-driven Clyde Barrow.

Easter Sunday, April 1, 1934. At the Shieffer farm just east of Grapevine, Texas, in northwestern Dallas County, a brand-new, light-grey Ford sedan stopped alongside the county road. Inside were at least two people, perhaps as many as four. They were laughing and talking among themselves, and at one point, one of them threw a whiskey bottle out the window. William Shieffer, the owner of the farm, paid no particular attention—young folks from Dallas stopped along his road all the time, and sometimes what they did while stopped—even in broad daylight—was embarrassing for an upstanding person to think about, much less witness.

The car had been stopped about twenty minutes when Shieffer heard the rumble of motorcycles and began to pay more attention. Texas Highway Patrol motorcycle officers E. D. Wheeler and H. D. Murphy had seen the Ford. Apparently thinking it was stalled, they stopped their motorcycles and approached on foot. According to Shieffer, neither man drew his revolver or even unstrapped it in the holster.

When Wheeler and Murphy got within ten feet or so of the car, the occupants suddenly opened fire on them, killing Wheeler instantly and mortally wounding Murphy. The front door of the car opened and a tiny, light-haired woman got out. She was carrying a sawed-off shotgun.

According to Shieffer, she was laughing and giggling as she approached the wounded officer. She pointed the shotgun at his head and continued to laugh as he tried to twist his head away from the muzzle. Finally, she tired of the game and fired twice. The loads of buckshot nearly tore Murphy's head off.

What she said as she ran back to the car, still laughing, has been reported two ways. Webb says she said, "Did you see his head bounce? Just like shooting a watermelon!" In *I'm Frank Hamer,* she's quoted as saying, "Did you see that? His head bounced like a rubber ball!" Authorities later identified the fingerprints on the discarded whiskey bottle as those of Clyde Barrow and Bonnie Parker.

This was too much even for Raymond Hamilton. He sent a letter to the Dallas County district attorney through an attorney's office in Dallas. He put his thumbprint on the letter to authenticate it. Hamilton denied any connection with Clyde Barrow, stated that he had not killed the two highway patrolmen, and claimed that he and Barrow had been quits for months and he had been nowhere near Grapevine on Easter Sunday. Hamilton's lawyer released the letter both to the D.A. and to the press.

The letter infuriated Clyde. He, too, wrote to the D.A., putting his thumbprint on the letter to authenticate it.

> Mr, King
>
> So Raymond Hamilton nev er killed anybody. If he can make a jury believe that I8m willing to come in and be tryed my self. Why dont you ask Ray about those two pol icemen that got killed near Grapevine? And while you are at it bwetter talk it ov er with his girl friend. Bonnie and me were in missouri when that happened but where was Ray? coming back from the West bankjob wasn8t he? Redhot too wasn8t he? I got it straight. And ask hi m about that escape at Eastham farm wherethat gard was killed. Guess he claims he doesnt know fire any shots there don8t ge? Well if he wasnt too dum to know how tp put a clip in a automatic he'd hace fired a lot m ore shots and some of the vrest of the gards would got killed too. He wrote his lawyer he was too good for me and didnt go my pace, well it makes a me sick to see a yellow punk like that playing baby ad making a jury cry over him. If he was half as smart as me o the officers couldnt catch him either/He stuck his fingerprint on a lett er so heres mine too just to let you k now thjis is on the leve;
>
> X Clyde
>
> P s AsK Ray why he was so dam jumpy to get rid of those yellow wh eels on his car and akshis girl friend how they spent easter

After Bonnie's death, her mother confirmed what everybody already knew—it was Bonnie Parker, not Raymond Hamilton's girlfriend, who fired the shotgun into Patrolman Murphy's head. Bonnie and Clyde had arranged to meet her on the Grapevine road, but she had been delayed. Bonnie had an Easter present for her mother. She was bringing her a white rabbit. The officers just happened to be in the wrong place at the wrong time.

Maybe a white bunny wasn't the only present Barrow and Parker were waiting to give somebody along the Grapevine road. Colonel Lee Simmons had his own theory. Hamilton robbed the bank at West on the afternoon of March 31. The morning radio reports carried the news. Clyde knew that Ray regularly ran for the maze of back roads around Grapevine and Roanoke, northwest of Dallas, to lie quietly while pursuit covered the main roads.

Hamilton was, in fact, headed for the very spot where Clyde's car was parked. Fortunately for him, he bogged his own car in a back road and kidnapped a farm wife, Mrs. Cam Gunters, who had a Model T Ford pickup. Mrs. Gunters was released on Monday, April 2, in Houston. Was Clyde waiting in ambush to kill his old partner? Colonel Simmons thought so—and he probably had inside information.

Bonnie and Clyde, accompanied by Henry Methvin, next surfaced near Miami, Oklahoma, on April 6. After a rainstorm, they got the car stuck in the mud. Two police officers, Constables Cal Campbell and Percy Boyd, drove up and offered to help pull them out. Their reward was gunfire—Campbell was shotgunned and killed instantly, Boyd was wounded. Boyd was forced to help Clyde and Methvin push the car out of the mud, then taken on a fourteen-hour ride before being released.

Strangely enough, Bonnie seems to have taken to Boyd. She and the lawman talked in the back seat while Clyde and Methvin alternated driving. She told him about her family, and he told her about his. The white rabbit was still in the car—would he, she asked, if anything were to happen to her while he was still in the car, see that her mother got the bunny? He agreed he would. When he was released, the outlaws bandaged his wounds, gave him a clean shirt, and supplied him with money to get home. He asked her, "Bonnie, what shall I tell the world when I go back?"

"Tell 'em I don't smoke cigars!" she replied. Bonnie's mother later reported that Bonnie said she liked Boyd, which probably saved his life. Boyd, incidentally, made it clear to the questioning press that he hadn't seen Bonnie smoking anything but Camels, and she said she didn't smoke cigars. It didn't do much to change the image.

Eight days after the kidnapping of Boyd, Frank Hamer was joined by his long-time friend and partner, Texas Ranger Captain "Manny" Gault. Bonnie and Clyde had thirty-nine days to live.

"In Louisiana," Hamer told Webb, "I made contact with Sheriff Henderson Jordan of Bienville Parish, and after I had informed him of my plan, he agreed to assist me and pay no attention to any other officers, state or federal. He brought with him Deputy (Bryan) Oakley."

Hamer knew that Barrow maintained a "mailbox"—a drop at which communications could be left from associates. Apparently, with the help of the family of W. H. Bybee, who had escaped from Huntsville with Hamilton, Hamer identified the location of the mailbox on a side road about eight miles out of the village of Plain Dealing, Louisiana. The next step was to lure Clyde to the mailbox.

"By the night of May 22, we had good reason to believe that Clyde would visit this mailbox within a short time," Hamer said. The mail drop was located under a board next to a tree stump about ten yards off the road. It was at the top of a knoll that commanded a good view of all the surrounding countryside—except for some woods on the east side of the road. In those woods, Hamer, Gault, Sheriff Jordan, Deputy Oakley, and two Dallas

County sheriff's deputies, Ted Hinton and Bob Alcorn, built a blind of pine boughs about thirty feet off the road. Hamer took up a position at the extreme left, armed with his .35 caliber Remington autoloader. Gault was next, armed with a .45 caliber Thompson submachine gun. Then came Jordan with a ten-gauge short-barreled automatic shotgun loaded with double-aught buckshot, Alcorn with a Thompson, Oakley with an automatic shotgun identical to Jordan's, and finally Hinton, also armed with a Thompson. All officers also had sidearms. Hamer, Gault, and Jordan were to take care of the front seat, Alcorn and Oakley the back seat, if occupied. Hinton was the reserve. The six officers settled in for a seven-hour wait.

At about 9:10 A.M., Hamer recalled hearing a "humming through the pines that was different from that made by other motors. A car was coming from the north at a terrific speed, singing like a sewing machine. We heard it when it must have been three miles away." There was little doubt that it was Clyde Barrow.

It came into view at about a thousand yards—a new light-grey Ford V-8 sedan. As it approached, Hamer's keen eyes picked out the license number—Barrow's car, without doubt. When it came closer, the officers could see a small, dark-haired man driving and a small red-haired woman in the seat beside him. There was now no doubt that Clyde Barrow and Bonnie Parker had driven into Hamer's trap. Would they drive out leaving dead officers behind them, as they had from so many other traps? That was something Hamer was determined would not happen.

The car stopped exactly where Hamer had decided it would. Barrow put the car in low and held the clutch in, and both he and Bonnie stared intently toward the stump where the mailbox was located. Hamer stepped into the road, completely in the open. "Throw up your hands!" he ordered.

Clyde grabbed for the ten-gauge sawed-off automatic shotgun he'd used to kill so many police officers, while Bonnie swung up the sawed-off twenty-gauge she'd used to murder Officer Murphy at Grapevine. Hamer, who had his Remington rifle at his shoulder, instantly opened fire. As he did, the car jerked forward. Ted Hinton later recalled hearing Bonnie "scream like a panther." The other five officers opened fire from the east, and in something less than twenty seconds poured over 100 rounds of .45 ACP and buckshot into the Ford.

When the car stopped in the ditch and the firing ceased, Hamer, who was left-handed, transferred the Remington to his right hand and drew a .45 caliber automatic pistol with his left. He walked to the driver's side door. "Be careful, Cap," Gault called. "They may not be dead."

As soon as Hamer could see inside the car, there was no question in his mind that the careers of Bonnie Parker and Clyde Barrow were over. He stuck the automatic in his belt and pulled the car door open. Clyde fell to the road, his shotgun tumbling out atop his body. Bonnie was slumped forward, her face in her lap. "I would have gotten sick," Hamer said, "but when I thought about her crimes, I didn't."

In the car the officers found three BARs and 100 twenty-round loaded magazines for them, Clyde's sawed-off ten-gauge automatic shotgun, Bonnie's sawed-off twenty-gauge automatic shotgun, seven .45 caliber automatic pistols, a .32 caliber Colt automatic, a .380 Colt automatic, and a .45 caliber double-action revolver, as well as 3,000 rounds of assorted ammunition. The car also contained fourteen sets of license plates from ten different states.

The car and the bodies were taken to Gibsland, Louisiana, where an inquest was held and Hamer identified the dead as Clyde Barrow and Bonnie Parker. The bodies were taken to Dallas, where both were autopsied. The movie *Bonnie and Clyde* implied that Clyde substituted cars and guns for sex, but the autopsy said otherwise—Bonnie was four months pregnant when she died.

Clyde Barrow was buried in West Dallas on May 25. At his funeral, his youngest brother was reported as ranting and making threats against all lawmen, and Hamer and Gault in particular. Both Hamer and Gault died natural deaths. Bonnie Parker, who had expressed a wish to be buried with Clyde, was instead buried in Fishtrap Cemetery in Dallas on the twenty-sixth.

Hamer was besieged with offers totaling in the thousands to tell his story. He turned them all down. When the state of Texas declared May 28 "Hamer-Gault Hero Day," Frank Hamer told associates he would be unable to attend the festivities. "I have a date with a man downtown that evening," he said, which is what he always said when he had an active case working.

Of the many letters and telegrams, Hamer kept few. One came from the White House, another from the office of J. Edgar Hoover, who later asked Hamer to chase John Dillinger. Hamer declined —he felt he had become too easily identifiable. A third, on the stationery of Sam B. Dill's Big Three-Ring Circus, he particularly prized. It was signed by an old and valued friend who'd once, back in 1918, when Hamer was recovering from two bullet wounds as a result of an altercation in Sweetwater, urged the ranger to become a movie actor, where the gunfire was all make-believe—Tom Mix.

JENNIFER IS WAITING

The McDow waterhole on Green's Creek in Erath County, Texas, is—from all appearances—the ideal place for a picnic. The quiet creek, running across gravel bars and then widening into a deep, clear, tree-shaded pool, is beautiful to look at—from a distance.

About twenty years ago, I went to the McDow waterhole. The horse I was riding was an old, steady mare, not prone to shy. I'm glad I'm a good horseman; if I hadn't been, I'd have been thrown. The mare definitely wanted no part of that place.

I walked, finally, to the water. It was quiet—eerily so. The only sounds were the soft rustle of the water over the gravel bars, the whisper of the breeze in the leaves, and the jingle of my spurs. No birds. No crickets. Only the water, the leaves, and my spurs.

It's cool there. The breeze through the trees feels good on a hot Texas day. The water is brisk and inviting. The grass is—or was, twenty years ago—lush and green.

I didn't stay long. The hair on my arms and the back of my neck kept rising and prickling. I *saw* nothing. I felt *something.*

Something was watching me—waiting. I wasn't sure what it was waiting for. I knew, instinctively—as you know if you've lived, from time to time, on the edge of danger—that whatever the *something* was, it didn't wish me well. I left—and I haven't been back.

Don't picnic at the McDow. And, above all—if you value your sanity and perhaps your life as well—*don't* spend a night camping on its grassy, inviting banks. You won't be alone—and you definitely *don't* want to meet what you'll have for company.

A little over a century ago now, Charlie Papworth brought his wife, Jennifer, his young son, and his infant daughter to the McDow waterhole to settle and live. They came from Alabama, or at least local legend holds they did. They built a small house—more of a cabin—near the banks of Green's Creek. The foundations of that cabin, overgrown with brush and weeds, are still there. Skeptics claim the cabin ruins are the only trace of the Papworth family still remaining in twentieth-century Erath County. Skeptics—at least skeptics living near the McDow—are few and far between.

Erath County lies, today, southwest of Fort Worth, pretty much off the beaten path to or from anywhere in particular. The main north-south road, U.S. 281, was once a major artery but today has fairly well succumbed to competition from the Interstate to the east. Stephenville is the county seat, and is home to Tarleton State, once a junior college, now part of the Texas A&M system. The major industries used to be dairy farming, cattle, and petroleum. With the bust in cattle and oil-and-gas, it didn't do too well for a long time.

In the 1880s, Erath County was "frontier," and it had a reputation for lawlessness. There was a band of local outlaws—horse and cattle thieves, mostly, who weren't above looting an unprotected homestead if they could find one—who had the local law buffaloed. They dressed, often, as Indians. It was usually easier (and safer) to attribute their crimes to Indians.

It wasn't long after Charlie and Jennifer arrived that Charlie, for reasons not recorded in local memory, was called back to Alabama. He left his wife and children at their new home on Green's Creek. Jenny and the kids were supposed to spend the days at their place, the nights with neighbors a couple of miles away.

One evening, Jennifer and her children didn't make it to the neighbors'. The next morning, the neighbors went to investigate. The house was wrecked inside, looted, and blood was spattered on the walls and floors. There were no bodies to be found. "Indians got them." That, at least, was the safest assumption.

Charlie came home from Alabama to find his home destroyed and his family apparently murdered "by Indians." Then, out of the brush came the eight-year-old boy, and he wasn't talking about Indians.

A bunch of men—white men, but dressed as Indians—came to the house, he said. He recognized some of them, and named them to his father. The child got away into the brush while they were brutalizing his mother. He didn't see what they did with his mother and sister—or their bodies.

Charlie Papworth went to the law. He made accusations and named names—and after several narrow escapes from ambushes and one from a lynch mob (led, local legend holds, by the very men who raped and murdered his wife), he took his young son and quit the country. The problem, or so the outlaws thought, was solved. Any witness not dead was scared off. They could rest easy.

They reckoned without Jenny!

Stories began to circulate about the house the Papworths once lived in and the McDow waterhole. People saw strange things—things they didn't like to talk about. Horses, mules, and dogs didn't like the place. People—especially men—felt uncomfortable there, even in daylight, as though *something*—something very unpleasant—was waiting there.

The first concrete indication came when a man moved into Jenny's house. He was warned—and he scoffed.

They found him there one morning, not long after he moved in. The door and the window were bolted from the inside and the window had to be smashed in to let folks inside. He was huddled against the back wall, facing the door. His eyes were wide open, his face frozen in an expression of horror. There was a six-shooter in his hand, loaded five beans in the wheel. All five had been fired. There were five bullet holes in the door, from the inside. They had to break his fingers to get the gun out of his hand.

He was dead, of course—without a mark on his body. Whatever "got" him so pristinely also entered a sturdy cabin with the door and window bolted from the inside and then left again without disturbing the locks and without leaving any *physical* trace of its presence. "Jenny," folks said. "Jenny got her first one."

"They say" that the leader of the band of "Indians" died in his bed in Dublin—but he didn't die peaceably. As he was dying, he suddenly sat bolt upright in bed and screamed, "Oh, my God! Don't let her get me! Don't let her get me!" The man at his bedside looked toward the foot of the bed and saw—*something*. He'd never talk, in detail, about what he saw there.

After the turn of the century, a railroad was built near the site of Jenny's house. There were a lot of unscheduled after-dark stops right about there—a shadowy figure, looking for all the world like a woman carrying a baby, would suddenly appear on the tracks in front of the engine. The train "hit" her countless times—but no one ever found any trace of a body. Jenny?

Well into the twentieth century, two young men—late teens, early twenties—were near the McDow as dark came on. They saw—*something*. One died very shortly thereafter. The other would never talk, in detail, about what they'd seen—and what had chased them, at impossible speed, as they whipped and spurred their horses to get away.

The only possible trace of Jennifer Papworth's body, so far as anyone recalls, was found in the 1940s. A local man found some small glass buttons—the kind used to fasten women's dresses in the 1880s—in the sand and gravel alongside the McDow, near where a long-caved-in seep well in the gravel bar had once been.

The McDow waterhole is still there, of course—still cool, tree-shaded, and inviting. Don't accept the invitation. Jenny's still there, too—and nobody along Green's Creek believes she's anywhere *near* through.

WHERE THESE STORIES CAME FROM

The following is a partial listing of sources that served to supply either the jumping-off place for further research into some stories, or the confirmation of a story already heard.

Bolton, H. E., ed. *Spanish Exploration in the Southwest, 1542-1706.* New York: Barnes and Noble, 1946.

Brann, William Cowper, "The Buck Negro," *The Iconoclast* (February 1895).

Carver, Charles. *Brann and the Iconoclast.* Austin: University of Texas Press, 1957.

Cook, John R. *The Border and the Buffalo.* Austin: State House Press, 1989.

Cunningham, Eugene. *Triggernometry: A Gallery of Gunfighters.* Boise: Caxton, 1980.

Frost, H. Gordon. *The Gentlemen's Club, The Story of Prostitution in El Paso.* El Paso: Mangan, 1983.

Green, A. C. *The Santa Claus Bank Robbery.* Dallas: SMU Press, 1988.

Hardin, John Wesley. *The Life of John Wesley Hardin.* Seguin: Smith and Moore, 1896.

Horan, James D. *The Pinkertons: The Detective Dynasty that made History.* New York: Crown, 1967.

Jenkins, John H., and H. Gordon Frost. *I'm Frank Hamer: The Life of a Texas Peace Officer.* Austin and New York: Pemberton Press, 1961.

Landrey, Wanda A. *Outlaws in the Big Thicket.* Austin: Eakin, 1976.

Miller, Rick. *Bounty Hunter.* College Station: Creative Publishing, 1988.

Paredes, Americo. *With His Pistol in His Hand.* Austin: University of Texas Press, 1958.

Simmons, Lee. *Assignment Huntsville: Memoirs of a Texas Prison Official.* Austin: University of Texas Press, 1957.

Skiles, Jack. *Judge Roy Bean Country.* Lubbock: Texas Tech University Press, 1996.

Sonnichsen, C. L. *I'll Die Before I'll Run: The Story of the Great Feuds of Texas.* Lincoln: University of Nebraska Press, 1988.

Sonnichsen, C. L. *The Life and Times of Judge Roy Bean.* New York: Bantam, 1965.

Syers, Wm. Edward, ed. *Ghost Stories of Texas.* Waco: Texian, 1980.

Walton, W. M. *Life and Adventures of Ben Thompson.* Austin: Edwards and Church, 1884.

Webb, Walter P. *The Texas Rangers: A Century of Frontier Defense.* Boston: Houghton Mifflin, 1935.

Weddle, Robert S. *The San Saba Mission: Spanish Pivot in Texas.* Austin: University of Texas Press, 1964.

Weddle, Robert S. *The Search for La Salle.* Austin: University of Texas Press, 1982.

Wilbarger, J. W. *Indian Depredations in Texas.* Austin: Hutchings, 1889.

And, of course, the Grasshoppers' Library, courtesy the Shadetree Historical Society.

Emphatically not seriously consulted, though thoroughly enjoyed:

Twist, Ananias. *Snide Lights on Texas History.* San Antonio: Naylor, 1959.

INDEX

A

Abbott, Alice, 80, 138, 139, 140
Abilene, Kansas, 111
Abilene, Texas, 162
Acme Saloon, 80
African Methodist Episcopal Church, 121
Alabama, 7, 10, 28, 73, 74, 75, 76, 205, 206
Alamo Plaza, 113
Albany, Texas, 61
Albuquerque, New Mexico, 140
alcalde, 29
Alcorn, Bob, 201
Allen Station, Texas, 97
Allen, James A., 150
Alligator Lake, 34
Allison, Clay, 110, 111, 169
Alma, Texas, 189
American Civil War, 52
American Protective Association, 125
American Society of Arms Collectors, 179
Amtrak, 113
Anson, Texas, 162
Apaches, 3, 23, 52, 164
Apalache, 9, 10
Apalachicola, Florida, 9
Aransas Bay, Texas, 14
Arizona, 2, 3, 10, 40, 45, 146, 163, 164
Armstrong, Sergeant John, 74, 75
Assignment Huntsville: Memoirs of a Texas Prison Official, 180, 191
Atascosa County, 49, 155, 156
Atlanta, Georgia, 140
Atoka, Oklahoma, 184
Austin Iconoclast, 120
Austin Statesman, 112
Austin, Stephen F., 29
Austin, Texas, 62, 76, 82, 86, 90, 101, 104, 110, 111, 112, 113, 114, 115, 116, 117, 120, 154, 164, 171, 179, 193, 195

B

Baffin Bay, 14
Baird, Texas, 177
Baldwin 4-4-0, 58
"*Ballad of Sam Bass*," 88
Ballinger, Texas, 150
Bandera, Texas, 82
banditos, 159
Bannister, John R., 103, 104
Baptist Standard, 124, 125
Barataria Island, 14
Barnes, Seaborn "Sebe," 98, 101, 107, 108
Barnum, P. T., 138
Barrow, Clyde Champion, 88, 179, 202
Bass, Sam, 88, 90, 91, 92, 94, 95, 96, 97, 98, 99, 101, 102, 103, 104, 105, 106, 107, 108, 109
Bass, Seaborn, 98
Bastrop County, Texas, 57
Baxter's Curve, 152

Baylor, General John, 45
Baylor University, 100, 119, 121, 127-133
Bean, Ann, 40
Bean, Fauntleroy, 40
Bean, James, 40
Bean, Joshua, 40
Bean, Jr., Phantly Roy, 40
Bean, Judge Roy, 39-51, 60
Bean, Major General Joshua, 43
Bean, Molly, 40
Bean, Sam, 40
Beanville, 47, 48, 49, 51
Beatty, Warren, 178
Beaumont, 29, 32
Beck, Ed (also known as Old Beck, Ole Beck, Ed Becker, Ole Becker), 151
Bedford, G. E. "Bit," 175–176
Bell, Major Horace, 42, 43
Belmont, Texas, 159
Belton, Texas, 196, 197
Bender Gang, 27–28
Berry, Jim, 91, 94, 96
Bettinger, Maggie, 128
Bexar County, 143
Bienville Parish, 194, 200
Bierce, Ambrose, 123
Big Horn River, 93
Big Spring Station, Nebraska, 93, 94, 96
Big Thicket, 27, 30, 32
Bill, Pecos, 154
Billy the Kid, 88
Biloxi, Mississippi, 14
Black Bess, 87
Boerne, Texas, 48
Bonham, Texas, 66
Bonnie and Clyde—A Love Story, 178, 179
Border, Lycurgus C. "Curg," 168–172
Border, George, 168
Border, Olivia, 172
Borger, Texas, 164
Borginnis, Sarah, 164
Bosman, Clem, 190
Bowen, Brown, 72, 73, 74, 76
Bowman, Joe, 111
Boyd, Percy, 199–200
Brann, William Cowper, 100, 119–135
brasada, 35
Brazil, 106, 127, 128, 130
Brazos River, 61, 67, 100
Brewster County, Texas, 106
Briant, Sheriff Elijah S. "Lige," 148–149
Broocks, Ben, 170, 171
Brooker, W. H., 120–121
Brown County, Texas, 72
Browning automatic rifle, 187, 190
Brownsville, Texas, 164
Brushy Creek, 22, 24, 26
Bryan, William Jennings, 169
Bucher Grocery, 183
Bucher, J. W.,183
Bucher, Martha, 183
Buckelew, Frank, 52, 53
Bull's Head, 111
Bullion, Laura (alias Delta Rose), 143, 149, 153
Buntline, Ned, 111
Burleson, Dr. Rufus C., 127–129, 133
Burr, Aaron, 42
Bushick, Frank, 91
Butch and Sundance— The Early Years, 141
Bybee, W. H., 190, 200
Byler, Viana, 146
Byron, Lord, 126

C

cacique, 12
Caddo Lake, 33
California, 40, 41, 42, 43, 44, 195
California State Militia, 40, 42, 43
californio, 43
Camels (cigarettes), 189, 200
Campbell, Cal, 89, 199
Canary Islanders, 48
Candelaria mission, 22, 23, 25
Capuchin priests, 12
Carver, William R., 142, 143, 144, 145, 146–149
Cassidy, Butch, 141
Catholic Academy of the Sacred Heart, 121
Cavelier, René Robert, Sieur de La Salle, 5–21
Cedar Bayou, Louisiana, 33
Cedar Key, Florida, 73
Central America, 7, 24, 95
Chandler, Charles, 28–29
Chapa, Juan Bautista, 16
Chávez, Leandro M., 48
Chávez, María Anastasia Virginia, 48
Chevrolet, 178–180
Chichimec Indians, 12
Chicken War, 21
Chihuahua City, Mexico, 41, 50
Chihuahuan desert, 40, 164
Chisholm, Dick, 68
Cibolo River, 160
Cimarron, New Mexico, 147
Clark, Etta, 138, 140
Clay County, Missouri, 90
Clear Fork Creek, 54, 55
Clements, Jr., Emanuel, 70
Clinton, Iowa, 125
Coahuila, 45
Coe, Phillip, 111–112
Coke, Richard, 74, 84, 85, 86
College Hill, Texas, 113
Collier, James, 28–29
Collier, Robert, 28–29
Collier, Susan, 28
Collin County, 97
Collins, Joel, 91–92, 94, 96, 109
Colorado, 10, 27, 93, 94 110, 113, 163
Colorado & Southern Railroad, 146–147
Colt, 71, 75, 76, 78, 117, 133, 187, 202
Colvin, Bessie, 138–140
Comanche, Texas, 72, 73, 76
Comanches, 52–56, 164
Concho County, 144, 145, 150
Confederacy, 45, 86, 89
Confederate General Albert Sidney Johnston, 86
Congress Avenue, Austin, Texas, 84, 90, 111
Conner, T. E. “Ted,” 51
Copprell's Store, 88, 101, 108
Coronado's Children, 34, 35, 37
Corpus Christi, Texas, 83, 86, 163, 164
Corpus Christi Bay, 10, 14
corrida, 158
Cortez, Crispín, 155
Cortez y Garza, Román, 154
Cortez y Lira, Gregorio, 154, 155, 156–162
Cortez, Mariana, 155, 158
Cortez, Severo, 155
Cotulla, Texas, 161
Creary, Captain Edward, 113
Crockett, Davy, 154
Crowson, Major, 190
Crystal City, Texas, 34
Cuero, Texas, 142, 143

Cunningham, Eugene, 71, 72, 95
Curry, Flat-Nosed George, 141
Curry, Kid, 142, 143, 144, 148, 149, 150
Custer, George Armstrong, 92–93

D

d'Aigron, Sieur, 8
Dakota Territory, 92, 93
Dallas, 73, 89, 96, 97, 164, 180, 182, 190, 194, 197, 198, 199, 202, 203
Davis Mountains, 34, 164
Davis Police, 68, 74, 83, 84
Davis, Edmund J., 70, 83, 84, 85, 90
Davis, J. L., 149
Davis, Jack, 91, 95, 105
Davis, Jeff, 169
Davis, Louis, 173, 175
Davis, Malcom "Mal," 186
Davis, Thomas E., 134
Dawes, Billy, 139
Day, Al, 69
de Agreda, Sister María de Jesús, 20
de Benavides, Father Alonso, 19–20
de Bienville, Sieur, 20
de Beaujeu, Sieur, 6, 7
de Graff, Laurens, 9
de Grammont, Michel (Lorencillo), 9
de la Garza, Abrán, 161
de León, General Alonso, 16
de Palacios, Gaspar, 10
de Piñeda, Alonzo Alverez, 10
de Rabago y Terán, Felipe, 24–26
de Salaz, Monsieur, 9
De Soto, 10
De Witt County War, 67,
De Witt County, 67, 77, 82, 142, 143,
Deaf Charlie, 142–143
Deno, Lottie, 61, 63–65
Denton, Texas, 89, 90, 96, 97, 98, 104
Denton County, Texas, 89, 90, 98, 104
Denton Mare, 89
Díaz, Leonor, 155, 156, 162
Díaz, Valeriano, 155, 158
Dillinger, John, 88, 185, 203
Dingus, 90
Division of Weights and Measures, 83
Dixon, Bud, 72, 73
Dobie, J. Frank, 34, 35, 36, 37, 88
Dolores mission, 22
Dodge City, Kansas, 71
Domingue, Saint, 7, 9, 18
Dominican Republic, 7
Don Juan, 126
Doña Ana County, New Mexico, 40, 43
Dooley, Tom, 88
Dowlearn, Bud, 69
Dryden, Texas, 152
Duderstadt, Ernst, "Mister Duder," 72
Duderstadt, Frederick, 72
Dula, Thomas, 87
Dunaway, Faye, 178
Duncan, Private Jack, 74–75

E

Eagle Pass, 11, 45, 46
Eagle's Nest Camp, 51
Earp, Wyatt, 63
East Lynne, 117
East Texas, 3, 67, 121, 169
Eastham, Texas, 190, 198
Eastland County, Texas, 176, 177
Eckhardt, Fred, 195–196
Eden, Texas, 144
Egan, Sheriff W. P. "Dad, " 89
El Parral, Mexico, 15

El Paso, 19, 50, 78–82, 106, 121, 137–140, 163–167, 179
El Paso del Norte, 163
El Paso Herald, 140
El Paso Historical Society, 179
El Paso Saddlery Company, 78–79
El Río de San Xavier, 34
El Sauz, 161
El Teco, 161, 162
Elgin, Texas, 57–60
Ellis Island, 165
Erick, Oklahoma, 189
Erisophesians, 131
Enrique, Juan, 12
Erath County, Texas, 204, 205
Espantosa Lake, 34–37
Espíritu Santo de Bahía, 19
Espiritu Santo Bay, 9, 10
estanciero, 95
Exodus, 137

F

Fat Alice, *See* Abbott, Alice
Fayetteville, Arkansas, 189
Ferguson, James E., 191–193
Ferguson, Miriam Amanda Wallace "Maw," 191
Fest, Jr., Mr. and Mrs. Simon, 51
First National Bank of Cisco, Texas, 173
Fisher, Jr., John King, 116–118
Fisher, Sr., John King, 116
Fishtrap Cemetery, 203
Flores, Cerefino, 160
Floresville, Texas, 161
Florida, 7, 9, 14, 22, 70, 73, 74, 75, 195
Floyd, Pretty Boy, 88, 185, 195
Floyd, Thomas, 103
Folsom, New Mexico, 146
Ford V8, 178, 184, 185, 186, 188, 189, 193, 201
Ford, Bob, 98
Ford, Henry, 184
Fort Abraham Lincoln, Dakota Territory, 92
Fort Griffin Flat, 61, 63, 64, 65
Fort Howard, 50
Fort Saint Louis, 14, 16, 18
Fort Worth, Texas, 95, 96–100, 105, 142, 143, 163, 164, 185, 205
Forty Thieves, 45
Foster, Joe, 114–115, 117
Fox, Red, 90
Franklin, Texas, 163, 165
Franks, George, 146
Free Rovers, 44–45
Frontier Times, 82
Frost, H. Gordon, 179
Fulcher, Walter, 151

G

Gainesville, Florida, 73
Galveston, Texas, 164
Galveston Evening Tribune, 119
Galveston News, 119
Galveston, Harrisburg, and San Antonio Railroad, 51, 152–153
Garcitas Creek, 4, 11
Gault, "Manny," 200, 201, 202, 203
George Holmgreen & Sons, 48
Georgia, 7, 76, 140
Gerald, Judge George Bruce "Big Sandy," 132–133
Gery, Jean, 12–13, 16
Gibsland, Louisiana, 202
Giddings, 86
Gila River, 40
Gillette, Jim, 106
Glover, Robert M., 159, 161, 162
Goave, Petit, 7–8

Goliad, Texas, 19
Gonzales, Texas, 69, 77, 78, 91
Gonzales County, 76, 77, 82, 159, 161–162
González, Anastacio, 50
González, Jesús, 161
Government Hill, 61
Grant, President U. S., 84
Grapevine, Texas, 197, 198, 199, 202
Greasy Grass, Montana, 93
Great Northern Railroad, 149, 150
Green's Creek, 204, 205–206, 208
Greene, A. C., 177
Grider, Nick, 151
Grigsby, Erwin, 152
Grimes, Henry, 101–102
Grollet, Jacques, 15, 16, 18
Guadalupe County, 82
Guadalupe River, 160
Guadalupe Mountain, 164
Gulf of Mexico, 7, 21
Gunters, Mrs. Cam, 199
Gutenberg, Johannes, 137

H

Haiti, 7
Hall Grocery, 185
Hall, Howard, 185
Hall, Lee, 77
Hall, Samuel, 87, 134
Hallettsville, 68
Hamer, Francis Augustus "Frank," 106–107, 179–181, 191, 192–195, 197, 200–203
Hamilton, Alex, 42
Hamilton, Floyd, 190
Hamilton, Raymond, 180, 182–185, 190, 198–200
Hanks, O. Camilla, 142, 143, *See also* "Deaf Charlie"
Hanks, Wyatt, 143
Haraszthy, Agustin, 42
Hardin, Elizabeth Dixon, 67
Hardin, Jane Bowen, 72, 73
Hardin, Jeff Davis, 67
Hardin, John G., 67
Hardin, John Wesley, 66–67, 69–82, 86, 89
Hardin, Joseph G., 67
Harrel, Geo., 103
Harrington, Frank, 147
Harris, J. W., 132–133
Harris, Jack, 114–118
Harrisburg, Texas, 46, 51, 152, 153
Harryman, J. W., 188
Headquarters Saloon, 42, 43, 44
Heffridge, Billy, 91, 94, 96
Heins, James, 18
Helgin, Texas, 57–59
Hell Again Hill, 59
Hellagin Hill, 58–60
Helms, Henry, 173, 175–176
Helms, Jack, 68, 69, 71
Henry, O., 150
Hickok, Duckbill "Wild Bill," 111
Hidden Lake, 33
Hidetown, 61, 62, 63
Highway Patrol, Division of Weights and Measures, 83
Hill, Bob, 175
Hill, Robert, 173, 175
Hillsboro, Texas, 183
Hinton, Ted, 201–202
Hobek, Ole, 151, 153. *See also*, Walsh, Ed; Welsh, Ed; Oldbeck, Ole
Hole-in-the-Wall Gang, 141–142, 152
Holliday, Doc, 63
Hollywood, 2, 141, 180
Holy Ghost Bay, 9
Honorius, 144

Hood, Robin, 87–88
Hoover, J. Edgar, 203
Houston, Texas, 27, 46, 57, 58, 119, 164, 192, 193, 199
Houston & Texas Central Railroad, (H&TC), 58, 60
Houston Post, 119
Howard's Well, 50
Hudson River, 111
Humphrey, H. D., 189
Hunter, J. Marvin, 82
Huntsville, Texas, 77, 155, 162, 182, 185, 190, 200

I

I'm Frank Hamer—The Life of a Texas Peace Officer, 179, 180, 197
Iconoclast, 120–135
Indiana, 88, 98, 107
International & Great Northern railroad, 113, 119
Iver Johnson Bulldog .44, 139

J

Jackson, Frank, 91, 98, 99, 101, 102–107, 109
Jackson, Wyoming, 141
Jacksonville, Florida, 73
James, Jesse Woodson, 88
Jefferson City, Missouri, 150
Jenkins, John H.,179
Jennings, Al, 88, 150
Jesús María, Chihuahua, 41
Johnson, Doyle, 185–186
Johnston, Albert Sidney, 86, 89
Joly, 6, 8
Jones, Thomas, 177
Joplin, Missouri, 194
Jordan, Henderson, 200-201
Juárez, 79, 163
Juárez, Benito, 163
Jumano Indians, 19, 20
Jumbo, 138, 140
Jumio, 138
Junction, Texas, 78, 81

K

Kahler, 188
Kansas, 27, 70, 71, 92, 93, 94, 95, 100, 110, 111, 112, 114
Karankawa "Kronks," 11, 17, 23
Karnes County, 68, 155, 156, 158, 161
Kelly, Henry, 68
Kelly, Machine Gun, 185
Kenedy, Texas, 155, 158–159
Kentucky, 40, 88
Ketchum, Tom "Black Jack," 146, 147
Ketchum, Berry, 146, 151, 153
Ketchum, Sam, 146, 147
Kilpatrick, Alice, 145
Kilpatrick, Benjamin A., "Blackie," 142, 144, 145, 148, 150, 153
Kilpatrick, Daniel Boone, 144, 145
Kilpatrick, Ed,145
Kilpatrick, Etta, 145
Kilpatrick, Felix, 145
Kilpatrick, George, 148
Kilpatrick, Ola, 145
Kilpatrick, Will, 145
King Kong, 139
King Ranch, 14
King Ranch Red quarter horses, 90
King, Captain Richard, 89–90
Kingston Trio, 88
Kirker, James, 41
Knoxville, Tennessee, 150

L

L'Aimable, 6, 8, 17
L'Amour, Louis, 18

L'Archeveque, Jean, 15–16, 18
La Belle, 6, 8, 11, 14
La Belle France, 21
La Louisiane, 21
La Mobila, 10
La Rochelle, 6
La Salle, René Robert Cavelier, Sieur de, 5-21
La Villa de Benito Juárez, 163
Lago de los Legartos, 34, 35
Lago Espantosa, 35
Lamont, Jimmie, 190
Langley Field, Virginia, 195
Langtry, Texas, 39, 40, 51
Las Cruces, New Mexico, 43, 44, 45
Lavaca Bay, 11
Law West of the Pecos, 39, 40, 60
Lea, Prairie, 55
Leahy, Harry, 176
Lehmann, Herman, 52–53
Lewis, Callie, 78
Liberty, Texas, 29
Lincoln, Freda Bullion, *See* Bullion, Laura
Lincoln, Maurice, 153
Lincolnshire, England, 168
Lipan-Apaches, 52
Lira y Cortinas, Rosalía, 154
Little Big Horn, 93
Little Etta, *See* Etta Clark
Lively, Mr., 47
Lockhart, Texas, 52, 54, 55, 110
Locksley, Robert, Earl of Huntingdon, 87, 168
Logan, Harvey "Kid Curry," 141, 142, 148
Logan, Lonny, 141
Lomax, John A., 103
Longabaugh, Harry, 141, 144
Longley, Bill, 86, 89
Longley, Campbell, 89
Lorencillo, 9, *See* de Graff
Los Angeles, California, 42
Los Frijoles, 41
Lost Lake, 33
Louisiana, 7, 21, 28, 29, 33, 75, 194, 200, 202
Louisiana State Police, 194
Louisville, Kentucky, 88
Love Me Tender, 89
Love, Albert H., 36–37
Lubbock, Texas, 137
Lubbock Avalanche, 137

M

MacDonald, Bill, 171
Malloy Land and Cattle Company, 144
Managua, Nicaragua, 95
Manor, Texas, 154, 159
Many, Louisiana, 28
Marlin, Texas, 68
Martínez, Francisco, 16, 18
Martinique, 7
Mason, Texas, 101
Mason County, Kentucky, 40
Massanet, Father Damian, 16, 19
Masterson, Bat, 63
Matagorda Bay, 4, 8, 9, 10, 11, 14, 17, 21
Matamoros, Mexico, 154
McBride, Lillie, 186
McCarty, Henry, 88
McDonald, Bob, 145
McDow waterhole, 204–208
McGinnis, Harry, 188
McGrath, 188
McKinney, Texas, 97
McLennan County, 127, 132, 181
McMillan, Neil, 73–74
McNelly, Captain Leander Henry, 77, 86

Memphis, Tennessee, 153
Menard, Texas, 21, 26
Mencken, H. L., 123
Mercier, Eva, 140
Mertzon, Texas, 150
mestizos, 24
Methodist Waco Female Academy, 121
Methvin, Henry, 190, 199
Metroplex, 97
Metz, Leon, 81
Meunier, Pierre, 18
Mexican Central Railroad, 79
Mexico, 3, 6, 7, 14–15, 18, 19, 28, 30, 34, 45, 50, 144, 163
Mexico City, 10, 13–14, 25–26
Miami, Oklahoma, 199
Micanopy, Florida, 73
Michigan, 185
Micipipi, 6, 9
Miller, Jim, 78
Milmo, Pat, 45–46
Milton, Jeff, 81
Mississippi, 6, 7, 28, 75
Mississippi River, 6, 7–11, 14, 15 20
Missouri, 90, 94, 98, 150, 186, 187, 189, 190, 194, 198
MKT railroad, 119
Mobile Bay, 10, 14
Model A ford, 196
Model T Ford, 164, 199
Monclova, Texas,16
Montana, 93, 150
Moore, E. C., 184
Moral Picture Film Company, 163–167
Morfi, Father, 19
Morgan, John Hunt, 87
Morgan's Raiders, 87
Morose, Beulah "Betty," 79, 80, 81
Morose, Martin, 79, 81
Morris, Brack, 155–162
Morris, Dave, 68
Morris, H. S. Steen, 127–130
Morris, Reverend Silas, 127
Mullin, James (alias Jimmy Lamont), 190
Murieta, Joaquín, 43, 88
Murphy, H. D., 197, 199, 202
Murphy, Jim, 91, 98–105, 109
Murrel, John, 28

N

Nacogdoches, Texas, 130
National Guard Armory, 190
National Rifle Association, 179
Navasota River, 15
Neuhoff Packing Company, 185
Nevada, 10, 142
New Albany, Indiana, 88, 89
New Mexico, 3, 10, 40, 41, 43, 45, 106, 107, 140, 146, 147, 163, 164, 185
New Orleans, Lousiana, 30, 73, 121, 165
Newman, Paul, 141
Ney, Elizabet, 86
Nicaragua, 95
Nixon, Tom, 91, 94, 96
Nobles, Sneed, 172
Noelke, Hub, 151, 153
Nogales, Arizona, 146
North America, 3, 5, 10, 22, 24, 33, 167
Nouvelle France, 10
Nouvelle Orleans, 21
Nova Scotia, Canada, 110
Nueces River, 34–35, 161
Nuestra Señora de Regla, 9
Nuevo Méjico, 10

O

Oakley, Bryan, 200–201
Oakwood Cemetery, 134–135
Ogden's Store, 148
Oklahoma, 111, 164, 171, 184, 185, 189, 194, 199
Ohio, 57
Ohio River, 40, 88
Ohio State Penitentiary, 150
Oldbeck, Ole, 151
Olive, I. Prentice "Print,"58
Olney, George W., 76
Onderdonk, Robert, 82
Ottine, Texas, 159

P

Padre Ganzabal, 25
Page, Frank, 134
Paint Rock, 145, 149
Palance, Jack, 168
Palmer, Joseph, 190
Papworth, Charlie, 205–206
Papworth, Jennifer, 205–206
Paredes, Dr. Américo, 155, 159
Parker County, Texas, 97
Parker, Bonnie, 178–203
Parker, Robert Leroy, 141, 142
Paul Quinn College, 121
Peak, Major June, 100, 102
Pecos, Texas, 78
Pecos County, Texas, 50, 151
Pecos Bill, 154
Pecos River, 3, 39
Pensacola, Florida, 74
Pensacola Railroad, 74
Philomathesians, 131
Plano, Texas, 97
Pinkerton National Detective Agency, 143, 144, 148
Plain Dealing, Louisiana, 200
Planche Spring, 144, 148
Platte City, Missouri, 189
Pleasants, Judge Henry Clay, 77
Pollard, Alabama, 73, 74
Poor Clare, 20
Populist Party, 169
Porter, William Sidney, 120, 150
Poverty Row, 111
Prairie Lea Road, 55
Presidio de San Francisco, 16
Presley, Elvis, 89
Price, Archibald "Arch," 169–172
Puerto Rico, 7

Q

Querquer, Petra, 41
Querquer, Santiago, 41
Quintana, Rafael, 46–47

R

Ranchería Grande, 22, 23, 24, 25
rancherías, 22
rancheros, 30
Ratliff, Marshall, 173–177
Reconstruction, 70, 73, 83, 84, 90
Red River, 21, 189
Redford, Robert, 141
Redwing, Rodd, 111
Reglita, 9
Regulators, 31
Remington autoloader, 201
Remington rifle, 62, 202
Remington semiautomatic, 193
remuda, 72, 158
Reno brothers, 89
résumé, 119
Reynosa, Mexico, 154
Rhodes, Eugene Manlove, 106
Riley, James Whitcomb, 126
Rio Grande, 10, 11, 12, 14, 16, 18, 79, 81, 99, 151, 154, 158, 161

Rio San Antonio, 19, 60
Ritter, Tex, 88
River of the Logs, 14
Riverside Drive, 193
Roberts, Noel G., 170–171
Robledo, Benifacio, 159
Robledo, Encarnación, 160
Robledo, Martín, 159–160
Robledo, Refugia, 160
Robledo, Tomás, 160
Rockdale, Texas, 22
Rodríguez, Ramón, 160
Rogers, J. H., 161
Rolling Stone, 120
Romain, Julien, 46–47
Romaldo, Cortez y Lira, 154, 155–158
Rose, Della, 143, 150, 153, *See* Bullion, Laura
Round Rock, Texas, 88, 99, 101–108
Round Rock's Sam Bass Cafe, 88
Round Top Mountain, 55
Rowena, Texas, 181
Runnels County Jail, 150
Ruston, Louisiana, 194
Ruter, 18

S

Sabine River, 29, 30, 75
Saint Domingue, 7, 9, 18
Saint François, 6, 7
Saint Louis, Missouri, 120, 150
Saint Louis Globe-Democrat, 119
Saint Louis Post-Dispatch, 120
Saint Paul's Episcopal Church, 134
Saint Xavier, 23
Salt Fork, 189
Sam B. Dill's Big Three-Ring Circus, 203
San Angelo, 146
San Antonio, Texas, 19, 22, 23, 26, 45, 46, 47, 48, 50, 51, 60, 82, 91, 92, 113, 115, 116, 117, 120, 121, 134, 142, 143, 160, 163, 164, 195
San Antonio Express, 120, 160
San Antonio Light, 120
San Antonio Number Nine, 152–153
San Augustine County, Texas, 168, 169, 170, 171, 172,
San Diego, California, 40–43
San Fernando de Bejar, 19, 22
San Francisco, Presidio de, 16
San Gabriel, California, 42
San Gabriel River, 23, 26, 35
San Ildefonso, 22
San Marcos River, 26
San Pedro Creek, 47
San Saba River, 21, 26
San Saba Street, 142
San Xavier, 23
Sanderson Canyon, 152
Sanderson Cemetery, 153
Sandoval, Cipriano, 43
Sandoval, Martín, 159
Santa Fe, New Mexico, 19, 41
Santiago de Monclova, 18–19
Santo Domingo, 7
Scarbrough, George, 81, 132
Scarbrough, John, 132
Schnabel ranch, 159
Schnabel, Henry, 159, 161–162
Schoate, Boone, 156–158
Schoate, Crockett, 158
Seguin, Texas, 36, 72, 82, 162
Selman, Rowdy John, 79–81
Senate Saloon, 111
Seno Mexicano, 7
Shadetree Historical Society, 57–59
Sharp, Boosie, 148

Sharp, Henry, 148
Sharps rifle, 62
Sheffield, Texas, 151, 152, 153
Sheridan, Major General Phillip H., 62
Sherman, Texas, 185
Shieffer, William, 197
Simmons, Lee, 180, 191–193, 199
Sioux, 93
Slattery, Joseph, 125
Smith & Wesson, 76, 117
Smith & Moore, 82
Smithville, Texas, 16
Sonora, Mexico, 144
Sour Lake, 29
South America, 7, 24, 144
South Carolina, 195
South El Paso Street, 166
South Flores Street, 47
South Joplin, Missouri, 187
South Mesa Street, 137, 164
South San Gabriel River, 35
South Santa Fe Street, 166
South Utah Street, 137–138, 164, 165, 166
Southern Baptist Church, 121, 124
Southern Pacific, 152
Spanish Florida, 21
Spanish Fort, Texas, 21
Springfield rifle, 62
State House Press, 82
Steen, Mary "Mamie," 145
Stephenville, Texas, 205
Sterling, Bill, 106
Stockdale, Texas, 160
Storyville, 165
"Suicide Sal," 188
Sundance Kid, 141, 142, 144, 148
Sutton County, 145, 148, 149
Sutton, Bill, 68, 69
Sutton-Taylor Feud, 67, 77, 158
Swain, John H., a.k.a. John Wesley Hardin, 73, 74, 75
Sweetwater, Texas, 203

T

Taino Indian, 8
Tall Texan (Benjamin Kilpatrick), 142, 143, 150, 151
Talmadge, T. DeWitt, 122–123
Talon, Pierre, 18
Tampa Bay, 10
Tampico, 9, 10, 14
Tanner, John, 131
Tarleton State College, 205
Taylor, Bill, 69
Taylor, Buck, 67–68
Taylor, Jim, 69, 72
Taylor, Mart, 68
Taylor, Pitkin, 69
Taylor, Scrap, 69
Teixeira, Antonia, 127
Tejas Indians, 16, 19, 20
Teleco, Texas, 180
Temple, Texas, 99, 185, 195, 196, 197
Ten Commandments, 137
Tennessee, 150, 153, 195
Tennessee Highway Patrol, 195
Terrell County, Texas, 151
Terrell County Historical Society, 153
Texas A&M, 205
Texas Bankers Association, 173–174
Texas Baptist General Convention, 129, 133
Texas Confederate troops, 45
Texas Department of Public Safety, 83, 106
Texas Highway Patrol, 83, 197
Texas Historical Society, 179
Texas Iconoclast, 120
Texas Panhandle, 40

Texas Rangers, 1, 76, 83, 84, 85, 91, 105, 171
"Texas Robin Hood," 88
Texas State Cemetery, 86
Texas State Police, 83, 84
Thirty-fifth District Court, 150
Thomas, Denis, 9
Thomason, Constable W. D., 149
Thompson submachine gun, 201
Thompson, Ben, 110–117, 169
Thorne, J. M., 105
Thornton, Oliver G. "Ollie," 144, 145, 148, 149, 150
Throckmorton, Texas, 61
Tipton, Wyoming, 147
Tonkawa, 3, 4, 16, 23
Travis County, 57, 76, 101, 154, 155
Travis Rifles, 84, 85
Triggernometry, 71
Trimmel, John, 156, 157, 158
Trinity County, Texas, 66
Trinity River, 190
Trousdale, David Andrew, 152–153
Turkey Canyon, 147
Turner Hall, 117
Turner's Lou, 30, 32
Turpin, Dick, 87
Tyler Telegram, 122

U

Uncle Sam, 62
Underwood, "Old Dad," 98, 105
Union Pacfic, 93, 95–96, 147
United States Army Air Corps, 195
University of Texas, 113

V

vaqueros, 155
Variety Theater, 111
Vaudeville Variety Theater, 114, 117
Vera Cruz, 10, 46
Villarreal, Andrés, 155, 156, 157
Vinegaroon, Texas, 51
Virginia, 195

W

Waco Daily News, 121
Waco News, 128
Waco Times Herald, 132
Waco, Texas, 100, 101, 107, 119, 121, 123, 124, 125, 127, 129, 132, 133-134, 164, 180, 181
Wagner, Montana, 150
Walker County, Texas, 176–177
Walker, Charles, 148, 149
Wall, Brune, 169, 171
Wall, Eugene Beauharnais, 169, 170, 171
Wall, George Washington "Uncle Buck," 168–169, 170, 171
Wall, Ney, 169, 171
Wall, Pez (Lopez), 169, 171
Wall-Broocks-Border feud, 168
Walsh, Ed, 151
Walton & Hill, 116
Walton, W. H., 113–115
War between the States, 52, 67
Ward, William H., 133–134
Ware, Richard, 103
Weatherford, Texas, 97
Webb, Charles "Charlie," 71–73, 76, 78
Webb, Dr. Walter Prescott, 179–180, 193, 197, 200
Weinert, F. C., 162
Wellington, Texas, 189
Wells Fargo, 152
Welsh, Ed, 151
West Texas, 34, 64, 79, 173, 177
Wheeler, E. D., 197

White House, 203
White, Matthew G., 29
Wichita Falls, 175, 183
Wicks and Hickman, 48–49
Wild Bunch, 141–142, 152
Wild Old Days, 91
Williamson County, Texas, 101, 107
Winchesters, 36, 58, 59, 60, 85, 117, 152, 160
Winnemucca, Nevada, 142
Winnipeg, Manitoba, Canada, 105
Woolem, Dee, 110
Wooten, Dr. Goodall, 117
Wright's Saloon, 72
Wurlitzer, 88
Wyoming, 2, 141, 148, 163

X

Xavier, Saint, 23
Xeble, France, 16

Y

Yankee, 42, 51, 70, 83, 89, 90, 167
yegua trigueña, 158, 161
Yocum, Christopher, 31, 32
Yocum, Matthew, 28–29
Yocum, Thomas D., 29–31, 32
Yocum's Inn, 30, 31
Yorkshire, England, 110

Z

Zevallos, Juan José, 23, 24
Zevallos, María, 24